A Baptist Manual of Polity and Practice

REVISED EDITION

NORMAN H. MARING
WINTHROP S. HUDSON

Revised by
Norman H. Maring

Judson Press ®
Valley Forge

A BAPTIST MANUAL OF POLITY AND PRACTICE
REVISED EDITION

Copyright © 1991
Judson Press, Valley Forge, PA 19482-0851
Statistics updated in September 1997.

All rights reserved. No part of this publication may be reproduced, stored in a retrieval system, or transmitted in any form or by any means, electronic, mechanical, photocopying, recording, or otherwise, without the prior permission of the copyright owner, except for brief quotations included in a review of the book.

Unless otherwise indicated, Bible quotations in this volume are from the New Revised Standard Version of the Bible, copyrighted, 1989 by the Division of Christian Education of the National Council of the Churches of Christ in the United States of America, and are used by permission. All rights reserved.

Library of Congress Cataloging-in-Publication Data
Maring, Norman H. (Norman Hill), 1914-
    A Baptist manual of polity and practice / Norman H. Maring, Winthrop S. Hudson. —Rev. ed.
      p. cm.
Includes bibliographical references and index.
ISBN 0-8170-1171-4
1. Baptists—Government. I. Hudson, Winthrop Still, 1911-
  II. Title.
  BX6340.M29   1991   91-18402
  262'06131—dc20   CIP

The name JUDSON PRESS is a registered trademark in the U.S. Patent Office. Printed in the U.S.A.

10 09 08 07 06 05 04 03 02 01 00 99 98

6 5 4 3 2

Contents

	Page
Foreword to the New Edition	vii
Foreword to the Original Edition	ix
Author's Preface	xiii

1. Identifying the Baptists 1
   The meaning of polity . . . Defining Baptist identity . . . Self-discovery in ecumenical encounter . . . Some typical ideas about Baptists . . . A look at Baptist origins . . . Historic Baptist emphases

2. The New Testament Concept of the Church 19
   The need for a doctrine of the church . . . The biblical doctrine of the church . . . The nature of the church . . . The mission of the church

3. The Church and the Churches 35
   Tensions between the church and the churches . . . The Baptist doctrine of the church . . . Historic doctrines in today's world

4. The Local Church 49
   The question of polity ... Marks of a local church ... Powers of a local church ... Church meetings ... Guidelines for an effective congregational meeting ... Procedure for organizing a church ... Special provisions on denominational relationships recommended for inclusion in church constitutions

5. Church Membership: Qualifications and Responsibilities 71
   Admission to church membership ... Members' responsibilities and privileges ... Termination of membership ... The question of open membership

6. The Baptist Ministry....................... 97
   Officers of a local church ... The ministry of the laity ... The changing nature of the pastoral office ... Roles of the pastor ... The authority of a pastor ... Qualifications of a pastor ... Ordination ... Withdrawal of recognition ... Lay preachers

7. Other Officers of the Local Church 121
   Drafting a constitution and bylaws ... General officers of the church ... Boards of the church ... Committees of the church ... Auxiliary organizations ... The Church Council ... A single-board plan

8. Baptism and the Lord's Supper 145
   Ordinance or sacrament? ... Understanding religious symbols ... A theology of baptism needed ... Baptism ... The Lord's Supper

9. The Associational Principle of Baptists........ 173
   Origins of the associational principle ... The Philadelphia Baptist Association ... The challenge of the society method ... Further erosion of the associations ... The revival of the association principle

10. Regional and National Organizations 195
    Varied ways of organizing for mission ... Drawing the churches together: the Northern Baptist Convention ... Moving toward community: the American Baptist Convention ... Creating a unified denomination: ABCUSA ... Relationships with denominational schools

11. Ecumenical Relationships.................. 227
    The modern ecumenical movement... Ecumenical organizations... Baptists and ecumenism... Cooperation with other Baptists

Appendices
1. Some Significant Dates in Baptist History............................. 249
2. Church Covenants.................... 253
3. Suggested Constitution and Bylaws 257
4. Selected Bibliography................ 275

Index...................................... 283

Foreword to the New Edition

When my distinguished predecessor in the general secretaryship of American Baptist Churches, Edwin H. Tuller, wrote the foreword to the original edition of *A Baptist Manual of Polity and Practice,* he contributed several insights which over the past three decades have proved to be accurate. First among these was his observation that Baptists have needed a manual that would help them to understand the biblical and historical basis upon which our church polity must rest. The many thousands of copies of the *Manual* that have found their way from the pressroom to the bookshelves of pastors and lay leaders bear a clear witness by their very numbers that the need has existed and is being met.

Dr. Tuller pointed out also that, though the preparation of this book was initiated by denominational action, it could not bear an "official stamp of approval" that would be binding in any way upon the churches or the denomination, but would gain its status only through acceptance and use. Such is still the case. The book still has no *official* authority, and yet the authority it has gained through the churches' acceptance over the years is unquestioned. This is the Baptist way.

Further, and perhaps most relevant to the present project,

Dr. Tuller pointed out that the original book was not the final word, for "some future generation will feel the need for additional modifications in order to keep pace with the dynamic movement so evident among a people whose paramount desire is to enable [Baptists] more fully to experience the power and presence of God in contemporary life."

That time has come. A new generation of Baptists has need for new insights and new understandings—but with the same biblical and historical rootage that they have cherished so long. We are indeed fortunate that Norman Maring has been able to give us this new and greatly improved edition. Like the earlier book, it does not attempt to prescribe exact patterns of church polity but rather to explain the basic principles by which each congregation may develop the forms most appropriate to its specific situation. Furthermore, going beyond the earlier edition, it outlines the current movement of Baptists toward a closer cooperation with each other and an increased sense of denominational unity. Thus the churches are carrying out the intent of their spiritual ancestors, who believed strongly in the associational principle by which churches supported and counseled each other as they worked toward common goals—a principle that became blurred by an excessive emphasis on local church independence in the nineteenth century but has been recovered in the twentieth.

I commend this book to those who lead our churches into the new millennium. At the same time I remind the readers that this *Manual,* like its predecessor, is only as official as they feel led by the Holy Spirit to make it, and that yet another day will come when it must be looked at afresh and again revised to meet the needs of still another generation.

> DANIEL E. WEISS
> *General Secretary*
> *American Baptist Churches*
> *in the U.S.A.*

April 15, 1991

Foreword to the Original Edition

Many Baptists have long felt the need for a new Baptist "manual" that would bring together traditional Baptist positions and practices and the modifications adopted over the years by Baptists in local churches and in larger groupings. Baptist organization is not static. It changes slowly in keeping with the needs of people to maintain a vital and personal relationship between the individual and God through Jesus Christ. The gospel remains our basis, and the Baptist genius as exhibited in history is our guide. The application of these considerations, however, undergoes almost constant change which, while neither rapid nor cataclysmic, is none the less persistent. Baptists have always placed more emphasis on personal faith and experience than upon uniformity of structure or organization. Because of this very fact, it is almost axiomatic that varieties of practice should be found within the churches and among them.

The General Council of the American Baptist Convention several years ago initiated procedures which, it was hoped, would result in the production of a manual such as the one here presented. It was fully agreed that the manual could not bear an "official stamp of approval" in such a way as to be considered binding upon the churches or the Convention.

Although it would be released only after having the constructive criticism of many groups and knowledgeable individuals, it would have to stand basically as the work of its authors themselves. It could take on an "official" stamp for Baptists in the only way any of its predecessors had: through acceptance and use over the years.

We feel deeply grateful in having secured the consent of two outstanding church historians to take the responsibility for writing this important document: Dr. Norman H. Maring, of Eastern Baptist Theological Seminary, and Dr. Winthrop S. Hudson, of the Colgate Rochester Divinity School. These two scholars know the great importance of historical handbooks in the development of Baptist thought and polity, and are quite aware of the process which brought these handbooks of the past into wide usage as "official" guides of faith and practice. A precise sense of historical perspective and value is the first requisite they have brought to this present task. But church historians occupied with the interpretation of history cannot live in the past. Dr. Maring and Dr. Hudson are thoroughly familiar with the modern scene. Their extensive studies of current procedures among our churches have qualified them fully to discharge their responsibilities of writing a new manual. They have sought and profited by the opinion of many others, but they bear full responsibility for the completed work.

Among those who have reviewed all or parts of the manuscript and have submitted written comments and criticisms of it are the Advisory Board for Theological Studies, the Executive Committee and most of the members of the Commission on the Ministry, the Executive Committees of American Baptist Men and the National Council of American Baptist Women, some members of the General Council, some officers of the Ministers Council, and selected staff members and leaders of the American Baptist Convention. Fully one hundred people in all have critically examined the manuscript. It must be obvious that the resulting criticisms and suggestions for change could not all be finally incorporated into the manual, for the simple reason that some were diametrically opposed to others. The authors have chosen the course of reviewing alternative views in connection with

FOREWORD TO THE ORIGINAL EDITION

issues that have proven to be complex and persistently difficult for Baptists. They were greatly aided by the stimulating criticisms. These have led to modifications which, in their opinion, have strengthened the book as a whole and clarified many portions of it. The final product, while remaining that of Dr. Maring and Dr. Hudson, does reflect, to this extent, the judgment of those considered most capable in this field.

I commend this book to the thoughtful reading of all who would like to become more familiar with the people called "Baptists." Those responsible for leadership in local churches, associations, and wider levels of organized witness and outreach will find this stimulating and provocative. It is hoped that many groups of Baptists at local, state, and national levels will make this work a subject of thoughtful inquiry and discussion.

Of course it is not the "final" word. Time alone will determine its proper place as far as an "official" expression of our policies and practices is concerned. One thing seems certain: Some future generation will feel the need for additional modifications in order to keep pace with the dynamic movement so evident among a people whose paramount desire is to enable man more fully to experience the power and presence of God in contemporary life.

EDWIN H. TULLER
General Secretary
American Baptist Convention

November 16, 1962

Author's Preface

In revising and enlarging this book, the general outline, much of the previous material, and the original purpose have been preserved. The original was written in the conviction that contemporary Baptist practice reflected confusion and distortion of what had long been central to Baptist identity, particularly with regard to their concept of the church and its implications for polity. There was no intention to offer an arbitrary plan of Baptist organizational patterns which should or could be applied to Baptists everywhere. The aim was rather to recover a biblical understanding of the nature of the church and its visible expression, which was also a central concern of Baptists at their origins.

Thus, the book begins by presenting a concept based on the biblical portrayal of the church as it is in God's purpose and also on early Baptist convictions as to its nature. Some of the organizational patterns are described by which Baptists have sought to give visible form to that vision of the church. They have exercised freedom and flexibility in adapting institutional forms to changing circumstances, but the doctrine of the church furnishes broad guidelines which limit that freedom. A good deal of attention is given throughout to historical developments and ecclesiology in the attempt to keep issues of polity in historical and theological perspective. Some may find such historical and theological discussion too theoretical, preferring a simpler how-to book. I am convinced, however, that the more pragmatic approach is self-defeating in the long run.

Because, in the course of Baptist history, forms of polity have become so diverse, especially at levels above the local church, it is difficult to describe Baptist forms in all their diversity. Therefore a narrower focus must be chosen, and in this case special attention is devoted to the American Baptist Churches in the U.S.A. While basic concepts and principles are pertinent to all Baptists, many of the specific institutional developments are different from those that have been shaped by other Baptists in the United States and elsewhere. Other Baptist groups have found the *Manual* helpful in the past, and it is hoped that it will continue to be useful to bodies other than the ABCUSA.

A considerable debt of gratitude is owed to a great many people who in some way shared in this work of revision. It is impossible to name everyone who had a part in it. Many of the students taught during my years at Eastern Baptist Theological Seminary have contributed criticisms and suggestions that have helped to develop my thinking on the subject matter of the book. More specifically, in the course of the rewriting, many other individuals have contributed to this revised and enlarged work. Regional ministers, national executives, seminary professors, pastors, and laypersons— both men and women—have been among my benefactors, as they have offered reflections out of their practical experience in the churches and in using the earlier edition of this book in seminary and church groups.

Beyond the more general expression of gratitude, there are a number of individuals whom I would be remiss not to thank publicly. In the first place recognition is due to those who urged the publisher to undertake a thorough revision of the *Baptist Manual.* Among the foremost of these was the late Clarence C. Goen, who was instrumental in calling attention of the American Baptist Historical Society to the need for a revised and updated volume. He had great interest in this work and anticipated involvement in producing the new edition, but death deprived us of his capable assistance and continued friendship. Others on the board of the Historical Society, for whom James C. Miller was a spokesman, also

AUTHOR'S PREFACE

helped to impress upon Judson Press the value of this book, and the need for updating it for the benefit of seminarians, new pastors coming into the ABCUSA from other denominations, and study groups in churches. I would also express thanks to my erstwhile collaborator and friend of many years, Winthrop Hudson, who made substantial contributions to the original edition. Although urging that a revision be made and being supportive of the project, he did not feel able to participate in the work of revision.

Thanks are due to those who did the laborious reading of the book, offering their critiques and suggestions, and then read the revised draft and made further comments. Appreciation for such help goes to William K. Cober, Blake E. Edwards, S. Mark Heim, Howard R. Stewart, and George D. Younger. Others who read parts and furnished useful information, ideas, documents, charts, sample constitutions, and/or other items were: William R. Belli, Beverly Carlson, Ralph H. Elliott, Moley G. Familiaran, Richard K. Gladden, Leland Hine, Harley D. Hunt, Parkes R. Johnson, Ralph H. Lightbody, Eric Ohlmann, Malcolm G. Shotwell, and J. Eugene Wright. Without such help the book would have more shortcomings than it does.

Appreciation is also expressed to Kristy Arnesen Pullen and Valerie Gittings, of Judson Press, who initiated this project and have helped to shape the finished product by their editorial scrutiny, and to Susan Casey whose helpfulness as editorial assistant did much to facilitate the process all along the way. I am grateful, too, to Frank T. Hoadley, who as book editor at Judson Press in the 1960s saw the original book through the various stages leading to publication, and who now in retirement has been willing to lend his expertise to do the copy editing again this time. Finally, I wish to acknowledge the help of Daniel E. Weiss, General Secretary of the American Baptist Churches, who lent his support to the project and contributed the Foreword to the new edition of this book as his predecessor, Edwin H. Tuller, did for the original one.

NORMAN H. MARING
Rock Hill, S.C.
January 1991

1

Identifying the Baptists

When the term "polity" is introduced into a discussion, people frequently ask what it means. While not entirely foreign to us, its meaning may be hazy. Therefore, some explanation may assist those who wish to study this subject. Originally used in connection with political theory, it has been applied for a long time to church order.

The Meaning of Polity

In a broad sense, polity is to be understood as organization. It is the way we order our resources to enable the church to be and do what God expects. It involves a pattern of relationships: ways of believing and acting, and ways of marshaling our forces to fulfill God's mission. It answers the question: How can we best accomplish God's purpose for the church?

Many feel that organizational structures conflict with the work of the Holy Spirit, but they need not do so. Organization is essential to the viability of the church and its ministry. God's grace is not bound by human forms; rather, God has condescended to use human instruments to work out the divine purposes. The Christian gospel must be incarnated both in individual lives and in corporate forms.

To develop forms consistent with the church's nature and

mission, we must have a vision of its purpose. Although it is a social institution, it is more than that by virtue of its divine calling and unique purpose. Created by the Holy Spirit, it is a fellowship which exists for the formation of a people who live by faith in God under the lordship of Jesus Christ. Through its message of reconciliation individuals are transformed and drawn into a nurturing community that witnesses to God's redeeming love and concern for justice, righteousness, and peace. The church thus exists as a constant reminder that all human lives are accountable to the sovereign God whose kingdom Jesus came to announce.

The kingdom that Jesus proclaimed, of which the church is an agent, was envisioned as a moral community that would be "the salt of the earth" and "the light of the world" (Matthew 5:13-16). This church would make an impact by proclaiming the kingdom of God and by exhibiting beliefs, values, and lifestyles shaped by the gospel. Cultivating the fruits of the Spirit, its members would manifest integrity in personal ethics and compassionate concern for fellow human beings. Thus the church is to be a continuing sign of God's kingdom, making an appeal to human beings to accept God's rule in faith and obedience. The forms and structures that the church assumes as it incarnates this vision is what polity is all about.

Polity forces us to ask specific questions such as: What is the Good News we are called to proclaim? How do we, in obedience to the Great Commission (Matthew 28:19-20), make disciples? What are the qualifications for discipleship and church membership? How do we admit new members? How can we best nurture those who seek a more mature faith? How can we facilitate the development of a fellowship of worship, witness, and service? What is the significance of an ordained ministry, and how is it related to the ministry of the laity? What other offices are needed, and how should they be chosen? Where is authority for making decisions located? What is our understanding of baptism and the Lord's Supper? How are they to be administered and by whom? How should local churches be related to each other, and what is the purpose of regional and national bodies? How can separate denominations give visible expression to the unity for which Jesus prayed (John 17:20-21)? What is the relationship of the Christian community to the larger society and to civil government? In this book we try to answer these and other questions from a biblical perspective as Baptists have understood them over the centuries.

As Stephen Brachlow makes clear in *The Communion of Saints*, ecclesiology was a major issue leading to the origin of the Baptists. Congregational polity (one centered in the local church membership), they held, best enables the church to fulfill God's intentions for his people. To be sure, Baptists have developed many diverse ways of doing things over nearly four centuries, but they have largely tried to maintain forms consistent with a congregational theory of church order. Problems can arise from a polity that locates authority in all the members of the church. It may be more vulnerable to fragmentation than some others, and it is sometimes less efficient in making decisions and acting of them. On the other hand, it provides a large measure of freedom and flexibility, which allows for adopting new forms to meet changing needs. Particular forms may vary, but basic principles persist. This book, therefore, will describe ways in which Baptist bodies today maintain fundamental concepts while they seek to balance freedom and order by adapting organizational forms to the fulfillment of mission in a changing environment.

Defining Baptist Identity

Who are the Baptists? What are their characteristic beliefs and practices? Scattered around the world, they number over 37,000,000 members in more than 157,000 churches. They are organized in 191 conventions/unions, which vary in size from the Southern Baptists who report almost 16,000,000 to the Australian Seventh Day Baptists with only 150 members in five churches. Baptists are concentrated in the United States, where nine-tenths of them reside, but they are divided into numerous groups based upon ethnic origin, region, language, and doctrine. Even within a single Baptist body there may be wide latitude of practice and doctrine.

Although most Baptist bodies have a common origin, some

groups use the name without having any resemblance to historic Baptists beyond the practice of believers' baptism by immersion. These have no relationship to the larger Baptist family and take no interest in Baptist history and heritage. The fact that they bear a common name, however, seems to imply a shared identity, and that is confusing to non-Baptists who assume that all who call themselves Baptists are related and share the same principles. Even among Baptists who are clearly in a direct line of descent from seventeenth-century beginnings, divergences have multiplied under the influence of varied cultural environments, tending to obscure the common marks which characterized this family of denominations. Even within a single Baptist group, a growing pluralism has produced tensions, as it has among other older denominations, and this condition has led to renewed attempts to recover a sense of identity that counteracts any tendency toward fragmentation. It is necessary to ask what constitutes the core of Baptist life and thought, which ensures an overarching unity greater than our diversity. Adherents of any Christian group need to know who they are, what are their "convictional genes," and what is their purpose and mission.

One such effort was the appointment of a Commission on Denominational Identity by American Baptist Churches in the U.S.A., which explored this question in the period 1984–1987. Out of their labors came *American Baptists: A Unifying Vision, Study Document and Commentary,* and an accompanying Leader's Guide, for use by study groups in churches. In a key statement the Commission declared; "Our identity is bound up with mission as well as memory. It looks to the future as much as to the past." We need to look back to see whence we have come and where we have been, in order to reach a unifying vision for the future. To be confused about one's identity is demoralizing. If a denomination is to maintain its integrity in the midst of changing times, it needs a clear concept of itself. The health and vitality of the Baptist denomination depends upon such clarity.

If self-definition is indispensable, it is also dangerous. In seeking to define ourselves, we may overemphasize our distinctiveness. The search for clearer identity requires that we see ourselves in relation to other Christians. It involves not only an understanding of our points of difference, but also of basic similarities. In the past we have been so preoccupied with defining our differences from other Christians that we have fostered a feeling of estrangement from them. It is a mistake to focus so much attention upon denominational "distinctives" that these obscure the more important elements which unite us as Christians.

Self-Discovery in Ecumenical Encounter

The ecumenical movement which has flowered in recent times has the great virtue of enabling us to experience the oneness of those who are in Christ. Brought face to face with Christians of diverse backgrounds, we learn to know them as kindred spirits who have also experienced the grace of our Lord Jesus Christ. Our eyes are opened to the unity which underlies our varieties of custom and thought. Moreover, we become aware of the need for a united Christian witness to the world. It would be wrong to stifle this sense of Christian unity by accentuating our differences.

The encounter with other Christians in cooperative movements has had a further healthy effect, for it has caused us to reexamine our denominational traditions. Not only are we invited to share a fellowship, but we are challenged to testify to our understanding of God's truth and listen to what others have to say. As a result of honest examination, our distinctive claims are discovered to be fewer and less important than we had supposed. Often we find that many of our apparent differences are more verbal than real.

Points of agreement are important. But, having become aware that our agreements are more significant than our differences, we may be tempted to fall into the opposite error. In our eagerness to stress our common faith, we may brush aside all differences as of no consequence. Although many differences are due to misunderstanding, there are some disagreements that have practical significance for Christian faith and life. Differences of doctrine and practice should be subordinated to the central issue of faith in Jesus Christ as Lord and Savior. It does not follow, however, that all convictions concerning the gospel and the way in which it is communicated and appropriated should be ignored. Denominations need to be faithful and obedient to God, in accord with the understandings to which they have been led.

Only as we are sure of our identity as Baptists can we participate responsibly within the larger church and share effectively in its witness to the world. Being clear about the heritage we share with other Christian communions, we should also understand and appreciate the inheritance we have as Baptists. With a clear conception of the characteristics of Baptist belief and life, we shall be in a better position to know which of those emphases are valid and relevant for today. Out of the integrity produced by greater self-understanding, we can play a more vigorous role within the church and be more articulate in addressing the need of the world.

To share in fellowship through a denomination does not mean to be sectarian. No denomination has the right to claim that it alone is the "true church." It can declare that it has some insight which must not be overlooked, but it should be willing to examine such a claim candidly and submit it to the criticism of others within the Christian community. To recognize the inevitability of different interpretations is realistic. They spring from limitations of ignorance and pride which are inherent within the human situation. So long as denominations can make it clear that their differences from other Christians are in matters of emphasis rather than in essential nature, they serve a legitimate and necessary purpose. They check the pretensions of one another, they keep alive facets of Christian truth which otherwise might be lost, and they remind us of the obligation to be true to the light which God has given to each of us.

Some Typical Ideas About Baptists

What, then, should be rightfully identified as characteristic marks of Baptists? Who are we, and for what do we stand? There is no lack of answers to these questions in books and pamphlets about Baptists, but there is an embarrassing lack of agreement among the interpreters. Although we speak confidently of "the Baptist witness," "our Baptist heritage," or "the people called Baptists," there is some confusion regarding the substance of these terms. Too often statements have been made about our unique character which will not bear close scrutiny. We have sometimes tried to explain ourselves with clichés and shibboleths which cause confusion instead of clarifying issues.

A typical list of Baptist distinctives is apt to include the following points: the Scriptures, or the New Testament, as the supreme authority for faith and practice; the priesthood of believers; freedom of conscience, soul liberty, and the right of private interpretation; congregational polity and the autonomy of the local church; religious liberty and the separation of church and state; believers' baptism by immersion; and a regenerate church membership. Some of them are not so much distinctive of Baptists as they are beliefs of Protestants in general. Others are distortions of some valid Baptist emphases. A few are closely related to the true genius of Baptists.

In view of the fact that there is a large amount of confusion about Baptist identity, it is necessary to restudy our heritage to gain a clear picture of ourselves. For this purpose we shall first examine some of the tenets which Baptists commonly regard as distinctive of themselves, and then we shall review our Baptist beginnings to see how our forebears understood themselves.

Authority of the Scriptures

There are many who believe that the uniqueness of Baptists is to be found in their loyalty to the Scriptures, but all Protestants affirm the Scriptures as their rule of faith and practice. Luther, Calvin, and the other Protestant Reformers vigorously asserted the authority of the Bible. In official doctrinal statements, such as *The Thirty-Nine Articles* of the Church of England and *The Westminster Confession* of the Church of Scotland and other Presbyterian bodies throughout the world, it is made clear that the Bible stands on a level above all creedal formulas and is normative for doctrine and life. Similar comments are applicable to "the priesthood of believers," a doctrine given classic formulation by Martin Luther.

Freedom of Conscience

It is frequently stated that the primary characteristic of Baptists is their love of liberty. "Soul liberty" and "the right of private judgment" are heralded as the special watchwords of the denomination. Although in our tradition there has been a cherished emphasis upon liberty of conscience, this has not always borne the same meaning that some modern interpreters give to it. Initially resting upon their belief in the sovereignty of God over the conscience, rather than upon human dignity and individual rights, early Baptists advocated a responsible freedom which had certain recognized limits. Today this doctrine of liberty is often taken to mean that individuals are free to adopt whatever views they will, without any restraints at all. Many Baptists thus take pride in their lack of agreement, boastfully asserting that where there are two Baptists there are at least three opinions. Early Baptists, however, would have regarded such a concept of freedom as unwarranted license, a view that can lead only to chaos. Thus, though liberty of conscience has been an important strand of Baptist tradition, the meaning of that concept today has been twisted beyond recognition.

Autonomy of the Local Church

For some people, the most prized doctrine of Baptists is "the autonomy of the local church." The notion of absolute independence of a local church, however, was foreign to the thinking of early Baptists. They adopted the congregational principle because they believed it would afford the possibility of fuller obedience to God, who is the only Lord of conscience. Especially in local affairs, such as the admission and exclusion of members and the choosing of a pastor, they needed to be free to seek and follow the will of the Lord. This right to "church power" represented a degree of independence, but it was balanced by a strong sense of *inter*dependence among congregations. Baptists recognized an obligation to maintain a wider fellowship within which they would give assistance, accept counsel, and work toward common ends. Today there is a widespread misconception of the "independent local church" strand of Baptist ideology. In its original form it is essential to the Baptist genius, but the present-day idea of "*absolute* independence" creates misunderstanding and fosters anarchy. It ignores the important values which are grounded in the associational principle.

Religious Liberty

Another characteristic of Baptist thought is the doctrine of religious liberty, along with its corollary: the separation of church and state. This principle grows out of a conviction of the necessity for the church to be free to obey God. Baptists have asserted that such liberty was impeded by the intervention of civil government in religious affairs. Since they presupposed that only Christians could offer true worship to God, and that God alone could effect regeneration by the inner witness of the Spirit, they insisted that the state should not interfere by prescribing religious belief or practice. The church, they said, must be left free to seek and to execute the will of God. Happily, this view is shared by most American Protestants today.

Believers' Baptism

The most important difference between Baptists and other Protestants is widely believed to be the practice of baptism by immersion. Many persons, on being asked about Baptist emphases, would probably mention this as the chief distinctive. Without minimizing the importance of immersion as a form of baptism, it must be said that this is not the *primary* mark of differentiation. Most informed Baptists would protest that the mode of baptism is not the chief distinction of their denomination. Indeed, the earliest Baptists seem to have baptized by pouring water upon the head rather than by immersion. Only a few years after their beginnings did they adopt immersion as the approved method.[1]

Much closer to the heart of Baptist concern is "believers' baptism"—the restriction of baptism to persons who make a personal profession of faith. Both from a theological and a

---

[1] Robert G. Torbet, *A History of the Baptists* (Valley Forge: Judson Press, 1978, 10th printing), pp. 42-43; H.L. McBeth, *The Baptist Heritage* (Nashville: Broadman Press, 1987), pp. 44-47.

practical point of view, this practice is significant. In the first place, Baptists believe that New Testament baptism signifies faith and repentance, and therefore it is to be administered only to those who are old enough to make responsible decisions. At the same time, by confining baptism to persons who have made personal professions of faith, the churches guard the entrance to membership and try to maintain regenerate churches. In so doing, they come close to the original emphasis which called the Baptists into existence.

The Need for More Adequate Definitions

This survey of Baptist self-interpretations makes it clear that more precise and more adequate self-definition is needed. Some current statements have distorted our tradition. Others indicate that the passage of time has blurred our image of ourselves. If we are to recover our authentic tradition, we must once again look at our historical roots. We may ask how the Baptists originated. Against what were they reacting? What were they concerned to protect? What were their chief concerns? A view of ourselves in the perspective of our historical beginnings will afford a vantage point for better understanding who we are as Baptists.

A Look at Baptist Origins

Serious students will recognize that historical investigation is not simply an antiquarian pursuit, although some people see little value in a study of the past. We are living in the present, some people say, and do not need to find out what our ancestors may have done. A knowledge of history, however, can be of great practical importance, and the reconstruction of the situation out of which Baptists emerged can contribute to our self-understanding. Only when we know our beginnings shall we be in a position to find clues to many of the questions pertaining to Baptist tradition and identity. When we have ascertained the historical point at which Baptists came into being, the groups with which they were associated, and the issues on which they separated, we shall be able to see how they viewed their own significance. Not only will we see what they considered to be their distinguishing marks, but we may also learn much about the theology and practices of our early Baptist predecessors.

IDENTIFYING THE BAPTISTS

Some Questionable Theories of Baptist Origins

Historians have sometimes differed in locating these Baptist beginnings, but it seems clear today that our denomination had its origin within English congregationalism. Although there is a widely circulated notion that Baptist churches have had an unbroken succession from the first century, there is no reason to give credence to such a fanciful theory. Historical evidence does not support the idea that a chain of Christian churches with definite Baptist traits has existed apart from the main stream of Christianity. Such an outward succession, even if it existed, would be irrelevant to the Baptist understanding of the church. Even an assertion of spiritual kinship between Baptists and a wide variety of schismatic and heretical groups over the centuries is meaningless. To try to establish special relationships between Baptists and assorted movements in the early centuries necessitates the ignoring of important differences and is bound to be misleading.

Another popular view connects Baptists with the Anabaptists on the continent of Europe, particularly with a Mennonite group in Holland. Although there are some similarities between Baptist and Mennonite doctrines, there are also great points of contrast. In spite of considerable research, no clear evidence has demonstrated that Baptist origins are traceable to a Mennonite source.

It should be acknowledged, however, that Baptists share with Anabaptists in general a vision of the believer's church.[2] The churches commonly called Anabaptist originated in the sixteenth century, but the historical links among the various strands of Anabaptists have been debated of late by their own historians. Nevertheless, there is a spiritual kinship between these pioneers of the Radical Reformation and Baptists. The Anabaptists suffered persecution for their advocacy of believers' baptism and the believers' church, as did Baptists. In the United States, Baptists have joined with descendants of the Anabaptists in conferences devoted to strengthening support for their common acceptance of the concept of the believers' church.

---

[2]McBeth, *The Baptist Heritage,* pp. 52ff.; Torbet, *A History of the Baptists,* pp. 21-29.

Baptist Relationship to Puritanism

There is really no need to look beyond the English scene to account for Baptist origins, for they were a natural outgrowth in the evolution of English Puritanism. If we wish to see Baptist beginnings in their proper setting, we must retrace the rather obvious stages by which they arose out of the Puritan background. At its inception, Puritanism was a reform movement within the Church of England. Having expected a thorough housecleaning in the Church of England when the break with Rome occurred, many were disappointed that Queen Elizabeth chose a middle way between Roman Catholicism and the stricter reforms inspired by Calvin's Geneva. Therefore, the Puritans sought to reform the English church more thoroughly "according to the Word of God," and their program called for the removal of certain practices reminiscent of what they called "popery." Objections were raised to much of the ritual of the Book of Common Prayer and to the wearing of special garb at the Lord's Supper. As the movement developed, its aims were expanded to include a demand that a presbyterial system of church government be substituted for the episcopal polity. The authority of bishops would then be transferred to presbyteries.

Although these Puritans stood for a deepened spiritual life in the churches, they did not reject two critical assumptions that were almost universally held in Europe. First, they expected everyone in a given geographical area to be a member of the parish church. Thus, they had no objection to laws requiring that all infants be baptized. Second, they acknowledged the right of the civil ruler to supervise the life of the church. In their view it was the duty of the state to support and protect the church by wise legislation, by financial support, and by the suppression of heresy. In both of these views the Puritan outlook accorded with that of the Church of England, as well as with those of the Roman Catholics and most Protestants in Europe.

Out of this Puritan wing of the Anglican Church, however, there developed a Congregationalist party which did not accept the idea that everyone automatically belongs to the church. Rejecting the concept of the "parish church" with its mixed multitude of believers and unbelievers, the leaders of this party declared that visible churches ought to be composed of "visible saints." They insisted that churches should admit to membership only those persons who could testify to their own Christian experience. With membership thus restricted, congregations were transformed into "gathered" instead of "parish" congregations. Having covenanted to form a congregation, the members of each church became responsible for governing their own affairs.

In taking this step, however, the early advocates of Congregationalist principles still stopped short of pursuing their basic contention to its logical conclusion. Although they wished to limit church membership to believers, they were reluctant to exclude children completely. Thus, they retained baptism for the children of the church members, and said that the churches are composed of visible saints "and their children." It was expected, of course, that when these children grew up they would be able to testify to God's saving work in their lives. They would then be admitted to the Lord's Table and to full membership. In actuality, however, when the children thus baptized became adults, many of them were unable to testify to any experience of conversion. The presence of such persons who had been baptized, but had been unable to qualify for full membership in the church, was embarrassing. The practice of infant baptism was inconsistent with the idea of a "gathered" church. Dissatisfaction also arose at another point. The Congregationalist party still adhered to the idea that the civil government was responsible for the welfare of the church. Although they claimed the right to withdraw from the Church of England, they hoped for a day when they would enjoy state support as the official faith. It soon became apparent to some, however, that this position was also inconsistent.

Those who advocated a clean break with the Church of England were dubbed Separatists. There were others who held a congregational theory, but were loath to secede from the Church of England. Out of the Separatist group came the Pilgrims who eventually founded the settlement at Plymouth in 1620, whereas the less radical Puritans started the

Massachusetts Bay Colony in 1630. In the New World both groups found opportunity to translate their theories into practice, unhampered by the civil government or the older church.

In the rise of a people with Congregationalist sentiments may be seen a movement which reached the very brink of adopting principles that would have made them Baptists. In the ferment of religious ideas in the seventeenth century, it is not surprising that some persons decided to take the next step. Consistent adherence to the gathered-church principle required the rejection of infant baptism and of the state church concept. When people were ready to take these two steps, the Baptists arrived on the scene.

Origin from English Congregationalism Illustrated

In some cases Baptists emerged from Separatists; in other instances their background was that of nonseparating Congregationalists. In many ways the Baptists continued to resemble Congregationalists. They maintained the idea of the "gathered church," and they emphasized the importance of the local church in governing its own affairs. *At only two important points did the Baptists take a different line: namely, by insisting that believers' baptism was necessary to the gathered-church idea, and by advocating the freedom of churches from the control of civil government.*

The first illustration of the transition from Congregationalist to Baptist principles is found in a Separatist congregation that had fled from England to Amsterdam.[3] When the pastor, John Smyth, concluded that infant baptism was wrong and persuaded the congregation of the correctness of his views, the church was reconstituted upon a basis of believers' baptism. Smyth baptized himself and then baptized

---

[3]It is of interest to observe in passing that the members of this church had been closely associated in England with a Separatist congregation of which John Robinson was the pastor. Both of these groups fled to Holland, where one took a route which led its members to become founders of New England Congregationalism at Plymouth, and the other followed a course which resulted in their becoming Baptists. This connection serves to show how closely connected Baptists and Congregationalists were in this early period.

the others. Smyth also was convinced that a church which is responsible to Christ as its head must have freedom from ecclesiastical and civil interference. This conviction led him to publish one of the earliest defenses of liberty of conscience.

Shortly after Smyth had baptized himself and his congregation, he was criticized by other Separatists-in-exile for his irregular action. If he insisted upon being rebaptized, they declared, he could have applied to local Mennonites who already practiced believers' baptism. Beginning to doubt the propriety of his self-baptism, he began to make overtures to the Mennonites that might have led to a rebaptism and perhaps to union with them. Some members of his congregation, however, saw no reason to question the validity of their baptism by Smyth. When their pastor persisted in his negotiations with the Dutch Mennonites, this group, now led by Thomas Helwys, returned to England. In 1612, they formed the first Baptist church on English soil.

These first Baptists had been affected by current theological discussions about the role of free will in the process of salvation, and they adopted an Arminian position supporting free will, which was anathema to the strictly predestinarian Calvinists. Because these Baptists asserted that the atonement of Christ was sufficient to save all human beings, not just the elect, their adherence to the concept of a general atonement led to their being called General Baptists. Although these General Baptists experienced some growth during the seventeenth century, their movement dwindled after 1700 and never had much influence upon the mainstream of Baptist development. It is important for our purpose to note that these Baptists limited baptism to those who had made a profession of faith and opposed all interference by the civil government. Thus they were differentiated from the Congregationalist party with whom they had been associated.

A second instance of Baptist beginnings, unrelated to that of the Smyth group, came about in 1638. Several people withdrew from a Congregationalist church in London to form a new church on the basis of believers' baptism. The parent church had been Congregationalist in its emphasis upon the concept of a gathered church, but it had shied away from complete separation from the Church of England. Sharing the general theological outlook of the nonseparating Congregationalists, these Baptists were more typical Calvinists than were the General Baptists. Holding the doctrine of a "particular" atonement (Christ having died only for the elect), they were known as Particular Baptists. Living in almost complete isolation from each other, the General and Particular Baptists developed in different ways. It was the latter who eventually represented the main line of Baptist history in England and in America. The principles that these groups had in common, distinguishing them from their fellow dissenters, were the practice of believers' baptism and a specific theory of religious liberty.

The third case of an independent Baptist beginning is of less moment for subsequent Baptist history, but it illustrates again the ease with which Congregationalist views could lead to a Baptist position. In this instance the leading spirit was an American colonist, Roger Williams. Having moved from being a moderate Puritan to a strong Separatist, he denied the right of civil government to interfere in matters of conscience at all. Expelled from the Massachusetts Bay settlement, he established the new colony of Rhode Island, where in 1639 he joined with others to form a church on the basis of believers' baptism. He himself was associated with the Baptist church at Providence for only a few weeks, and the Providence church exercised little influence upon the spread and development of the Baptist cause in America. Once more, however, it may be seen how Baptists emerged logically and naturally out of the Congregationalist setting by refusing to baptize infants and by affirming the freedom of the church from the authority of the state.

Historic Baptist Emphases

Our excursion into Baptist origins should enable us to recognize more clearly both the common heritage that Baptists shared with others and the points that set them apart. From what the early Baptists wrote and did, it is plain that most of them were not sectarians. This fact was notably true of the Particular Baptists. They did not cut themselves off from fellowship with other Christians, nor did they feel that they had an exclusive claim to truth. That they regarded themselves as Protestants is indicated in many statements, and their close kinship with Presbyterians and Congregationalists is reflected in early confessions of faith.

The doctrine of the church is where the Baptists began to diverge from other Protestants. Indeed, a modern Baptist historian has asserted that "the distinctive feature about Baptists is their doctrine of the church."[4] It was not the nature and mission of the church which provided the point of disagreement; rather, Baptists differed with their fellow Protestants concerning the way in which the church finds visible expression and does its work in the world. Even at this point they had much in common with early Congregationalists.

Like the Congregationalists, Baptists believed that the visible churches should approximate the invisible by maintaining a regenerate membership. The Baptists added, however, that such gathered churches are possible only when the door to membership is guarded by baptizing exclusively persons who have made a personal profession of faith. It is this view that regenerate churches can be realized only in conjunction with believers' baptism which distinguished Baptists in the beginning. Like the Congregationalists, the Baptists believed that each local congregation had power from Christ to govern its own affairs, but the Baptists early developed the associational principle to give visible expression to the interdependence of local churches. The other point at which Baptists differed from Congregationalists was in their insistence upon complete separation between spheres of church and state. *In summary, then, we may say that the distinguishing marks of the Baptists, historically speaking, were: a regenerate membership safeguarded by believers' baptism; congregational polity, coupled with an associational principle; and the necessity of freeing the church from interference by the civil government or ecclesiastical officials.*

We began this chapter by asking: Who are the Baptists?

---

[4]W. T. Whitley, *A History of British Baptists* (Philadelphia: J. B. Lippincott, 1923), p. 4.

It is easier to answer the question: Who were the Baptists? It should, however, be of some help to know where we began. Knowing where we started, we may trace the path by which we have traveled; we may see what alterations have been made, either deliberately or unconsciously. We are then in a better position to judge whether or not the changes have been justified.

An understanding of the way in which early Baptists viewed themselves also helps us rid ourselves of false notions about our distinctiveness. As indicated earlier, some Baptists have preempted general Protestant teachings and claimed to make them peculiarly Baptist. This has often led to an exaggerated sense of uniqueness and has contributed to isolation and provincialism. Indeed, when we consider the situation today, the area of disagreement has been narrowed considerably. At the present time, congregational ideas, the concept of regenerate membership, and the ideal of religious liberty have permeated American Christianity. Therefore it is questionable whether there is any value in using the term "distinctive" in these issues, which unduly enhances the idea of differences and encourages too much separateness. There are certain emphases which Baptists have historically championed, and they will do well to continue to witness to the importance of these through their own teaching and practice.

Before we proceed to a further discussion of the Baptist doctrine of the church and to assess its worth for today, it is necessary to devote a chapter to the biblical doctrine of the church. In order to make decisions we need criteria of judgment, and for us the biblical view of the church must be our norm.

2

The New Testament Concept of the Church

The search for a clearer sense of Baptist identity is not ended when we have uncovered our historical antecedents. It is still necessary to ask whether the distinguishing ideas of our forebears are still important. If not, we need not perpetuate them. On the other hand, if they still testify in significant ways to the gospel of Christ, then we must continue to cherish them.

The Need for a Doctrine of the Church

The distinctive character of Baptist life, as we have learned, springs from a particular understanding of the church. The question we must now face is whether that understanding is true, adequate, and significant. Is the historic concept of church polity and practice appropriate for our day?

Biblical and Theological Tests

By what tests of adequacy, then, are we to answer this question? History can show us how Baptists organized to express their faith, but it cannot furnish criteria for judging the adequacy of such views. Nor can practical needs be the chief guide in judging a church polity. When expediency becomes the primary consideration in determining its form and program, the essential character of the church may be obscured. There is also a perpetual risk that the desire to achieve influence as an institution may lead the church to deny its own nature. Therefore, although both history and practical considerations should be taken into account, the ultimate standard must be theological. In other words, all church order must grow out of an understanding of the nature and mission of the church, and should be so designed as to fulfill God's purpose for it. Moreover, such an understanding of the church can only be derived in any ultimate sense from the Scriptures which testify to God's intention in Christ.

Thus, our question about Baptist identity leads to the biblical doctrine of the church. Having begun by asking who the Baptists are, we must now come to a prior question, namely: What is the New Testament concept of the church? Before we can proceed far in the discussion of polity and practice, we must have some answer to this prior question. Out of our concept of the church will come deductions as to matters of practice. Our next step, then, is to inquire about the church as it is depicted in the Scriptures. We shall then be in a better position to examine traditional Baptist ideas to see whether they are in accord with this biblical portrayal.

A High View of the Church

The doctrine of the church is a matter of vital importance. After years of neglect, Baptists as well as other Protestants have been rediscovering how crucial is the place of the church in God's redemptive purpose. Unawareness of the divine dimensions of the church has often led us to treat it as an institution which could be explained in sociological terms alone. An inadequate concept of the church encourages members to be careless about their responsibilities, to attend its services only when convenient, and to give leftovers of money and energies.

When a low view of the church is held by those within its ranks, it is natural that the world should have a similar estimate of its worth. Although the little volume by C. S. Lewis, *The Screwtape Letters*, is fantasy, there is truth in

Satan's message to his emissary, Wormwood. Having chided his underling for allowing his human charge to become converted, Satan then consoled him with the hope that the man might return when he found out what churches are like: "One of our great allies at present is the Church itself. Do not misunderstand me. I do not mean the Church as we see her spread out through all time and space and rooted in eternity, terrible as an army with banners. That, I confess, is a spectacle which makes our boldest tempters uneasy."[1] There can be no doubt that we often treat the church as though it were of second-rate importance. The weakened impact of the church upon the world today is partially due to the fact that Christians have had an inadequate understanding of its role. Therefore, it is a hopeful sign that we are coming to accept the high view which the New Testament has of the church of Christ.

The Biblical Doctrine of the Church

To recover the biblical teaching about the church is not as easy as it might seem. The fact that in our usage we assign several meanings to the same word "church" enhances the difficulty of defining it. When we speak of "the church on the corner," we are likely to mean a building. Again, the word may be used to refer to a worship service, when one remarks, "I am staying for church today." We speak of the Episcopal Church or the Presbyterian Church, and thereby we designate a denomination. At other times, our conversation may include some mention of "our church," and thus we signify a local congregation. The same term is employed to speak of the universal church of the past and present, the totality of believers. It is little wonder that there is confusion about the word "church."

What then does "church" mean? What is its meaning in the New Testament? When we turn to find an answer to this question, we are faced with a number of secondary problems. Did Jesus found the church? When was the church founded—when Jesus chose the Twelve? at the Last Supper?

---

[1] C. S. Lewis, *The Screwtape Letters* (New York: The Macmillan Company, 1943), p. 15.

at Pentecost? Did the church exist prior to the incarnation? What is the connection between the Israel of the Old Testament and the church of the New Testament? Is the kingdom of God preached by Jesus the same as the church? What is the relationship between the church and the churches? Is the local church primary, and the concept of a universal church an abstraction, derived from adding together all of the local congregations? Or is the universal church primary, and each local congregation an expression of it? All of these subsidiary questions are involved in the discussion of the church.

If we expect to find in the New Testament a concise passage describing the nature of the church, we will be disappointed. At first, there was no one standardized term by which the Christian community was designated. It was referred to by equivalent terms, such as brethren, the way, assembly, family, household, people, body, etc. It was not until later that the term *ecclesia* (meaning, in its broad sense, a "calling out" or "assembly," and translated "church" in the English versions of the Bible) came to be accepted as the standard term. There is no special reason why a word meaning "people" or "household" could not have been adopted instead. Certainly such words occur frequently in the New Testament. It is necessary for us to get behind these varied terms and to uncover their common underlying assumptions if we are to arrive at a clear understanding of the nature and purpose of the church.

In the following discussion, we shall approach our question from three directions. First, we shall look at the message of Jesus to see its implications for the church. Second, the letter to the Ephesians will be summarized to get a Pauline view of the church. Third, the relationship between the church and the "people of God" of the Old Testament will be noted.

Jesus and the Church

Since there were various terms in the Greek language for the reality we now call the church, it is not surprising that only one of the four Gospels uses the specific word *ecclesia*. It is mentioned only in Matthew 16:18 and 18:17, and in the second of these places it seems to be referring to the synagogue. The fact that Jesus seldom employed the term has led some interpreters to infer that he had no intention of establishing the church. Some New Testament scholars have declared the church was a later invention of Jesus' disciples. This interpretation, however, is to mistake a word for the reality. It is now clear to biblical scholars that he expected to establish a people who should bear his name and continue his work.

The terms that Jesus used expressed his expectation that a community of disciples would succeed him, and the major part of his ministry was directed to the preparation of a company of disciples who would continue his mission. Two synonymous phrases, "the kingdom of God" and "the kingdom of heaven," implied the creation of a community or fellowship. The emphasis in these terms is not so much upon a temporal kingdom as upon human relationship to the sovereign rule of God. To proclaim the kingdom was to bid humans to accept God's rule, to enter God's fellowship, to receive God's saving power, and to yield their lives in obedient service. The sovereign God announced by Jesus was a loving parent who invited lost men and women to accept forgiveness and become reconciled to the family as children of God. Thus the kingdom announced by Jesus was a new set of relationships, vertical and horizontal. It was a community uniting humanity with God and with one another, which was being proclaimed by Jesus Christ and created through the power of the Holy Spirit. Inaugurated by the messianic ministry of Jesus, the kingdom was present then, but not in its fullness. It had a future aspect—beyond history—when the kingdom would be consummated.

What Jesus did was to establish a community of persons who were united by their loyalty to him and by the indwelling of God's power. Other terms that he employed pointed to the same close-knit fellowship as when he referred to his followers as "little flock" (Luke 12:32), "my mother and my brothers" (Luke 8:21), or "the branches" (John 15:5). The creation of this community was a primary object of his earthly ministry. It appears that he gave surprisingly little attention to institutional forms. He left no written instructions; he developed no elaborate system of ritual. What he left was a fellowship of those who had been convinced that Jesus was the long-awaited Messiah in whom God was uniquely manifested to human beings once for all.

The purpose of this community was to carry on the ministry that Jesus had begun. To his disciples Jesus stated their mission in these words: "As the Father has sent me, so I send you" (John 20:21). In the closing verses of Matthew is given the Great Commission: "Go therefore and make disciples of all nations, baptizing them in the name of the Father and of the Son and of the Holy Spirit, and teaching them to obey everything that I have commanded you. And remember, I am with you always, to the end of the age" (Matt. 28:19-20). The phrase "the extension of the incarnation" is sometimes used to describe the mission of the church, but it makes too close an identification between Christ and the church. The gospel needs to be incarnated in us, but we must beware of any figure that might convey the idea that the church in its sinfulness is one and the same with Jesus Christ, its head. It is better to express the work of the church by saying that it is intended to carry on the ministry of Christ in preaching, teaching, and serving.

The Church in Paul's Letter to the Ephesians

The clearest exposition of the nature and purpose of the church is Paul's letter to the Ephesians. Against the background of a world deeply involved in evil, the writer portrays the church as a body which has a redemptive mission. A summary of the Ephesian letter will help to bring the New Testament doctrine of the church into focus.

"Blessed be . . . God," begins the author, ". . . he has made known to us . . . the mystery of his will, according to his good pleasure that he set forth in Christ" (Eph. 1:3,9). That eternal purpose, hitherto a secret, has now been revealed—namely, that God intends to "gather up all things in [Christ]" (1:10). In the life, death, resurrection, and exaltation of Jesus Christ, God has invaded human history and in principle has defeated the power of sin and death. Having completed the mighty acts of redemption in Jesus Christ, God now continues to work in this divided, sin-sick world by the Spirit, through the church which is "his body" (1:23).

Indeed, the writer of the letter asserts, the process of uniting all things has already begun with the reconciliation of Jew and Gentile. By the same power with which God raised Christ from the dead, he has also made these two elements of the population alive with Christ (2:1). He has "broken down the dividing wall, that is, the hostility between us" (2:14). In order to "create in himself one new humanity in place of the two" (2:15), God has reconciled Jew and Gentile. Thus the church has been called into being.

The "therefore" of Ephesians 4:1 reminds the readers again that they have been chosen by God, made alive with Christ, set apart to "live for the praise of his glory" (1:12), and to make known "the wisdom of God in its rich variety" to all the universe (3:10). "I therefore," appeals Paul, "... beg you to lead a life worthy of the calling to which you have been called" (4:1). In effect, he is urging the church to be the church! He wants the people of God to be clear about their identity and their mission, to know what God has called them to be and to do. God's call to the church is a call to unity and holiness, so that its life will be a persuasive witness to the world.

The rest of the letter deals with some specific ways in which the church can fulfill the vocation to which God has called it. The ministry belongs to the entire church and not just to a special ministerial class. To every person God grants gifts for use in the community. Some special gifts, to be sure, have been bestowed for leadership in the church, but this leadership is provided "to equip the saints for the work of ministry, for building up the body of Christ" (4:11-12). Led and informed by those who are endowed with special gifts and appointed to offices in the church, the whole body is to grow up "until all of us come to the unity of the faith and of the knowledge of the Son of God, to maturity, to the measure of the full stature of Christ" (4:13).

Furthermore, the instructions of the last three chapters of Ephesians indicate that our ministry as members of Christ's body, the church, involves a many-sided witness. Love is to be expressed in all of our human relationships. Personal integrity is demanded ("putting away falsehood," "give up stealing," etc.). Relationships in the home (husband-wife, parent-child) and at work (servant-master) are to be brought under the lordship of Christ. The church witnesses not only by what it says, but by what it is. Through the depth of its fellowship, the Christian community is to make clear the power of God which makes for unity: "making every effort to maintain the unity of the Spirit in the bond of peace" (4:3).

Thus God works in and through the church, which is the body of Christ. As the relationships and quality of life within the Christian community express love, unity, and dedication, the Holy Spirit uses the church to fulfill God's purpose to unite all things in Christ. The practical implications of this letter are many, and call for a church different from much of the institutional life that characterizes the churches today.

The Church as the Israel of God

The letter that the apostle Paul wrote to the Ephesians makes explicit a concept of the church that is implicit throughout the Bible. It is important, therefore, to see this idea as it appears within the context of the whole biblical record. Throughout the Old and New Testaments run certain motifs that give unity to the record, and these furnish a framework in which the church must be understood. The first of these primary themes is that of God as Creator; another is that of humankind whom Pascal called "the glory and the scandal of the universe." Made in the divine image and endowed with freedom and responsibility, men and women have persistently misused that freedom in revolt against the will of their Maker. To the concept of God as Creator, then, is added that of Redeemer, seeking to win people to acknowledge divine sovereignty and to find their fulfillment in God. Thus begin the parallel strands of the biblical narrative: human sinners unwilling to accept their status as creatures, and God as the Redeemer whose mercy is everlasting.

The story of God's purpose to redeem humanity from alienation and bondage to sin is connected in the Old Testament with a particular people. The history of Israel (the corporate name given to the people chosen for this special mission) became the history of God's redemptive work. Speaking to them through mighty acts, God welded them into a nation conscious of being called for a divine mission. To this covenant people, God spoke repeatedly in judgment and mercy, in warning and promise.

In the New Testament the story of God's redemptive purpose continues, centering in the person of Jesus the Messiah, who called to himself a people in whom God's purpose would be realized. Thus, Israel was reconstituted; the church of Jesus Christ became the new Israel of God, the people of the new covenant. That re-creation of Israel in the church was taking place when Jesus called the Twelve, reminiscent of the twelve tribes of Israel, and when he instituted the Lord's Supper, which signified the new covenant ratified by his blood. However, it was only after the crucifixion, resurrection, and exaltation that the messianic work was completed and a new power was released. Then came Pentecost, when, in the fullest sense, the Israel of God was reestablished in the form of the Christian church.

That the church considered itself the heir of Israel's vocation as God's chosen people is attested in many passages. In the letter to the Galatians, for example, Paul spoke of the church as "the Israel of God" (Galatians 6:16). In the same epistle he wrote: "Those who believe are the descendants of Abraham" (3:7). To the Romans he said: "Not all Israelites truly belong to Israel . . . but the children of the promise are counted as descendants" (Romans 9:6,8). The same idea is addressed to Christians in 1 Peter: "But you are a chosen race, a royal priesthood, a holy nation, God's own people, that you may declare the wonderful deeds of him who called you" (1 Peter 2:9). Here in unmistakable language it may be seen that the early church regarded itself as closely identified with the old Israel and the inheritor of its promises and responsibilities.

Against the background of this holy history, the features of the church stand out in clearer outline, and the relationship of the church to the total purpose of God is thrown into sharp relief. The church is then seen to be no afterthought of the apostles, no mere interim makeshift to fill a stopgap in the present age. It is the nucleus of the kingdom of God, the realm of redemption, the agency in and through which God accomplishes his purpose for the world.

Although this connection between the old and the new Israel needs to be stressed, we should not forget that there is more than simple continuity here. There are differences as well as resemblances. What had been a vaguely defined hope was now fulfilled. Instead of peering with hopeful eyes into a dim future, the new Israel could look back to recall what God had done in Christ. Under the New Covenant, the establishment of the people of God no longer was based upon birthright, but upon personal response. There was a new emphasis upon inwardness and depth in the requirements of those who became the disciples of Jesus Christ.

The Nature of the Church

Several conclusions may be drawn from this discussion of the church. In the first place, the church is *a people*. Early Baptists sought to remind themselves of this fact by calling the places in which they met "meeting houses." The word "church" was reserved to apply to men and women in the divine-human fellowship. Our varied use of the term "church," however, makes us lose sight of this fact and makes it apply to something impersonal. An experience with an overseas student in a seminary provides a forceful illustration of this tendency. Having become acquainted with a certain congregation, he asked the pastor if he could get a picture of the church to take home with him. The minister said that he would take care of it later. After the service, when the congregation had dispersed, the pastor said that now they could take a picture of the church. "But," protested the student, "how can we take a picture of the church? The people have gone home!"

Second, not only is the church people, but it is the *people of God*. The phrase "people of God" is synonymous with "the church of God" or "assembly of God." Indeed wherever the word "church" is used in the New Testament, the words "of God" are implied when they are not expressed. The church is not simply a voluntary association of good people who have banded themselves together to help God. Although their human response to God's gracious offer is not to be denied, the divine initiative is of first importance. It is God who has *called* the church into being.

The third point to be drawn from the discussion is that the church is to be seen as *a close-knit fellowship,* not simply as a collection of loosely related individuals. Indeed, one of the most impressive terms by which the inner meaning of the church is expressed in the New Testament is "fellowship" *(koinonia).* Fellowship is not simply something which the church sometimes enjoys; the church *is* a fellowship. Emil Brunner emphasized that fact by saying that the church is "nothing other than a fellowship of persons."[2] In our common usage, the word "fellowship" has been debased, so that it means the good times we enjoy when there is a church supper or gathering for recreation. In the New Testament, however, "fellowship" signifies participation in the divine life and power, a life which is characterized by sharing. Beginning with the sharing which we experience in the salvation of God, it goes on to include sharing the good news with others and even sharing one's property. The church then *is* a fellowship, or community, a participation in the life of the Spirit.

Another way of reiterating this idea is to insist that the church is not simply a means to an end, not a crutch to assist individual growth. To consider the church in that way is the same as to say that the family exists only in order to assist the development of individuals. The relationships that make up family life are important in themselves. The individual self becomes a real person in relationship with others, and selfhood is intricately involved in a complex network of interrelationships. Likewise, the individual Christian cannot rightly be severed from the context of the Christian community. The individual is important, of course, and the fellowship is important, but they are inextricably intertwined. It is a mistake to try to separate them and to make one simply an instrument for the development of the other.

In the fourth place, the church acknowledges Jesus Christ as Lord. He is "the head of the church," wrote Paul (Eph.

---

[2]Emil Brunner, *The Misunderstanding of the Church* (Philadelphia: Westminster Press, 1953), p. 10.

5:23), identifying the church itself as Christ's body. The heart of the apostolic preaching centers upon Jesus as God's promised Messiah whose life, teachings, death, resurrection, and exaltation have ultimate significance for human redemption. Not only do his remembered teachings furnish guidance for the life of the church, but the Holy Spirit makes Christ present as its living Lord. His will supersedes all human claims.

The Mission of the Church

Further, this close-knit community gathered by God is called to be *a servant people.* If it becomes so preoccupied with analyzing its own nature and conducting its internal affairs that it forgets its mission to the world, it ceases to be the church. As the body of Christ, the church is the sphere in which God's Spirit operates in a special way; through this body, God's presence and power are communicated. The Christian community represents the demonstration project in this world of what can be done through God's power. It is the spearhead of God's reconciling movement. Here is the place where God is creating that "one new humanity" out of discordant elements, a community in which the barriers that separate people are removed. By what it *does,* what it *says,* and what it *is* the church proclaims the grace of God which makes men and women alive and incorporates them into the new society. It is thus a people called to worship, witness, teach, and serve in the name of Christ and to be a sign of God's kingdom.

Worship, first of all, is an indispensable part of the life of the church. Called "to live for the praise of his glory" (Eph. 1:12), the church is bidden to sing "psalms and hymns and spiritual songs . . . making melody to the Lord with all your heart" (5:19). Although ritual may easily drift into mere formalism, yet the use of such rites serves an important purpose in keeping the church in vital touch with Christ. As branches must remain in connection with the vine, so must the Christian fellowship keep closely related with the source of its life. Unless there is constant renewal of the sense of God's presence and power, there will be no spiritual resources for ministering to the world. The church must continually offer itself in gratitude to God, and from God it must receive renewal of faith and power, if it is to be the bearer of revelation and a redemptive fellowship.

Second, the church is also called to be *a witnessing community.* Its responsibility for evangelism is so clear that there should be no need to remind Christians of it. The fact that God makes use of the church in the process of redemption indicates that the words "church" and "evangelism" are inseparably connected. The entire church is included in the commission to witness to the world, although not everyone shares in the same way in this ministry of reconciliation.

Unfortunately, for many people the word "evangelism" is associated with sensational methods and an atmosphere charged with emotion. Evangelism means essentially the outreach of the church to persuade men and women to acknowledge Jesus Christ as Savior and to obey him as Lord in the totality of their lives. In this sense, missions and evangelism have the same meaning. They are not to be identified with particular methods of winning persons to Christ, for methods vary with time and place. The point that needs to be emphasized is that evangelistic witness is integral to the life of the church. We must seek the most effective means of communicating with a world which is being attracted by secularism, nationalism, and materialism. For this kind of witness we must learn how to live as Christians in the common life of our workaday world, in the home, in the community, in the sphere of the intellect, and in our churches. Whatever the method or the occasion, the church is called to be a witnessing fellowship.

In the third place, the church is called to be *a ministering community.* Actually, no clear lines can be drawn between the church's witness and its service. By our concern for others and our ministry to their need, we witness to the love of God and seek to point people to Christ. For purposes of analysis we may distinguish between evangelism and service, but in reality we witness by what we are and what we do as well as by what we say.

To call Christ Lord is to accept his claims upon our lives and to acknowledge that we are his servants. In the New Testament the servant role of the church is emphasized by the figure of stewardship. The image of a steward stresses that we are not our own, but are God's. We are dependent upon God for our very lives, and our abilities and possessions are entrusted to us for temporary use. To accept the lordship of Christ over the church is to imply that all of life is to be lived under the direction of the One who is its head. Somehow, then, the church must learn to live responsibly with regard to the world and its needs; it cannot bypass social issues of our times as the Levite ignored the suffering man on the road to Jericho. Christ has bidden his disciples not only to love God, but to manifest that love by a sense of responsible concern towards those whom he has given to be our neighbors, whether the neighbor next door or the one on the other side of the world.

Finally, *the church must teach* if it is to live. Failure to teach produces weak churches which can hardly be distinguished from the world. Only as the Christian community understands its nature and mission can it maintain its identity. Its values, its ideals, and the power of God must therefore be transmitted to each generation, not just as a set of ideas, but as attitudes and loyalties essential for carrying out its role.

To be faithful in its teaching, the church has to take a serious interest in theology. If Christianity were simply a matter of emotions, we could dispense with the attempt to develop a fairly consistent theological rationale. But a firm faith requires the total commitment of the whole person, where heart and mind are in accord. Theology is the backbone of religion; it steadies and stiffens it. Without it, Christianity grows flabby and sentimental, and finally becomes laden with superstition.

Therefore, the church must accept responsibility to teach its members. It must formulate its own convictions in order to instruct the children and youth committed to its care. It must enable members to develop criteria for making ethical judgments, for one cannot act consistently over a period of time without guiding principles by which to make decisions. Also the church has an obligation to prepare its members to make an articulate Christian witness in their roles as citizens, workers, and members of families. Some members need more intensive instruction than others, for they are called to share in the actual work of teaching in the church school and other educational agencies. To some extent, however, all who belong to the church share in the responsibility of the church as a teaching community.

Conclusion

Biblically oriented and biblically grounded as they were, the early Baptists were in general accord with the New Testament understanding of the church. In the following chapter, we shall look at the way in which Baptists tried to develop a polity that would give outward form suitable to the inner being of the church. We shall then be better able to understand and to evaluate the validity and relevance of the Baptist witness.

3

The Church and the Churches

From the biblical view of the church, we turn our attention to specifically Baptist thought on this subject. Is Baptist ecclesiology in harmony with biblical teaching about the church? Do our formulations of doctrine parallel the vision of the church as seen in the light of God's intentions for it? Does our polity and practice faithfully express this concept of the church in visible forms? Such questions are crucial, since the historic emphases of Baptists revolve around them.

Tensions Between the Church and the Churches

By this time the reader will have asked, "What is the relationship between the church as depicted in the previous chapter and the actual churches with which we are acquainted? How is the *church* related to the *churches?*"

The church, as God intends it to be, is one and universal. In one of our favorite hymns we acknowledge this oneness as we sing:

Elect from every nation, yet one o'er all the earth;
Her charter of salvation, one Lord, one faith, one birth.

Actually, there is nothing more apparent than the fact that outwardly we are not one, but many. Herein is the first of three embarrassing contrasts. Instead of one catholic, or universal, church, we see a multitude of local congregations and denominations. Sometimes these are independent and unrelated to each other; sometimes they are connected along national, linguistic, class, racial, or confessional lines. Denominations and congregations compete with each other; and, within particular churches, factions strive for preeminence. On the surface it is difficult to recognize either the unity or the catholicity of the church.

Equally obvious is the contrast between the membership of the true church of Jesus Christ and the membership of the churches with which we are familiar. Surely, the church—as God knows it—is made up only of those who have been captivated by his Spirit. Yet within the membership of our churches are people who readily acknowledge that they are not committed Christians. Even those who are most dedicated show many marks of human sinfulness. Frequently our churches give the impression that they think of themselves as religious clubs, with overtones of a fraternal order or civic organization. Meeting with congenial people of their own kind, the members often reflect the social cleavages of the surrounding society instead of transcending such barriers.

A third contrast is found in the source of power. The church as a community derives its power from the Holy Spirit, whereas our churches often have depended upon institutional structures of power. In our eagerness to promote the work of the church we devise methods which frequently obscure the leading of the Spirit. Forgetful of our calling, we allow buildings, budgets, and programs to become ends in themselves.

One can sympathize with Dr. J. H. Oldham, when he remarks: "Christianity has no meaning for me whatsoever apart from the church, but I sometimes feel as though the church as it actually exists is the source of all my doubts and difficulties."[1] Although it is easy to bring such an indict-

---

[1] J. H. Oldham, *Life Is Commitment* (New York: Association Press, 1959), p. 70.

ment, we must remember that God works in and through the churches despite all the inevitable weaknesses of human material.

These contrasts all point to the need for a definition of the relationship between the church as it is in God's purpose and the actual churches in which wheat and tares are mingled. This question is what has been called "the unsolved problem of the Reformation." How are the many separate churches related to the one church? How can earthly churches with defects and imperfections be the church which is the instrument of God's purpose? We cannot treat the church and the churches as though they are completely identical, for the contrasts are too great. On the other hand, it is not possible to separate them completely, for then we rob the institutional churches of all significance. To state this question in a pointed and practical way, we may ask, "How can the church of Jesus Christ be expressed in such a way as to manifest its unity, catholicity, and holiness?" All Protestants including the Baptists have addressed themselves to this question, and *it is in their answer to it that Baptists have made their primary contribution.*

Like the other leading reformers, John Calvin faced this difficulty. Appealing to the distinction between the "visible church" and the "invisible church," he worked out an answer to the relationship between the two. Since the latter is made up only of the elect, and God alone knows who they are, Calvin concluded that we have no way of knowing who its members are. Inasmuch, then, as the boundaries of the true church are invisible to us, he held that there is little point in trying to draw those boundaries by a precise definition of membership. In his understanding, there is no reason, therefore, why everyone should not be required to belong to the outward churches. In that way everyone would be exposed to the means of grace, including the discipline of the church. Such a line of argument led to the continuation of the parish-type church, in which everyone within a given geographical area was included in its membership. Everyone was enrolled by baptism as an infant. With a somewhat similar rationale, all the major Reformation churches justified their practice of infant baptism. Baptists have traditionally rejected this viewpoint.

Although such terms as "visible" and "invisible" may have some convenience in discussing the church, they are misleading. They seem to suggest that the church has no visible existence on earth. This concept is not true, however, for in the church are real people who are "knit together in love through faith," and they share a common life. Their life in fellowship is created and sustained by the presence and power of the Holy Spirit. As a company of those who have been forgiven and who also forgive and forbear others, and as a fellowship in which Christ lives and works, they are a redemptive community where the grace of God is mediated to sinful people. It is merely the *limits* of the church that are considered as "invisible."

The Baptist Doctrine of the Church

The most distinctive emphasis of the early Baptists was their threefold solution to the problem of the relationship of the church to the churches:

1. They believed that the latter should reproduce, as nearly as possible in this imperfect world, the life of faith, obedience, and fellowship which characterizes the former. To this end, they rejected infant baptism, insisting upon believers' baptism.

2. Holding firmly to the primacy of the universal church, they also insisted that each individual church represented the larger church in its locality, and had all necessary powers of self-government.

3. At the same time, they devised ways to express the interdependence of local churches, so that the tendency to an isolated self-sufficiency would be avoided. Around these three points the Baptist doctrine of the church revolved.

Regenerate Membership and Believers' Baptism

Basic to all of their thought was a stress upon a regenerate church membership. They did not presume to play the role of God, realizing that God alone knows with exactitude who are Christians and who are not. They did believe, however, that an approximate judgment could be made regarding those who belonged in a Christian fellowship. At least they were confident that no one who could not relate a convincing profession of faith should be admitted to the visible churches. In this respect they were at one with congregational theory, but Congregationalists retreated from the full logic of their position by including the children of regenerate believers within the membership of a church. It was on this basis that Congregationalists retained the practice of infant baptism. Baptists, however, rejected this practice as inconsistent with the conviction that visible churches should strive to approximate the invisible church in the quality of its life. Nothing less than individual conversion would do as a qualification for membership; and baptism, they insisted, should therefore be restricted to those who "by a judgment of charity" were believed to be regenerate. As a guard against subsequent defection, moreover, a continuing discipline was to be exercised within the churches.

These Baptists were not perfectionists. They did not pretend that the boundaries of the visible churches correspond exactly with the invisible boundaries of the true church. Errors of judgment were not uncommon. Nor did they pretend that even the saints were free from human sinfulness. They were quite aware that imperfection taints everything human, even when the greatest care is exercised. "The purest churches under heaven," they said, "are subject to mixture and error."[2] What they did attempt to do was to restrict the membership to committed Christians, to those who made an open profession of faith in Jesus Christ as Lord and Savior. This was what they understood when they sought to achieve a regenerate church membership—not a sinless community, but a committed community.

The Associational Principle

Besides the regenerate church membership, there is another main strand of the Baptist doctrine of the church. This is the attempt to magnify the importance of the local church without losing sight of the primacy of the universal church. The Presbyterian wing of Puritan dissent had emphasized

---

[2]The Assembly or Second London Confession of Faith. W. L. Lumpkin, *Baptist Confessions of Faith* (Valley Forge: Judson Press, 1959), p. 285.

the universal church to the neglect of the particular churches, while the Congregationalist party in New England had so stressed the place of local churches that they tended to obscure the view of the universal church.

The General Baptists

For the most part, it appears, agreement prevailed among General and Particular Baptists on these major issues regarding the doctrine of the church. In reading the confessions of faith put forth by the early Baptists, one will be impressed by their clear convictions on these matters. It is instructive to read the following excerpt from "The Orthodox Creed" published by the General Baptists in 1678:

> There is one holy, catholic church, consisting of, or made up of the whole number of the elect that have been, are, or shall be gathered, in one body under Christ, the only head thereof. . . .
>
> Nevertheless, we believe the visible church of Christ on earth is made up of several distinct congregations, which make up that one catholic church, or mystical body of Christ. And the marks by which she is known to be the true spouse of Christ, are these, viz. Where the word of God is rightly preached and the sacraments truly administered, according to Christ's institution, and the practice of the primitive church; having discipline and government duly executed, by ministers or pastors of God's appointing, and the church's election, that is a true constituted church; to which church, and not elsewhere, all persons that seek for eternal life should gladly join themselves. And altho' there may be many errors in such a visible church, or congregations, they being not infallible, yet those errors being not fundamental, and the church in the major, or governing part, being not guilty, she is not thereby unchurched; nevertheless she ought to detect those errors, and to reform, according to God's holy word, and from such visible church, or congregations, no man ought, by any pretence whatever, schismatically to separate.[3]

---

[3]*Ibid.*, pp. 318–319.

From the foregoing quotation it can be seen that these General Baptists stressed the importance of the local church, while maintaining a proper appreciation of the universal church. The particular congregation was a focal point of the life of the church; it represented the church in a particular place. They were convinced that the fellowship of the Spirit is apt to be experienced most deeply in the smaller close-knit group. In the face-to-face relationships of the particular congregation, they saw a possibility of developing a corporate life where the Spirit can work more freely than in looser associations of people. Because the opportunity for members to know one another intimately is of such importance to the life of the church, an early confession states: "And therefore a church ought not to consist of such a multitude as cannot have particular knowledge one of another."[4]

To give visible expression to the universal character of the church, the General Baptists formed associational bodies in which delegates of the churches could meet. They also considered such a representative assembly to be a church: "Churches appearing there by their representatives, make but one church, and have lawful right and suffrage in this general meeting, or assembly, to act in the name of Christ."[5] Thus the power of the local congregation to act as a church is balanced by a recognition of the interdependence of the churches and of the right of assembled delegates of several churches to act as a church in the name of Christ.

The Particular Baptists

In spite of the fact that the General Baptists and Particular Baptists differed in some matters of theology and practice, their basic doctrine of the church was practically identical. A reading of the confessional statements of the Particular Baptists reveals the same concern to preserve a judicious balance between the universal church and the local churches. Certain powers inhered in the local body, and these were jealously protected from encroachment by larger associations, but each congregation was to act responsibly in its relationships with others. As it was put in the earliest of

---
[4]*Ibid.,* p. 121.
[5]*Ibid.,* p. 327.

the Particular Baptist confessions of faith in 1644: "Although the particular congregations be distinct and several bodies, every one a compact and knit city in itself, yet are they all to walk by one and the same rule, and by all means convenient to have the counsel and help one of another in all needful affairs of the church, as members of one body in the common faith under Christ their only head."[6]

A similar point of view is echoed in the confession of faith generally accepted by the majority of the Particular Baptist churches in England and in America. Known as the London Baptist Confession in England, it was called the Philadelphia Baptist Confession in America. Of great interest is the fact that the Baptists were so desirous of showing their affinity with other Dissenters that they adopted the Westminster Confession of Faith as a basis for their own statement. Quoting the Westminster Confession verbatim, page after page, they made significant modifications only in the articles which dealt with the church, the ministry, baptism, and the relationship of the state to the church. Not only does this document help us to see the close relationship which existed between Baptists and other Protestants, but it shows again the points at which they were conscious of their differences. The divergencies are centered in believers' baptism and church polity.

This confessional statement affirms a belief in the "catholic or universal church." With respect to the internal work of the Spirit, the Philadelphia Baptist Confession states that the church may be called invisible. It becomes visible to us, however, to the extent that it is made up of visible saints gathered in individual congregations. "To each of these churches thus gathered," it continues, Christ has given "all that power and authority which is in any way needful, for their carrying on that order in worship and discipline which he hath instituted for them to observe."[7] While each church has power to order its own affairs, it is not to live in isolation: "The churches . . . ought to hold communion amongst themselves for their peace, increase of love, and mutual edifica-

---

[6] *Ibid.*, pp. 168-169.
[7] *Ibid.*, pp. 286-287.

THE CHURCH AND THE CHURCHES

tion. In cases of difficulties or differences, either in point of doctrine or administration . . . it is according to the mind of Christ that many churches, holding communion together, do by their messengers meet to consider, and give their advice in or about that matter in difference, to be reported to all the churches concerned."[8] The associated churches, to be sure, could not "impose their determinations on the churches," for the assembly of delegates did not have "church power." Nevertheless, a church was expected to heed the advice of the association or else be subject to exclusion from its fellowship.

The doctrinal statements of both General and Particular Baptists sum up the Baptist solution to the problem of the church and the churches. By requiring a public profession of faith and repentance prior to baptism and reception into the fellowship of a church, they sought to make the visible churches approximate the membership of the invisible communion of saints. In reply to the question of where the church may be seen here on earth, they said that it becomes most visible in a local congregation of professed believers. Each individual congregation was considered as a local expression, or outcropping, of the universal church, and each had power to govern its own affairs in consultation with others under the leadership of Christ its head.

In asserting that the church becomes most visible in local congregations, Baptists did not deny that it is also visible in larger bodies. The General Baptists specifically affirmed that the assembly of representatives of local churches should also be regarded as a church. The Particular Baptists made much the same point in their Discipline of 1798, by implication treating the association as another visible representation of the church. It is true that they denied that such a meeting of delegates had "church power," but that denial meant that this large body had no coercive powers to impose its will upon the local church. They were emphatic, however, in declaring the obligation of churches to join in a wider fellowship in which they should seek and accept the counsel of others. Moreover, both the statements (in their confessions) and their actions indicate that they did not limit their

---

[8]*Ibid.*, p. 289.

fellowship to others of their own denomination, but acknowledged themselves to belong to the catholic, or universal, church, which transcends all denominational lines.

A Baptist Definition of the Church

A useful and concise modern definition of the church is the one formulated by the British Baptists in 1926, which is as follows:

> We believe in the Catholic Church[9] as the holy society of believers in our Lord Jesus Christ, which He founded, of which He is the only Head, and in which He dwells by His Spirit, so that though made up of many communions, organized in various modes, and scattered throughout the world, it is yet one in Him.
>
> We believe that this holy society is truly to be found wherever companies of believers unite as churches on the ground of a confession of personal faith. Every local community thus constituted is regarded by us as both enabled and responsible for self-government through His indwelling Spirit who supplies wisdom, love, and power, and who, as we believe, leads these communities to associate freely in wider organizations for fellowship and the propagation of the Gospel.[10]

Such a statement is a faithful reflection of historic Baptist views. It takes account of the larger church as well as the local congregations where that church is embodied. It indicates the freedom of local churches in their responsibility to Christ, but also the interrelatedness of congregations to each other. Without the use of terms which restrict the definition of the church to Baptists, or to a small segment of the church, it succeeds in making clear both the inclusiveness of the church and the Baptist interpretation of the visible churches.

---

[9] The reference, of course, is not to the Roman Catholic Church, but to the total fellowship of all Christian believers everywhere.

[10] Ernest A. Payne, *The Fellowship of Believers* (London: Carey Kingsgate Press, 1952), p. 143.

Historic Doctrines in Today's World

We may now again ask the question with which we began: Is the Baptist concept of the nature and purpose of the church faithful to the New Testament understanding of the church? In the light of the foregoing survey of historic Baptist ideas, we may readily reply that the Baptist concept of the church accords with that of the Scriptures.

There remains, however, a corollary question. Is this concept also adequate to today's shifting sociological demands? Can it meet the practical requirements of the modern world? Its adequacy has been questioned at two points: (1) Is it possible to retain a consistent emphasis upon a regenerate membership? and (2) Does Baptist theory provide satisfactory foundations upon which to develop an organization that is able to meet the challenge of a mobile and dispersed society?

Maintaining a witness to regenerate church membership has always been difficult. It must be acknowledged that our present practice is not consistent with our theory. Many influences have brought about a relaxation of standards for admission to church membership and permitted church members to treat their responsibilities lightly. If we were to take seriously the idea of regenerate churches, we would not ordinarily baptize children who are too young to make responsible decisions. The acceptance of persons into the fellowship of the churches would also involve a commitment to participate responsibly in the life of the church.

Although churches under these circumstances would become smaller, their witness might be more persuasive because of the committed, informed, and disciplined membership. Baptists have basic decisions to make. The temptation to be "successful" is strong, of course, and we may feel with Luther and Calvin that it is impossible to insist upon regenerate church membership. On the other hand, statistical success ought not to be our criterion. If we are convinced that faithfulness to God requires us to be true to the basic features of our Baptist heritage, then we should renew our effort to make the membership of our visible churches approximate the church as it is known to God, which is truly the body of Christ.

With regard to denominational organization, there can be no doubt but that our loose structural relationships have often hindered our effectiveness. But such weak organization is not necessary. It has rested upon distorted ideas regarding biblical teaching and of historical Baptist traditions.

As we have seen, the original Baptists tried to maintain a balance between the wider church and the local churches. Their successors were unable to keep this balance, but often stressed the local congregation to the near exclusion of the larger church. In nineteenth-century America, Baptists developed an exaggerated view of the autonomy of the local church. This distorted view was further encouraged by the promulgation of the New Hampshire Confession of Faith, which completely omitted any reference to the church universal. Although this confession was never formally adopted by the New Hampshire Baptist Convention, which had initiated the committee to draft it, J. Newton Brown published it in 1853 upon his own authority after he became head of the American Baptist Publication Society. It quickly gained popularity and was widely used. Landmarkist particularism, which began with J. R. Graves about 1850, taught that the New Testament envisioned no other church than the local congregation. Landmarkist ideas, as well as other forms of individualistic thinking, had wide circulation through popular Baptist manuals of E. S. Hiscox, J. M. Pendleton, Francis Wayland, and others, which have exercised a powerful influence upon the development of Baptist denominational organizations ever since. Only recently have American Baptist churches attempted to recover an older, more biblical concept of the church as a basis for developing a national organization. These recent developments will be described in detail in chapters 9 and 10.

Conclusions

The emphases which distinguished Baptists at the outset of their history were valid insights into the scriptural doctrine of the church. By recovering these insights and implementing them, we may develop stronger churches. To stress the importance of regenerate church membership—undergirded by believers' baptism, mature discipleship, and a holistic vision of Christian mission—may lead to renewal and more effective witness.

4

The Local Church

In order to fulfill its responsibilities under God, the church must be embodied in some visible shape in the world. Organizational structures are indispensable for expressing the life of the church and for carrying out its mission. No community can long retain its character and achieve its aims without established patterns of operation. Therefore, orderly procedures must be adopted, and leaders must be designated and their functions defined.

The Question of Polity

The meaning of polity in general was described in the opening chapter. In what follows, attention will be devoted to polity for a local church. Assuming that polity means the way in which we incarnate our vision of mission, by what criteria do we decide on a polity for a Baptist church? How is a new church constituted? How does it define its purpose? What are the requirements for membership? Where is authority vested for making decisions? What officers and organizations are needed to conduct its work? When and for what reasons does the church gather for meetings?

No Blueprint in the New Testament

It is commonplace for biblical scholars to observe that no single pattern of church government is prescribed in the New Testament. Christ laid down no detailed instructions for its organization, nor is any uniform organization reflected in the New Testament documents. In this respect, life under the New Covenant differs from the minute prescriptions by which the life of Israel was ordered under the Old Covenant. The absence of precise regulations, however, does not mean that questions of church order are unimportant. Several alternative systems exist today, but some may be less suitable than others to allow full scope to the concept of a priesthood of believers engaged in Christ's mission.

Criteria for Determining Local Church Polity

Since the New Testament does not prescribe a detailed polity for a local church, how do we decide what organizational forms are best suited to the use of a church? It is evident that early Christian communities adapted their organizational life to meet existing circumstances. The nature and purpose of the church are set forth in the Scriptures, and they are guidelines for today's use in developing an organization. Here, as elsewhere, form follows function. Structures of Baptist churches need not be all the same. The important thing is that they adhere to basic marks of the church. Specific mission goals, size of congregations, available leadership, financial resources, and other factors may affect the particular shape of a congregation, but a biblical picture of the nature and mission of Christ's church should guide the local church in whatever plan it develops.

Marks of a Local Church

There is a mistaken notion that any "two or three" gathered together in Christ's name constitute a church. Christ, to be sure, may be present in the midst of any "two or three" gathered in his name, but such a company is not necessarily a church. To be a church, according to the major historic Baptist confessions, a community in Christ must be prepared "to walk together before him in all the ways of obedience which he prescribes" and must so order its common life that it may act responsibly in his name.

The first characteristic mark of a Baptist church order is that it is *made up of committed, informed, and disciplined Christians.* For this reason a particular local church has traditionally been defined among Baptists as a company of faithful people, separated from the world by the Word and Spirit of God, who have been baptized upon their own confession of faith, and consent (or covenant) "to walk together according to the appointment of Christ, giving themselves up to the Lord and one another by the will of God in professed subjection to the ordinances of the gospel." This language may sound quaint, but it expresses a fundamental concern which Baptists express by the term "regenerate church membership."

In the second place, a community in Christ to be a church *must possess the means of grace appointed by Christ for ministering himself to the world.* All major Protestant bodies growing out of the Reformation have required that the Word of God be rightly preached, and that baptism and the Lord's Supper be truly administered. Baptists, in keeping with the Reformed tradition, have added "and for discipline to be duly executed."

In the third place, a truly constituted church *must be an ordered fellowship with officers of God's appointment and the churches' election, and with specific procedures for determining God's will by the inquiry of the whole congregation.* Administrative procedures are necessary in any community, if only to avoid confusion and disorder. In the Baptist view of a church it is also necessary to ensure that each member of the community participates as fully as possible, and that God's guidance be truly sought.

In the fourth place, a church *must always be aware that its very existence is bound up with its mission.* God has not called us to enjoy privileges of security and comfort, but to a vocation of witness and service to the world. Like its master, it is here not to be served, but to serve. The ministry is carried out partly within the church and partly outside its boundary. It invites people to enter the company of believers by repentance, faith, and baptism, and it nurtures them in fellowship, worship, and instruction in the meaning of the Christian faith for relationships and conduct. Beyond the church itself, all Christians are to live out their faith in the home, the workplace, and in public arenas where their influence is needed.

Finally, a truly constituted church *cannot exist in isolation from other churches.* It is but one particular manifestation of the whole church of Christ, and it must seek to maintain fellowship with other Christians. Baptists have maintained that churches should hold communion with one another—meeting together through their representatives—for mutual edification, increasing love, preserving peace, bearing witness to their common unity, and whatever may tend to the furtherance of the gospel and the interest of Christ. And since, as they put it in early confessions, "the purest churches under heaven are subject to mixture and error," each must seek counsel and admonition of many other churches meeting together for the correction of its own life. While this fellowship and counsel is most immediately shared with fellow Baptists, it extends also to other Christians through organizations that facilitate cooperative Christian action.

Powers of a Local Church

Baptists have maintained that Christ has given local churches "all that power and authority which is in any way needful for their carrying on that order in worship and discipline which he hath instituted for them to observe." This was also the teaching of the Protestant Reformers. Martin Luther, for example, declared that "a little group of pious Christian laymen" who had been "taken captive and set down in a wilderness" could constitute themselves a church and choose one of their number to preach and administer baptism and the Lord's Supper. Luther was insisting that the basic constituent element of a church is a faithful people and not any outward institutional succession. He was also insisting that, since all the faithful are priests, they may designate the person who is to act on their behalf as pastor. If these two contentions are true, there is no need for a company of Christian people to derive spiritual authority from any other source than Christ himself.

And yet, no church is a law unto itself. A church is subject to Christ. Congregational polity insists that all members must be permitted to assume the responsibilities of their mutual priesthood. That is to say, each member participates not only in the worship and work of the church, but also in making decisions which affect the common life of all members. Therefore, in a sense the church may be called a democracy, and it must utilize democratic procedures. But it is a democracy only in a qualified sense, for *Christ is the head of the church, and members are his subjects.* He is the king and lawgiver, and members are to render obedience to him.

The image of king and subjects has an unfamiliar ring to American ears, accustomed to thinking about individual rights and majority rule. Moreover, concern for the use of inclusive language makes it difficult for many to accept the term "king" because of its masculine gender. Since we cannot properly attribute gender to God, it is appropriate to speak of the "realm" or "reign" of God to avoid the language problem. The reign of God, however, was central to Jesus' preaching, and is a fundamental biblical concept. The church is a manifestation of God's realm which is a present reality, though not fully realized. This point is emphasized in the report of the Commission on Denominational Identity:

> The world belongs to Christ, its rebellion and fall notwithstanding. The reign of God is present here and now, even though it is also yet to come in its fullness when Christ returns. Though the visible church in any form cannot equate itself with "the kingdom of God," it is called to ... be an agent or sign of the kingdom and to order its life accordingly.... Each day we hear the Lord's Prayer: "Thy kingdom come, Thy will be done on earth. . . ." Nothing should be allowed to infringe upon the "crown rights of the Redeemer."[1]

---

[1]*American Baptists: A Unifying Vision* (Valley Forge: Judson Press, 1988), p. 10.

Judicial and Executive Powers

With that controlling idea in mind, Baptists have often employed the analogy of human government to describe the relationship of the church to Christ. As the divine ruler, they said, Christ is the lawgiver, and the church has *judicial* and *executive* powers only. *Its role is to discern the mind of Christ in both temporal and spiritual affairs and to obey his will.*

Baptists advocated a congregational form of church government, but not because a show of hands was a convenient method of reaching decisions. They did so because they believed that an assembly of committed Christians could be "a sensitive and delicate instrument," which can be led by the Holy Spirit to discover God's will. They were conscious that a congregation could not infallibly determine God's will in all matters, but they believed that full participation of all would provide a check to the distortions occasioned by self-regard, human limitations of knowledge, and vested interests.

Pursuing this analogy, the local church can have no legislative powers that supersede the fundamental teachings of the gospel, but it can and does interpret and implement those teachings. This way of distinguishing the powers of a church is not so simple as it may sound, for it is often difficult to be certain of the mind of Christ in specific matters. Christians are bidden to worship God, but within limits they have freedom to choose the forms they use in worship. Making disciples and teaching them are functions mandated by Christ, but methods of evangelism and Christian education are devised by human beings. To "love your neighbor as yourself" is "the royal law," according to James (2:8), but what that teaching means in particular cases is left to the judgment of Christians guided by the Spirit. Seeking justice and peace are part and parcel of God's will for people, but responsibility for making judgments about complex social issues or about a particular potential for war is left to human discretion. Discerning the leading of the Spirit takes time and sensitivity, and a group may fail to reach agreement and have to follow majority decisions. In a practical sense, therefore, a church is a spiritual democracy in which all may express their judgments. Indeed, there is a thin line between implementation and legislating; but it must never be forgotten that ultimate authority belongs to Christ, and we are called to obey his sovereign will.

Church Meetings

Churches gather for a variety of purposes, and the number and kinds of meetings differ from church to church. There are some meetings, however, that fulfill central functions of the church and are common to every congregation.

Worship

At the heart of any church's life is worship, and this involves most of the members. Forms of worship among Baptists vary considerably. For instance, a worship service in a predominantly white church may differ significantly from that in a predominantly black church. Among all churches there is a wide range of types of worship, from quite formal orders of service to those which seem to have no logical (or theological) order. One cannot say categorically that one pattern is authentic worship and that another is not, but that does not mean the style of worship makes no difference. The question is whether the intent of worship is realized for the particular group of participants.

Baptists have traditionally looked askance at formal liturgy. They come out of a tradition which eschewed all but the most elementary symbols, such as Bible, pulpit, Communion table, and baptistry. All candles, crosses, stained-glass windows, pictures, clerical garb, and altar cloths were taboo; and churches even refused to celebrate Easter and Christmas. More recently, however, attitudes have changed, and it is now common to see a cross and candles on the Communion table and even acolytes who light the candles. Much that is helpful can be learned from the historic liturgies, but such forms should not be appropriated indiscriminately. They must have meaning to those who worship. Only after careful instruction and deliberation in the congregational meeting should new modes be introduced.

What are a church's criteria for suitable ways of worship? There is always the danger that public worship may become an escape from encounter with the Word even while seeking to enter God's presence. In the Old Testament there are many examples of prophets who denounced formalism in worship, two of the most notable being Amos (5:21-24) and Isaiah (1:11-17). Both declared that God despises superficial piety and ceremonial worship, when it does not eventuate in concern for the poor and oppressed. True worship is closely linked with caring.

It must be asked, then, whether a particular form of worship serves to focus attention on God or on self. Does it evoke awe, adoration, and praise of God's great power and mercy? Does it deepen a sense of fellowship with other worshipers? Does it open hearts and minds to the searchlight of the word of God? Does it inform the conscience and increase compassion? Does it motivate people to greater faithfulness and more willing service? If not, our so-called worship may be empty and self-deceptive ritual.

Christian Education

Another fundamental aspect of the life of any church is its program of Christian education. The same Great Commission, which mandates that we make disciples, also charges that we teach them to observe all that Jesus commanded. Usually, the Sunday church school is the principal place where instruction is given, although its work is supplemented by vacation church school, midweek Bible study, retreats, and meetings of organizations involving different age and interest groups.

Many adults think of Sunday church school only in terms of children, and of course the Christian education program for girls and boys is of major importance. Children benefit greatly from competent teaching applied to their levels of understanding. Excellent curriculum materials are published by the denomination for study appropriate to the various age levels. From nursery age upwards it is important for children to develop awareness of God's love and care for them, of Jesus Christ as their Lord, Guide, and Savior, and of the basic principles of a caring relationship with others. As adolescents, however difficult it may be for them to recognize it, Christian education grows in importance, providing teenage boys and girls with understandings and spiritual strength to deal with the sometimes overwhelming challenges and temptations of a secular environment.

The need for Christian education is not limited to children, however. There is no justification for the indifference many men and women have toward the study opportunities afforded by adult Sunday church school classes. Such courses greatly enhance one's understanding of the Bible and its implications for living. Numerous surveys have shown that many church members are poorly informed about the Bible, and that many professing Christians see little connection between their religious beliefs and the affairs of daily living. There is indeed urgent need for serious attention to adult Christian education.

Even when Baptists utilized confessions of faith, they always (like persons in other denominations) insisted that the Bible was the primary authority for faith and practice. Today, when confessions have fallen into disuse, it is commonly asserted that the Bible is the only creed of Baptists. Indeed, they have long prided themselves in being "people of the Book." But what does that mean? It behooves those who make such affirmations to engage in serious study of the Scriptures and to seek guidance in them for living. Unfortunately, many Baptists have devoted more energies to controversy about the Bible than to study and application of its teachings.

Thus, a church needs a strong program of Bible study not only for children and youth, but especially for adults. The Bible is not a simple book to understand and interpret. Even though humble Christians led by the Holy Spirit may receive many insights into biblical truths, the ability to understand the Bible requires serious study. Written many centuries ago in very different cultures from ours, the Scriptures comprise poetry, history, wisdom literature, gospels, occasional letters, and other literary genres. It should be obvious that anything more than a superficial knowledge of the Bible requires some understanding of ancient cultures, diverse types of literature, and principles of interpretation. Admittedly understanding the Bible and its meaning for our lives is more than an intellectual task, for an understanding of both the original meaning and the modern application of a passage depends upon the guidance of the Holy Spirit.

After ascertaining what a passage meant when it was written, it is necessary to interpret its significance for the issues of modern life. Most of the Bible's theological, moral, and ethical teachings are in forms that need interpretation in order to find their present applications. We have often been reminded that correct interpretation of the Bible requires us to put a passage into its ancient context. It is also necessary that our application of biblical teaching take account of modern contexts. Meaningful theology is not developed in a vacuum, but must be contextual. Churches therefore should make provision for serious Bible study, utilizing the best resources available, and relying on the guidance of the Holy Spirit.

The Church Meeting

Besides meetings for worship and Christian education, the "church meeting," or "congregational meeting" has had a prominent place in the life of Baptist churches. It has been the means by which God's will has been humbly sought and Christ's rule acknowledged. While certain executive responsibilities are assigned to the pastor, diaconate, and other officers, the church has held that the entire membership is responsible to discuss, debate, and decide matters of basic concern to the life of the church. Thus the congregational meeting is the place where basic decisions and policies are made. Only by such participation will there be a genuine sense of ownership of policies and programs.

In contemporary church life, however, the church meeting has often been neglected. In part, this is because the growing complexity of life and its demands on people's time makes it more difficult to schedule such meetings. It is also because powers are often delegated to small groups or individuals when others were unwilling to accept responsibilities. On the other hand, members have too often been frustrated when trivial matters that might better be dealt with in other ways have been brought before the meeting. Questions of spiritual, moral, and social significance have been left to private reflection and decision rather than being brought to the corporate consideration of the church body.

The church meeting, then, is the place where the whole church gathers to consider matters of importance to its common life. Some business matters should come before it, but it is not just a "business meeting." Calling it that is a symptom of the restricted conception of its purpose which has come to prevail. The adoption of a budget, the admission of members, and setting of policies fall within its necessary competence, but execution of decisions and policies should be left to the designated boards and committees. The church meeting includes relating worship to the internal life of the church, the personal concerns of its members in daily living, community needs, and public policy.

Since congregational polity presupposes the full participation of members, there is some advantage in being a small church. On the other hand, if a church is too small, it may be handicapped by inadequate facilities, insufficient leadership, and a curtailed program. But size is not the overriding factor in determining the effectiveness of a church. A small congregation may lack full participation of its members, whereas a larger church may find ways of compensating for its bigness.

Where circumstances make the frequent town-meeting type of assembly impossible, there can be a modification of the church-meeting plan. Small fellowship groups can become a context for face-to-face relationships and an opportunity for thorough discussion of pertinent issues. Channels of communication can be established to relate these smaller groups to the entire church. After such groups have considered matters of common concern, a larger representative church meeting may be better prepared to seek further light on such questions. As many members as possible should participate in the final, all-church stage of such church meetings. If the spirit and values of the congregational system are to be preserved, ways such as these are needed to foster Christian fellowship, to involve individual members in worship, study, and decisions of the church, and to prepare members to make informed Christian judgments in personal and social issues.

Experience would indicate that a monthly church meeting

is desirable, but when that frequency is not feasible the meeting may be quarterly. Where there is a regular midweek service, it might be preceded by a church dinner, sometimes using this time as an occasion for a church meeting to discuss common concerns. Some churches have experimented with an older pattern, having a dinner at the church following the Sunday morning worship, and then holding the church meeting in the afternoon. This has two advantages. It places the church meeting within the context of the common worship of the church, and it provides an opportunity for the pastor in the sermon to provide instruction pertaining to the topic to be discussed. The church meeting may deal with a particular theological point that needs to be clarified in terms of the church's witness; it may consider the church's missionary obligation in some specific fashion; it may discuss some moral issue facing the community in order to provide guidance for members. Whatever the subject to be considered, the discussion needs to be informed by whatever light the pastor can bring to bear upon it from his or her understanding of God's Word.

Guidelines for an Effective Congregational Meeting

The congregational meeting has had a place of special emphasis in Baptist church life. Therefore, Baptists in the past were careful to define certain procedures necessary to a properly constituted church meeting. The intention was to make it as clear as possible that the entire congregation was engaged in seeking the mind of Christ.

A Competent Moderator

In the past, Baptists almost always held that the pastor should be the moderator. They spoke of "presidential authority," by which they meant the pastor's right to preside at all meetings of the church. Occasionally, it was regarded as wise that someone else serve in such a capacity, but only in exceptional circumstances.

The reason for such a requirement was that it seemed necessarily related to the pastoral office. The pastor had been chosen to be the leader of God's people in a particular church; and to permit someone else to preside might obscure the pastoral image. Furthermore, the pastor was the expert interpreter of the Scriptures, and as chairperson could give the competent theological guidance needed in the determination of questions. Among Southern Baptists and National Baptists this practice is still standard.

Most American Baptist churches today select someone from the congregation to preside at such meetings. The arguments in support of this arrangement are twofold. In the first place, such service enables laypersons to be more involved in the life of the church. This responsibility can be assumed by those who have gifts of leadership, but not formal theological training. Second, the pastor is free to take a more active part in the meeting than if she/he were the chairperson. Ordinarily the presiding officer does not have liberty to participate in discussions, and thus the pastor who does not preside can make a larger contribution to the meeting. In the role of a resource person, the pastor can give a kind of leadership which is better adapted than that of moderator to developing an informed and working church. Another consideration to keep in mind is that when the moderator is a layperson, there is continuity of leadership during a period when there is no pastor.

Each church will do well to weigh the foregoing arguments for and against the pastor's serving as moderator, and make a decision based on its own local situation.

Rules of Order for the Meeting

An orderly procedure. The meeting should be opened with a prayer invoking God's presence and the guidance of God's Spirit in all the deliberations. The minutes of the previous meeting should be read and approved. Routine business should be quickly dispatched so that discussion of such matters is not unduly prolonged. The major subjects to be considered by the meeting should then be clearly stated, so that there may be a proper division of time allotted to each. The meeting should be closed with prayer, asking God's blessing upon decisions which have been reached.

Opportunity for all to be heard. The church meeting is an

inquiry by the entire church, and the possibility must always be kept in mind that the Holy Spirit may speak through the humblest member. The more articulate and self-assertive members should not be allowed to monopolize the discussion to the exclusion of others. Each person must be given full opportunity to speak, and the words of each person should be carefully pondered.

Consensus to be sought. The principle of unanimity has been important in congregational theory, for the church is not just a political organization which can be satisfied with a mere majority vote. *The objective of the church meeting is not to win a vote, but rather to discern the mind of Christ.* When a decision is not concurred in by the whole church, the mind of Christ has evidently not been made clear. Such a decision would have dubious spiritual authority. The difficulty in involving a large number of people in a deliberative process leads to the temptation to delegate all important decisions to small committees or boards. In matters of basic policy which affect the church as a whole, however, every effort should be made to find time to reach a clear consensus before a decision is made.

Dividing the church to be avoided. A primary obligation resting upon the church is to "maintain the unity of the Spirit in the bond of peace." If a consensus cannot be reached, it is usually preferable to delay the decision, rather than risk dividing the church. Often a church may feel that it must make a decision on a controversial matter before it reaches a common mind and before unanimous consent can be reached, but under such circumstances no action should be taken which cannot command at least a two-thirds affirmative vote. Even then the action can be taken only with grave misgivings and regret. Furthermore, if such action threatens to divide the church, the decision should be postponed until the counsel and advice of the association, the area minister, or the executive minister of the region can be obtained.

Counsel and advice to be sought. It was once the custom of Baptists when confronted by perplexities to address inquiries to an association or regional body in order to secure counsel and advice. In response to such inquiries, either the matter was discussed and the requested advice given, or a committee was appointed to counsel with the church. Today, area ministers and executive ministers are usually persons of experience and wisdom, who can often shed light on questions at issue and facilitate the process of reaching a decision. Especially in cases where something threatens to divide a church, the regional office should be invited to send representatives qualified to act as consultants to help reconcile opposing parties and reach satisfactory conclusions.

Procedure for Organizing a Church

New churches come into existence in a number of ways. Sometimes an association or a regional or national agency initiates the process. Sometimes it emerges from a mission of another church; and sometimes an individual or several interested persons take the first steps toward forming a church. Although a church may be gathered in various ways, there is an orderly procedure which should be followed in the actual formation of the church.

Obtaining Preliminary Advice

Prior to drawing up a constitution, an attorney should be consulted to make sure there will be full compliance with the requirements of state laws. In some states there are requirements connected with receiving charters. Such incorporation sometimes specifies that there be a board of trustees, and that may mean that this board be created even where a single-board system is contemplated. Sometimes, also, there are requirements regarding notice to be given of church meetings for certain purposes. Even when the laws do not impose restrictions, it would be wise to include a rule concerning such announcements in the constitution or bylaws.

Furthermore, unless the regional body is already involved by virtue of being the instigator, persons seeking to organize a church would be well advised to consult the area minister or the executive minister of the region. He/she can furnish helpful information about steps to be taken, available resources, and services from regional and national agencies. Useful information concerning the developing of a constitution, financing the building, literature for the Sunday church school, and a sponsoring group can be secured in this way. An explanation of the American Baptist Personnel Services may be helpful in securing the services of a pastor. A sponsoring church may be found, which might dismiss some members to become part of a nucleus of trained leaders for the proposed new congregation. Its minister might then serve as convener or moderator of the incipient church, although it is equally possible for one of their own number to serve in that capacity.

Forming a Temporary Organization

Under the leadership of the appointed moderator, the church is formed into a *conference* which can meet in orderly fashion in advance of the actual organization of the church. The group will seek to ascertain their common understanding of the Christian faith and of the purpose, goals, and objectives of the new congregation. Then they will proceed to consideration of a covenant and confessional basis, and the drafting of a constitution and bylaws. Small groups of six to nine members can be responsible for framing these documents, but at every step they should keep the entire group informed and allow full discussion of every point calling for decision. When the constitution, bylaws, and covenant are completed, it would be well to have small groups meet to study them before the larger group meets to vote on their adoption.

Statement of Purpose

Prior to beginning the framing of the constitution, the prospective members should spend time considering the nature and mission of the church of Jesus Christ. The Bible, books about the church and its mission, and a minister or teacher who is knowledgeable on this subject will be resources used by the group to think about God's intention for the church in relation to the divine redemptive purpose for the world. It is important that the entire group take part in these discussions to establish the basic direction and spirit of the new congregation.

Out of the understanding of the nature and mission of the

church and a consideration of the needs and opportunities for service in the particular context of the community should come a statement of purpose. Some things are common to every church, such as worship, evangelistic witness, instruction and nurture of members of all ages, fostering healthy home life, enabling members to relate the gospel to all aspects of life, ministry to the immediate community, and sharing in the Christian world mission. There are also likely to be some specific concerns which should be emphasized in the purpose statement, which may include a desire to be racially inclusive, to identify and cooperate with Christians of other denominations, and to take responsibility for ministering to identifiable groups with special needs within the community.

Covenant and Doctrinal Basis

A statement of purpose should be supplemented by a covenant and statement of doctrinal basis. Covenants have had a long history among Baptists, dating back to the seventeenth century, but for many churches they fell into disuse in the twentieth century. Some congregations have revived the practice of covenanting together, and this instrument has become a bond uniting different parts of the American Baptist Churches. It is a means of acknowledging the relationships of members to one another and pledging to accept certain responsibilities as church members.

Covenants have sometimes contained doctrinal affirmations, but this content has not been typical. There ought to be, however, some affirmations of a doctrinal nature. Although Baptists at one time used confessions of faith, even requiring members to subscribe to them when they joined, contemporary Baptists have commonly shied away from anything suggestive of creedalism. They have been content to affirm the Scriptures (or perhaps only the New Testament) as their source of authority for faith and practice, leaving individuals free to interpret them for themselves.

A church may prefer to make such a general statement in its constitution, but there are beliefs which are inherent in Christianity, and no church ought to hesitate to adopt a set of affirmations which constitute a common core of beliefs held by the congregation. Such a statement should be kept simple, and it should be a means of corporately affirming convictions as well as a guideline for new members. There are simple affirmations in existence, such as the Apostles' Creed or more modern statements, or one can be carefully designed for a particular congregation.[2]

Designing a Constitution and Bylaws

Appendix 3 of this *Manual* contains a sample constitution and bylaws, as well as a variation for a single-board plan of organization. Examination of the constitutions and bylaws of other churches will also provide suggestions. It is unwise, however, to adopt any ready-made plan without critical scrutiny in the light of the stated purpose of the new church. There is no generic model applicable to every situation, although certain elements are common to all churches. Each situation is unique in some respects, and organization should be tailored to meet internal and external conditions. The size, age distribution, available leadership, and financial resources of a congregation will affect the organizational plan, as will the type and needs of the community in which it is located. Existing patterns of organization need to be modified and creatively adapted to fit the situation, so as to bring to reality the vision of ministry for a particular context.

Governance and Affiliations

The constitution should include a section regarding organization, specifying the nature of the church's governance and its denominational affiliations. With respect to governance it should be stated that the congregation has authority to admit and dismiss members, choose its officers, and determine matters of policy and program; also, that it may overrule decisions of any individual, board, or committee. Clear statements should be included as to responsibilities and relationships for each board and officer. There should also be a statement of affiliation with an association or cluster (or equivalent), region, and national body. It may also be appro-

---

[2] Further information on covenants may be found in chapter 5. Sample covenants appear in Appendix 2.

priate to express an intention to support ecumenical bodies such as the National Council of the Churches of Christ, National Association of Evangelicals, World Council of Churches, and/or other cooperative agencies (see Chapter 11 of this manual).

Single-Board or Multiple-Board System?

At an early stage in drafting a constitution and bylaws there will need to be a decision whether the church will operate with a single-board or a multiple-board plan. The single board is especially suitable for small congregations because it can work with a smaller number of persons; but it may be also used to advantage by medium-sized or even large churches.[3]

The multiple-board system involves more people in order to function well, and care must be taken to see that subgroups are related to major boards in ways that provide clear lines of accountability. In such a plan, it is also necessary to have some coordinating group, which will draw together the overall work of the church. This coordinating group is often called the Church Council, but some prefer to name it the Executive Committee, Advisory Council, or Congregational Council.

Constitution, Bylaws, and Standing Resolutions

Another decision to be made pertains to constitution, bylaws, and standing resolutions. Many churches make no distinctions between constitution and bylaws, but place everything in the constitution. The constitution, however, should be thought of as giving a basic shape to the operation of church affairs. It deals with fundamental matters that are expected to be more or less permanent in nature. Bylaws contain details of organization, such as times and frequency of meetings, membership, staff, board and committee structures, and other things which may need to be changed from time to time. This distinction is expressed in the fact that

---

[3] See chapter 7 for discussion of single-board organization; also see Appendix 3, pp. 271–273, for a suggested adaptation of bylaws to provide for this type of organization.

amendment of a constitution usually requires a two-thirds vote, whereas a simple majority is adequate to amend the bylaws.

Standing resolutions state policies decided by the church, and new ones will be added from time to time, while others will be dropped when they cease to be applicable or when so voted by the church. These may cover a wide range of matters, such as goals adopted for planning efforts, participation in a denominational program, use of literature in the church school, financial policies, use of buildings and equipment, rules of order, etc.

Completing the Organization

When the proposed covenant, constitution, and bylaws are completed, arrangements need to be made for the baptism of new converts who purpose to become members of the new church, and to secure letters of dismissal from other churches for those entitled to such letters. A committee should be appointed to examine, with the assistance of the person appointed to act as convener or moderator, both the letters and the candidates. These proceedings will normally take several months.

After preparations have been carefully made, all who wish to become members of the new congregation should be invited to attend a meeting specially convened for the purpose of constituting the new church. After prayer invoking God's presence, the covenant previously agreed upon shall be read and accepted by a show of hands. Those accepting it shall then proceed to sign their names to it, thus forming a church *essential*. The moderator shall then ask the guidance of the Holy Spirit in their further deliberations. A constitution for the orderly government of the church shall then be adopted, and the officers of the church—including pastor and deacons—shall be elected, thus constituting a church *completed*. The meeting shall be closed with prayers invoking God's blessing upon the newly constituted church.

The new church shall then petition the local Baptist association (area, cluster, or region) for admission into its membership. Upon favorable action by the wider body, the church becomes a church *recognized,* in full and regular standing. It is desirable that there shall be a service of recognition, at which the congregation is formally welcomed into the fellowship of the association or regional body.

Addendum
Special Provisions on Denominational Relationships Recommended for Inclusion in Church Constitutions

Denominational Affiliation

Since churches have sometimes been taken out of their denomination either by minority groups at sparsely attended church meetings, or by virtue of misinformation used to mislead the members, some churches have found it highly desirable to include a provision like the following in their constitutions:

> This church shall adhere to and be a member of the American Baptist Churches in the U.S.A., the American Baptist Churches of ___[name of region]___, and the _____ Baptist Association [or cluster], and shall not resign or withdraw from any of these bodies except by a duly adopted amendment to the Constitution of this church upon petition for such withdrawal signed by two-thirds of all the members of this church; nor shall such action be taken until at least thirty days have elapsed following a consultation thereto by the Board of Deacons and the Board of Trustees [or whatever appropriate terms are used for the equivalents of these] of this church with the Executive Minister of the Region and the Moderator of the Association [Cluster] or their representatives.

Notice to the Region Prior to Calling of a Pastor

Churches have sometimes called pastors, much to their later regret, on the basis of insufficient information. It is desirable that the bylaws contain a requirement that the pulpit committee meet with the area minister when the search for a new pastor begins. This person can put the committee in touch with American Baptist Personnel Services, which keeps up-to-date files on all ministers in the denomination and some other qualified persons seeking to enter the denomination. The area minister can help the church to evaluate its needs, resources, and requirements in a pastor. Personnel Services can then furnish names of available ministers who have the priority characteristics that the church needs. Seeking such advice does not mean that the committee may not consider names from other sources, but if the committee does consider calling someone who is not listed with the Personnel Services of the denomination, the bylaws should require that the area minister be asked to investigate the person in question. Some provision such as the following may be put in the bylaws of the church:

> This church shall not call a minister until thirty days after the pulpit committee has requested the office of the American Baptist Churches of ___[name of region]___ to supply information concerning the record and qualifications of the candidate it proposes to recommend to the church.

Reversionary clause

As a further protection of the church's denominational relationship, it is proposed that the following reversionary clause be included in the deed of the church's property:

> In the event that the church ceases to be a cooperating church of the American Baptist Churches in the U.S.A., this property shall revert to the [choose one] _____ Baptist Association, the American Baptist Churches of ___[name of region]___, one of the national program boards of the American Baptist Churches in the U.S.A., or any combination of these organizations.

5

Church Membership: Qualifications and Responsibilities

Baptists emphasize that the membership of visible churches should include only those persons who are sincere Christians. But they have also been ready to acknowledge that an infallible judgment of a person's relationship to God is impossible. For this reason various Baptist confessions conceded that even "the purest churches under heaven are subject to mixture and error."

It is not necessary to conclude that if we cannot do something perfectly we should not try to do it at all. We need not give up all efforts to determine who are fit material for church membership. To do so would be to surrender the claim that Christ has laid upon us and to give up all endeavor to express the true life of the church in any visible, tangible way. Although one's profession of faith cannot be tested in any ultimate sense, that fact does not mean that a profession of faith should not be required of those who wish to enter the fellowship of the church. Persons who have yielded their lives to God in Christ should be able to state simply what it means to them to be Christian, and their lives should give some evidence of the sincerity of their profession of faith. Thus an individual is baptized only after making a public profession of faith and having been examined by the church. In this way, and by explicit provision for subsequent nurture and discipline within the fellowship of the church, Baptists have tried to realize the ideal of fully committed churches composed only of believers.

Admission to Church Membership

Baptist churches receive members in three ways. First, new members are received *by baptism*, after having made a profession of faith. Second, a person coming from another church may present a letter of commendation, and be admitted then *by letter*. Third, there are some people who have once manifested faith in Christ and been baptized, but through carelessness their contact with the church was not maintained and their relationship with God grew cold. A person who repents of the lapse which has occurred should not be rebaptized, nor can one be certified by the former church as a member in good standing. He or she is received after making a statement of previous Christian experience, expressing repentance and an intention to dedicate his/her life anew to Christ. This practice is called receiving people *upon experience*, because its basis is their statement of previous Christian experience. Sometimes a fourth category of admission is used, namely, *by restoration*. This indicates that a member is received back into fellowship after having been excluded from the church. Such a case, however, is not essentially different from one who is accepted upon experience and need not be treated as a distinct classification.

A good many churches make provision for *associate membership*. This term has two entirely different connotations, which share only the fact that associate members usually are limited as to positions they may hold in the church and matters on which they may vote in congregational meetings. One type of associate membership is a substitute for open membership and will be considered later in this chapter in relation to that subject. The second type, often known as *watchcare*, is intended for persons who have come to a new community, presumably on a temporary basis, and expect to return to their former church. Therefore, as in the example of a college student, they may wish to retain membership in their home church and become associate or watchcare members of the church in their temporary location. A few churches reverse the procedure and retain as associate members persons who have moved away but wish to maintain sentimental ties with their former congregation, but this status is more difficult to justify. In general, it seems wise to keep the exceptional types of membership at a minimum, lest the concept of membership become blurred.

Preparation for Membership

Baptist churches of previous centuries used to require those wishing to join a church to appear before a congregational meeting to give a testimony to their experience of God's grace. Although not everyone had had a dramatic conversion, each person was expected to have made a decisive commitment and to tell simply what it meant to her/him to accept Christ as Savior and Lord. After a declaration of faith, an opportunity was presented for the pastor and others to ask questions to clarify points about which they wished further information. The candidate was then asked to withdraw, so that the congregation could discuss the question of admission. If the testimony had been convincing, the congregation voted to approve the applicant into the fellowship. While not claiming the ability to discern perfectly the mind of God, after careful deliberation the members made what they called "a judgment of charity."

Modern practice differs considerably from the early way. As congregations became larger and the residences of members were more scattered, the bonds of fellowship tended to weaken. In many churches, particularly in the South, it is common for a congregation to vote upon the reception of a member immediately after that person signifies a desire to join the church. A person may indicate that desire by coming to the front of the sanctuary at the end of a service, and the congregation is asked to vote without requiring further information. So forgotten is the original purpose of such a vote that the nays are usually not even asked for. In American Baptist churches, it is more usual to have a person appear before the Diaconate or a membership committee prior to a congregational vote, and there may be some preparatory course of study for the prospective member.

If a church is to act responsibly before God, it should exercise all reasonable care to see that those who are received are sincerely committed to Christ. It is therefore imperative that those who ask to become members of the church receive instruction and be examined. A sincere profession of faith in Jesus Christ as Savior and Lord is the only real test of eligibility for church membership. The only theological knowledge which can be expected of a new convert is an understanding of the rudiments of the gospel. In order to be as sure as possible that a candidate has these qualifications, however, a church should provide for instruction in the meaning of Christian discipleship and should try to ascertain the genuineness of a profession of faith.

Discipleship classes for those seeking membership should be standard practice in all churches. Such training is necessary both for young people and for older persons who are entering upon the Christian life. Even those who come from other denominational backgrounds need to be acquainted with general Baptist emphases, the relationship of the congregation to its own denomination, the way in which it perceives its mission, and what expectations it has of its members. The fact that people may have been church members elsewhere for years does not ensure their grasp of the essential elements of the gospel or of the meaning of church membership. Therefore, it is highly desirable that all prospective new members attend a preparatory class taught by the pastor before being received into the church. Study materials for such classes are published by the denomination.

It is difficult to know at what age children should be admitted into church membership. Many Baptist churches today encourage the baptism of children at age eight or even younger, particularly in the Southern Baptist Convention, but it is doubtful that those who are so young are prepared to make the significant decision which is required. There was a time when Baptists seldom baptized people under sixteen, and usually those who came into their churches were older than that. There are exceptions to most rules, but the rule should probably be to expect youth to reach at least age twelve or thirteen before admission to church membership. One reason why we have so many nominal Christians today may be our lax admission standards. To be so careless is tantamount to treating the faith itself with contempt, and to baptize children too early is virtually to return to a practice of infant baptism.

Examining Applicants for Membership

After instruction, *candidates should be examined by the Diaconate,* acting as a membership committee; or there may a special membership committee elected by the church. This meeting with candidates for membership (for baptism when it is a new convert) should not be thought of as an interrogation, which might be frightening to children or others. Rather it should be an affirming experience which will be remembered with pleasure. At that occasion, applicants should be given an opportunity to state simply what it has meant to them to become Christians, to affirm their intentions to live under the lordship of Christ, and to engage actively in the life of the church. Questions should be asked, if necessary, to elicit responses indicating their understanding of the step which is being taken and the desire to be loyal to Christ and his church.

Congregational Approval of New Members

When the Deacons (or membership committee) are satisfied with the statements of a candidate, they recommend to the church that he/she be received as a member, following baptism or receipt of a church letter. *The entire congregation should approve or reject a candidate in a regular church meeting.* Ordinarily, there should be unanimous agreement before a new member is admitted. In open meeting opportunity should be given for anyone to express any reasons for opposing the admission of a given individual. No one has a right to vote against a person without communicating good reasons to the church. So that the bond of fellowship will not be broken, there ought to be unanimity among the members in this matter.

Soon after the church has signified its approval, a baptismal service should be held for those who have not already been baptized. *The "hand of fellowship"* (Gal. 2:9)—the formal welcome of the person into the membership—is then extended at the first Communion service after the baptism, although it may be done at some other time if necessary. The hand of fellowship is a family greeting to a new member, but is not essential to membership.

Members' Responsibilities and Privileges

Church membership involves responsibilities, but that fact unfortunately has not been always made clear to everyone. By joining a church we become a party to a covenant in which we acknowledge our relationship to God and to one another.

Church Covenants[1]

During the seventeenth century, as indicated in chapter 4, it was the normal custom of Baptists to form a new congregation by covenanting with God and one another to walk together in all the ways which God would make known to them. The persons who were to be constituent members of a church would draw up a covenant, and at a formal meeting would sign their names to the document. The act of covenanting made explicit the vows implied in baptism, and their act was the means of constituting the church. New members consented to accept the terms of the covenant, and periodically entire congregations renewed their covenant vows. Although not uniformly adopted by all Baptists, the practice of forming a church by covenanting with God and with one another was a common pattern in America.

The use of covenants in forming a church is reflected in a seventeenth-century definition of a church. Benjamin Keach, a Baptist minister of that period, described a church as "a congregation of godly Christians, who at a stated assembly (being first baptized upon profession of faith) do by mutual agreement and consent give themselves up to the Lord, and one to another, according to the will of God." Although the word "covenant" is not used in this statement,

---

[1]Charles Deweese, *Baptist Church Covenants* (Nashville: Broadman Press, 1990) presents a history of Baptist use of covenants and a collection of many covenants from all periods and various countries.

the writer is describing the covenanting by which a visible church was constituted.

Although the language in which early covenants were couched differed somewhat, the general outlines were much the same. The essential idea was expressed as follows: "We do hereby give ourselves up to the Lord and to one another, agreeing to walk together in all of the ways which he does make known to us." In some cases the covenant contained little more than this simple statement; more often it mentioned specific duties which a member accepted as binding upon him or her as a member of a church. Three sample covenants appear in Appendix 2.

It is not uncommon for Baptists to read a church covenant today in connection with their observance of the Lord's Supper, but this usage is often little more than a formality. Few people know the significance of the covenant idea in the history of their churches, and little attempt is made to impress upon them the significance of their words when they read this document together. It used to be customary for Baptists to hold a covenant meeting on a weekday prior to the monthly observance of the Lord's Supper. At that time the church family gathered to testify to their religious experience and to renew their covenant with God and one another. The recovery of such a practice today could help to impress upon us the significance of our covenant obligations and prepare us for a more meaningful celebration of the Lord's Supper.

The use of such covenants is a most suitable means of impressing upon church members the sacred obligations which accompany their Christian profession. A church may draw up such a document for its own use, or it may adopt one prepared for general use in the churches. A covenant should include only things which inhere in the Christian life. Trifling things and customs based upon peculiar cultural conditions ought not to be included in its obligations. The covenant which is most common among Baptists today is an adaptation of earlier ones, particularly of one which was framed in connection with the New Hampshire Confession of Faith (Appendix 2, Type B).

In one paragraph, that covenant affirms a responsibility to

cooperate in the work of the church. Beginning with the words, "We engage . . . to strive for the advancement of this church," it enumerates ways in which its life will be supported. When one becomes a church member, it should be clearly understood that he or she is going to participate actively in the church's life. It is a travesty upon the nature of the church when members attend worship services irregularly and exhibit little or no interest in its work.

Responsibilities of a Church Member

In a large church, programs are often so complex that no individual can be involved in every activity. However, everyone can and should participate as fully as possible in the life of the church. As a minimum, members should attend worship services weekly, unless hindered by illness or disability or absence from the vicinity. They should also be enrolled in some regular group for Bible study to explore implications of the gospel for the church's worship, witness, and ministries. Those who are negligent toward their duties should be reminded of them. There is no more justification for having inactive members of a church than for having inactive soldiers in an army.

Members are responsible for sharing the work of the church when given the opportunity to do so. Those who have ability to teach, to hold office, to prepare meals or repair equipment, or to perform some other task, should gladly devote the time and energy to do the job thoroughly. There are varieties of gifts, and there are many kinds of service, all of which contribute to the smooth operation of the whole body.

Everyone is obligated to contribute generously to the financial support of the church. Stewardship involves not only the investment of our personal talents, but the use of our material possessions. What is liberal giving for one person will not be so for another, and a comparatively small contribution may represent a really sacrificial offering for a person of limited means. The New Testament does not lay down a rule requiring everyone to give a tenth of one's income to the church and the service of others, but that is a good proportion for an average family to strive for. Many people could reduce their spending for things which are unnecessary in order to increase their giving to the multiple ministries supported by their churches. A person who is grudging in giving to the cause of Christ evidences a spirit that runs counter to the love of God and neighbor which Christ has enjoined upon us.

Besides an interest in the work of the local church, Christians are concerned for the cooperative work of churches through their own denomination and interdenominational agencies for cooperative Christianity. We are often so preoccupied with immediate local interests that our outlook becomes provincial, but we also need to take part in the larger church of Christ as it presents its witness and shares common tasks. A church budget should include support for local agencies that minister to the homeless, the disadvantaged and needy, hospice ministries, and many other worthwhile causes. When the budget takes these needs into account, it is well to channel one's contributions through the church. When it does not do so, giving must be direct. The same applies to international ministries for world hunger, refugee relief, victims of natural disasters, and other ever-present needs. When denominational or interdenominational agencies are available for our giving through church channels, it would seem appropriate to make our contributions through them. If such means are not available, however, it is a part of our Christian stewardship to see that such needs are not neglected.

In another section of the usual covenants we "engage to watch over one another in brotherly love," thus acknowledging our duty toward those who are of the household of faith. Having been assured by their testimony that they are Christians, and having accepted them into the fellowship of the church following baptism, we receive them as Christian brothers and sisters. Our kinship is through a common participation in Christ; and our love is based upon higher considerations than the ties of blood or the sharing of common background and interests. Within the Christian community we have our opportunity to express most fully that love by which Christ said that the world should recognize his disciples. It is the mark which sets the church apart as a demonstration of that new society which God is creating and of which the church is the nucleus.

Love toward fellow Christians is expressed in many ways. Among other specific things mentioned under this heading are these: "to remember each other in prayer; to aid each other in sickness and distress; to cultivate Christian sympathy in feeling and courtesy in speech; to be slow to take offense, but always ready for reconciliation, and mindful of the rules of our Savior, to secure it without delay."

To pray for each other is an obligation and a privilege of church members. Our interest in our brothers and sisters should be expressed in intercessory prayer, as we seek God's blessing upon God's people. For those in need of material things, for those who are bereaved or lonely, and for those who through weakness have lapsed into sins, we must offer our prayers to God. For the corporate witness of the church, for the work of our congregation in its community, and for the pastor and other leaders of the church, we lift up our hearts and voices to God.

When prayer represents a sense of responsible concern, it will be accompanied by efforts to minister to the needs of others. Hence, there must be a willingness to bear burdens, and to share joys and sorrows. Today, when government assumes responsibility for assistance to the needy at so many points, there is a tendency to lose all sense of personal interest and responsibility for aiding others. Although we should rejoice that such relief is made available to those in need, we should not lose all personal interest in them. Most churches can have some share in ministering to families and individuals within their own ranks who are faced with hardships. Where the possibilities of giving financial aid end, there is still a place for sympathetic understanding and a ministry of Christian friendliness.

Furthermore, members are duty-bound to promote the unity and harmony of the church. Wherever human beings associate closely, tensions and conflicts arise, but in the church every effort should be made to resolve the conflicts and remove the tensions. Although truth and right are not to be disregarded, there should be a willingness to forbear and forgive, and a ready acceptance of persons in spite of their shortcomings. Made up of human beings who have known God's pardon, the church is to be a community where forgiveness and sympathetic understanding are readily offered.

As individuals in every family must often subordinate their own desires to the interests of the group, so within the church self-interest must be curbed. Here is the place to express best that love which does not envy and is not arrogant or conceited. Although we are familiar with churches where there is party strife and where unhappy divisions have occurred, such a spirit is a denial of Christian love and should be shunned. Even though we who compose the church are subject to human limitations, a power is available through the presence of Christ which enables us in some measure to overcome our human tendencies toward pride and selfishness.

Moreover, in the covenant we pledge ourselves to use aids available for the cultivation of our spiritual and moral development. While Christianity is not to be confused with moralism, it nevertheless involves a way of living and has a concern for ethical conduct. We do not seek to merit God's approval by our achievements, but in gratitude for God's goodness and mercy we seek to obey. This obedience includes the development of integrity, courage, concern, love, purity, and faith.

Membership in the church should inevitably make us open to God's leading. Thus, we try to ascertain how our Christian vocation may be fulfilled in all of the relationships and roles of life. If we are to learn God's will in these matters, and to have the resources of faith and courage to act accordingly, we need to increase our understanding of the Scriptures, to share in the worship and discipline of the church, and to maintain a private devotional life. Honest self-examination and humble confession of sins are necessary to growth in Christian life, and these are to be followed by the endeavor to alter our lives for the better at points of acknowledged weakness.

Finally, membership in the church implies willingness to bear witness to Christ. The ministry belongs to the church as a whole, and all members have a duty to share in that ministry in their own way. The New Testament makes no distinction between ministers and laypersons, for all are ministers and all are of the laity.[2] There is, however, a difference between "pastor" and "layperson," for the former term signifies one who is chosen by the church to occupy a position of leadership. Hence, we all share in the ministry of the church, but we do it in different ways.

Every Christian represents the church in the world; in fact, church members may be thought of as being at work on the frontiers between the church and the world. They make their testimony clear by what they do, say, and are, whether on the job, at home or in the community. Through the church they should receive insight and strength to live as Christians in their vocations, not simply through verbal means but through attitudes and relationships. Accepting responsibility for the nurture of their own children, they seek to provide the kind of environment in the home that will encourage children to become Christians. This kind of witness is something which occupies every day of the week, and involves all of life.

Privileges of a Church Member

Church membership involves privileges as well as duties. There are certain rights which accompany membership in a Christian church. A member has a right to participate in the whole range of the church's activities—its worship, witness, service, and decision making. As one who has a part in governing the church, a member has a right to be heard and to vote on any issue under consideration. Full opportunity should be afforded for all who wish to declare themselves on matters relevant to the life and faith of the church. If time does not permit all to be heard at a particular meeting,

---

[2]*Laos* is the Greek word from which we get "laity" and "laypersons." It means "people," and all members are included among the "people of God." In our common parlance, we use the term "layperson" to distinguish specialists from those who do not have special training in a particular field. In that sense, it is proper to speak of "laypersons" in the church, meaning thereby those who do not have the special training for exercising the pastoral leadership. Nevertheless, the term tends to be misleading.

another occasion should be appointed when they can express their views. It must be remembered that God does not automatically speak through majorities, and may even speak through a minority of one. Everyone who speaks and acts in good faith has a right to a hearing.

Termination of Membership

Having discussed the admission of members into a church, we need also to consider the ways in which members are dismissed. There are three main methods by which dismission is effected—by letter of commendation, by request, and by disciplinary action.

Letter of Commendation

The most common means is the transfer of membership from one congregation to another by letter. When persons move from one community to another, they should present themselves for membership in a church near enough to their residence to participate regularly in its life. The church to which they thus apply requests a *church letter* from the church where they are members. Such a letter indicates that a person is in good standing, and is being dismissed from their fellowship to that of the new church. If the person in question is not in good standing, the church letter should provide that information. When a church has received the letter, it should acknowledge receipt of it.

It is the practice of some churches to grant letters of dismission to individuals, so that they may present them somewhere at some future time to a church where they may move. However, many times such letters are retained by individuals for a period of years, because the person does not affiliate with any church. These people have been called "trunk Baptists," because their letters are packed away in their luggage. Such procedures are not very satisfactory. After the passage of months or years, these persons can hardly be said to be members in good standing of the church to which they formerly belonged. Any church to which they present themselves ought to raise serious questions as to their reasons for neglecting to identify themselves with a church for a prolonged period of time. It is better to grant letters of commendation only upon the direct request of another church. Then persons who move away and break their ties at home and remain unaffiliated will have to be received into membership on some other basis. The receiving church would then have an opportunity to impress upon them the responsibilities of church membership before accepting them into its number.

Request

A member may make a request to be dismissed from the church's membership without stating any reason for doing so. The pastor should try to ascertain the reason for the member's wish to withdraw from the fellowship of the church without indicating an intention to unite elsewhere, in hope of persuading the person either to continue as a member or to transfer to some other congregation. If this individual insists upon ceasing to be a member of this or any other church, his or her name shall be removed from the church roll. A letter from the pastor should express regret at this decision and indicate a continuing interest in the individual (or family).

Disciplinary Action

Membership may also be terminated by action of the congregation because of scandalous behavior, teachings which embarrass the church of Christ, or failure to live up to covenant obligations. This action is commonly called *exclusion*. Although such radical surgery should be taken only after great care and patience have been exercised, there are times when such suspension of membership may need to be invoked. Every effort should be made to win such persons back to repentance, reconciliation, and active Christian commitment.

Inactive Membership

There is another category which leaves people suspended between membership and dismissal. It is not consistent with strict expectations that members should be committed and disciplined, but it has grown out of a pastoral concern for persons who have become indifferent to the life of the church for a time. There was a time when disciplinary action would have resulted either in reclaiming the delinquent member to active discipleship and participation in the church's life or in exclusion from membership. Whatever the reasons, every church of any size has on its rolls the names of persons who have been members, but whose attendance has become infrequent and interest has waned. There are apt to be others whose whereabouts has become unknown to present members, or who have moved away long ago and have manifested no intention of affiliating with a church elsewhere.

Out of practical and pastoral considerations, the *inactive membership list* has been devised, and most churches have both an active and an inactive list. It is therefore incumbent upon a congregation to formulate a policy with respect to those who were active participants but who have ceased to support the church by their presence at services or their contributions without any physical incapacity or other valid reason. The names of such persons may be placed on inactive status after a year of evident indifference and lack of positive response to visits, letters, and telephone calls eliciting their renewed commitment to the covenant relationship. This kind of suspension is a form of disciplinary action. In many churches, further lack of interest for a stated period of time will lead to a vote to drop these persons from membership. Some churches, however, allow names to remain indefinitely on the inactive list, in the hope that eventually there will be a restoration to active membership in this church or another one. Such persons may be received to membership by *restoration* as noted above as one way of receiving members.

It should be noted, however, that persons on the inactive list should not be counted when making reports of membership to the association or other body. Also, inactive members are not eligible to vote in church meetings or to be elected to church office.

The Question of Open Membership

By the end of the twentieth century, new problems had emerged concerning the dismission and reception of members. According to traditional Baptist practice, letters were always granted only to churches of "like faith and order," and only those persons who had been immersed on a profession of faith were admitted as members. Baptists were convinced that their doctrine of a regenerate church membership could not be maintained if members were transferred by letter to and from other denominations which practice infant baptism (paedobaptism). To receive members from these paedobaptist churches by means of letter, they held, was tantamount to giving approval to infant baptism; and infant baptism seemed clearly incompatible with the concept of a regenerate membership. For generations, therefore, Baptists adhered to their historic stand. They stated that letters were granted only to churches of like faith and order. When a letter to a church outside the Baptist family was requested, they responded by writing that the person in question was a member in good standing, and that the name would be erased if the other church were to accept him/her on a statement of Christian experience.

Changing conditions, however, brought a challenge to Baptist practice. The mobility of families and the growing consciousness of a need for Christian unity led many congregations to reexamine their policy regarding the admission of paedobaptists. As it became more common for families to change denominational affiliations when they moved to new communities, there were more frequent requests for Baptist churches to grant letters to, and to accept letters from, churches of other denominations. In some cases, Baptist congregations, for a variety of reasons, joined with non-Baptist congregations in union or federated churches or in dual alignments. Most important of all, a pervasive ecumenical spirit has also made people more aware of the essential unity of the church of Jesus Christ.

In the face of this situation, an increasing number of Baptist churches have adopted an open-membership policy. That is, they admit persons from paedobaptist communions without requiring them to be rebaptized subsequent to their profession of faith. In the United States this practice is more the case in American Baptist churches than in other Baptist bodies. Open-membership churches expect the applicant to give evidence of a sincere profession of faith in Jesus Christ and of having been baptized *and confirmed* in a former church. Many Baptists have resisted such changes and consider them a betrayal of Baptist principles. On the other hand, a standing resolution of the American Baptist Churches since May 26, 1925, which stated that "only immersed members will be recognized as delegates to the Convention," has been rescinded.

The Case Against Open Membership

Many Baptist churches today still insist upon believers' baptism by immersion as a requirement for membership. They defend their position by an appeal to the Scriptures, to Baptist history, and to practical considerations. On these grounds they offer a strong case for continuing to insist upon believers' baptism by immersion as a requirement for membership in Baptist churches.

Approaching the question of baptism from the standpoint of the Scriptures, they insist that the rite must be associated with a decisive experience of faith and repentance on the part of the one baptized. Only by going beyond the evidence, they say, can one make a case for baptizing a passive individual on the grounds of the faith of someone else. Moreover, the evidence strongly supports immersion as the mode of baptism practiced in the apostolic era. Therefore, on scriptural grounds alone they regard the question as settled. They go on to point out that, with only a few exceptions, Baptists through the years have regarded believers' baptism by immersion as the only acceptable form of the rite. Since this practice seemed inseparably connected with the ideal of a regenerate membership, Baptists in the past have insisted that the latter could be maintained only by retaining an emphasis upon believers' baptism.

Some have also bolstered the arguments from Scriptures and from Baptist history with pragmatic observations. Pointing to the experience of Protestant Europe, they argue that the scandalous situation there illustrates the inevitable outcome of practicing infant baptism over a long period of time. In several countries, the state churches claim memberships which comprise the majority of the citizens, but only a small minority takes any serious interest in the life of the churches. Indeed, many Protestants in Europe seem to have had uneasy consciences with regard to infant baptism. Therefore, these Baptists declare, it would be foolish to abandon a position which has such strong biblical and historic support, and substitute one which has such demonstrable shortcomings.

The Case for Open Membership

There are other Baptists, however, who are not satisfied to uphold the traditional Baptist practice to this extent. They contend that more problems are raised by refusing to admit paedobaptists to membership in Baptist churches than by admitting them. They, too, are concerned to be faithful to the witness of Scripture, but they explain that we are closest to the mind of Christ when we emphasize the spirit and purpose which underlie outward forms of ecclesiastical practice. In support of their stand in favor of open membership, they appeal to the essential meaning of baptism in the New Testament and to its significance for Baptists. By such consideration, these Baptists believe that it is possible to preserve the scriptural intent of the rite and the historic Baptist emphasis of believers' baptism without conforming to the outward form in all details.

Those who espouse this position agree that baptism should be related to the repentance and faith of the person who is to be baptized. Since they are advocating the reception by letter of persons baptized as infants, the question is raised: Can infant baptism have a connection with faith and repentance? Many Protestant churches staunchly maintain that it can and does have such a meaning. The baptism of infants is tacitly acknowledged by such Protestants to be incomplete until the individual has personally accepted the baptism and made a public confession of faith. Vows of confirmation, or something corresponding to these, are regarded as the completion of a process begun at baptism. Only after confirmation is the person fully a member of the church and eligible to partake of the Lord's Supper. In a sense, it is held, the two acts become a single event, and baptism becomes associated with faith and repentance. The sequence of events is admittedly awkward, many say, but they add that this reversal and separation of the parts of baptism began fairly early in the history of the church and Christians today must make the best of the situation. Feeling that it is presumptuous to declare most Christians unbaptized, some Baptists are willing to admit therefore that infant baptism *followed by confirmation* constitutes a valid form of baptism.

Second, turning to the question concerning the significance of baptism in relation to regenerate church membership, it is asked: Can regenerate membership be realized without strict adherence to the practice of believers' baptism? Admittedly, most of our Baptist forebears would have returned an emphatic negative to that question. But early in our history, we are reminded, there were a few voices among Baptists which dissented from the prevailing opinion on this point. John Bunyan, for example, held that "the church of Christ hath no warrant to keep out of the communion the Christian that is discovered to be a visible saint." In examining this matter, it is stressed, one should clarify the issues and base conclusions upon principles rather than upon expediency.

Contrary to the general assumption, argue those who favor open membership, believers' baptism is not an indispensable prerequisite to regenerate churches. To make it so, they contend, would impart a "magical" quality to baptism which most Baptists would find unacceptable. Unless we are willing to contend that believers' baptism by immersion is essential to salvation, they say, we cannot very well assert that regenerate church membership depends upon that form of baptism. No one questions that there are in paedobaptist churches many persons whose vital Christian experience and deep consecration leave no doubts that they are twice-born. The history of the church offers ample evidence that God has not withheld the Holy Spirit from those who have been baptized as infants. Therefore, it seems necessary to concede that regenerate church membership is not inseparably tied to believers' baptism.

It frequently happens that persons who have been committed Christians for many years begin to attend a Baptist church. They may have moved to a new neighborhood and live near the Baptist church, or they marry a member of the Baptist church and wish to belong to the same church as their spouse. For whatever good reason, they wish to become a member of this congregation. Since they have long been Christians and see no reason to receive a second baptism, can we insist that they do so? What reason can we give for such a requirement, which implicitly calls for a rejection of their former baptism? To say simply that they must submit to baptism merely because that is the Baptist practice reduces the rite to a formal procedure which lacks significance. It is no more than the equivalent of an initiation ceremony for membership in a lodge. It is difficult to justify a demand that persons be baptized when they consider their previous baptism meaningful.

The quality of church membership, state the advocates of open membership, depends more upon the kind of preparation and examination of those admitted into it than upon the kind of baptism which is administered. Baptist experience, they contend, demonstrates that churches of poor quality can result even when believers' baptism is strictly adhered to but inadequate attention is paid to examination, nurture, and expectations of members. An emphasis upon the quality of Christian commitment by applicants, therefore, is more important than the requirement of a particular form of baptism.

It is not the intention of those who hold such views to minimize the importance of baptism. Their purpose is to focus attention upon what they regard as primary, so that we shall not be diverted by a preoccupation with secondary things. It is neither believers' baptism nor infant baptism which is the decisive factor, they assert, but faith in Jesus Christ as Savior and Lord. According to their position, baptism is an external form which is intended to signify a deeper reality. While no command of Christ is to be dismissed as trivial, we must not mistake form for substance. In the matter of baptism as with other ceremonies, they say, one may be so careful about proper compliance with ritual requirements that the act is reduced to legalism. If such a reduction is to be avoided, they conclude, and if we are really interested in the ideal of regenerate membership, our emphasis must be upon the care with which we admit members and the subsequent nurture which is provided for them.

To support open membership, say those who favor it, is not to propose that Baptists abandon believers' baptism. In our own practice, they explain, we must adhere to believers' baptism by immersion. Although another baptism may be accepted for Christians from other churches when their lives testify to a genuine Christian commitment, there is no reason for Baptists to adopt such a form for their own usage. Moreover, there is a vivid symbolism in immersion which is lacking in either sprinkling or pouring; immersion dramatically portrays one's identification with Christ in his death, burial, and resurrection. Therefore, from the standpoint of the New Testament, believers' baptism by immersion is the appropriate form, and it ought to be retained by Baptist churches.

An Intermediate Position: Associate Membership

Some Baptist churches, preferring neither to accept unimmersed persons into full membership nor to deny membership to Christians wishing to transfer from paedobaptist churches, have taken a compromise position in the form of associate membership. This practice became common in the early decades of the twentieth century as cooperation among denominations was increasing and many Baptists desired to be more open to fellowship with other Christians. So long as Baptist churches insisted that those who had been baptized as infants must be immersed upon a profession of faith in order to become members of a Baptist church, there were many from other denominations who became regular attenders but objected to what they considered a re-baptism in order to join. Although some churches responded to this need with open membership, others regarded this as too drastic a departure from Baptist practice and took the alternative road to associate, or affiliate, membership, thus accepting these persons at least partially, though with somewhat restricted privileges. Ordinarily, there were some church offices such members could not hold and some matters on which they could not vote in church meetings.

As open membership has been more widely accepted, the need for an associate membership has diminished. There are, however, still many church constitutions which provide for this category of member. There is considerable variation in church constitutions as to the restrictions which will govern such membership. Where open membership is not practiced by the church, associate membership with some limitations upon privileges may still be a useful option. The sample constitution in Appendix 3 contains one possible pattern for this (Article V, Optional Paragraph E).

A Relevant Ecumenical Study

Since baptismal practice has been a point at which Baptists have often been at odds with other Christians, it is heartening to note how much closer most Christian traditions have come together. Since the first edition of this *Manual* was published, the Faith and Order Commission of the World Council of Churches has sponsored consultations and published a document entitled *Baptism, Eucharist, and Ministry*[3] (BEM), which represents a major breakthrough. Although there is no claim to have reached a consensus, the participants speak of convergence on many hitherto stubborn points of division. Over three hundred denominational bodies engaged in a series of consultations, bilateral and multilateral, which have resulted in remarkable agreements on a broad range of issues pertaining to baptism, the Lord's Supper, and ministry.

Most of the participants in dialogues were from member churches of the Council, but nonmembers shared in some of the gatherings, including Roman Catholics and Southern Baptists. One important consultation, for example, on infant baptism and believers' baptism took place in 1979 at Southern Baptist Theological Seminary, Louisville, Kentucky. While the participants—Baptists from the United States and Europe, representatives of Reformed, Lutheran, United Church of Christ, and other Protestant bodies in the United States—did not agree on everything, there was a surprisingly high degree of understanding and convergence.

The *Baptism, Eucharist, and Ministry* document, was the result of years of studies, conferences, and dialogue within

---

[3]*Baptism, Eucharist, and Ministry,* Faith and Order Paper No. III (Geneva: World Council of Churches, 1982).

many churches. At the meeting of the Faith and Order Commission in 1982, the document was finally approved. Over one hundred of the church bodies had sent detailed responses to the preliminary draft, and it was recommended to the World Council for action. At the Assembly in Vancouver in 1983 it was adopted, and then sent to the churches for further comment and suggestions. Inasmuch as these areas had long been roadblocks to fuller unity of the churches, the agreements reached were indeed a notable achievement.

Baptists can resonate with most of the section on baptism. The biblical exposition dealing with New Testament images of baptism and the interpretation of the rite offer rich insights with which most Baptists can agree, and from which they may also have their understanding of baptism deepened. This ecumenical document acknowledges that believers' baptism "is the most clearly attested pattern in the New Testament," but allows the possibility that there may have been infant baptism in the early church (p. 4, par. 11). A good balance is maintained between two opposite tendencies in baptismal theology, affirming that "baptism is both God's gift and our human response to that gift" (p. 3, par. 8). It looks towards a growth into "the measure of the full stature of Christ" (Eph. 4:13). It declares that a personal profession of faith is essentially connected with baptism: "When one who can answer for himself or herself is baptized, a personal confession of faith will be an integral part of the baptismal service. When an infant is baptized, the personal response will be offered at a later moment in life. In both cases, the baptized person will have to grow in the understanding of faith" (p. 4, par. 12).

It is conceded that "in many large European and North American majority churches infant baptism is often practised in an apparently indiscriminate way," and that this fact "contributes to the reluctance of churches which practise believers' baptism to acknowledge the validity of infant baptism" (p. 7, commentary 21b). At the same time those who practice believers' baptism may not always put sufficient emphasis upon continuing nurture. Thus, "in order to overcome their differences, believer baptists and those who practise infant baptism should reconsider certain aspects of their practices. The first may seek to express more visibly the fact that children are placed under the protection of God's grace. The latter must guard themselves against the practice of apparently indiscriminate baptism and take more seriously their responsibility for the nurture of baptized children to mature commitment to Christ" (p. 6, par. 16).

Many Baptists will find themselves in accord with most of the section on baptism and will rejoice that so much common ground has been found for the doctrine and practice of baptism among Christians over the world. Of course, it is recognized by earlier discussion in this chapter that most Baptists are still not ready to accept the validity of infant baptism, while many others will find reinforcement in the BEM document for their practice of open membership. These will be among those churches "which unite both infant-baptist and believer-baptist traditions," and are able to accept "both a pattern whereby baptism in infancy is followed by later profession of faith and a pattern whereby believers' baptism follows upon a presentation and blessing in infancy" (Commentary, 12).

There are naturally some points at which Baptists feel uncomfortable, such as the suggestion that baptism effects an ethical cleansing. The response of American Baptist Churches, in 1986, noted that point of objection, but it also pointed to another matter of more substantial disagreement: "American Baptists, however, would have continuing difficulty with . . . Paragraph 13, in which it is stated that any practice 'which might be interpreted as "rebaptism" must be avoided.' American Baptists certainly wish to avoid unnecessary scandal or offense to their Christian sisters and brothers of other traditions. But we are generally unwilling to accept any assertion that in such a matter as this, 'appearances' should be the ruling consideration. Though sometimes persecuted as 'rebaptizers,' Baptists have never so understood themselves. Yet they have been—and largely still are—unwilling to commit themselves to deny the ordinance of baptism to those who may in all sincerity seek it in accordance with the biblical practices, whatever the 'appearance' may be in light of an earlier infant baptism." It is on this point that Baptists have often found themselves at odds with other Christians in ecumenical discussions. While many are willing to accept persons baptized as infants, they are unwilling to deny the rite to those who say that their baptism as infants has no meaning for them and who therefore desire to be baptized upon a profession of faith. Baptists do not consider this a rebaptism, and this is a sticking point which will not soon be removed.

Individual Churches Must Choose

With respect to the question of open membership, there seems to be no simple, neat solution of the problem. Although traditional Baptist practice which insists upon believers' baptism by immersion may be able to make a strong case, there is also both logical and theological force in the open-membership position. Until the impasse can be broken, both viewpoints, as well as the compromise of associate membership, will continue to find expression in Baptist churches. Meanwhile Baptists need to seek further light under the guidance of the Holy Spirit, as they try to reach a clear consensus on this issue.

Whatever position is adopted, it is necessary that the essential meaning of baptism be kept in mind. To continue to stress regenerate membership in local churches requires that we take care at the right places. Churches should seek to ascertain whether the baptism and confirmation of persons coming from other churches does represent a sincere commitment to Christ. The same careful scrutiny that is given to new converts should also be given to those who ask to be received by letter from another church. Such care should be exercised, whether the applicant comes from another Baptist church or from a church of another denomination. No church should succumb to the temptation to make standards of membership easier simply in order to increase its size. Moreover, it should give careful attention to continued nurture and discipline of the member, encouraging Christian growth and enlisting all in its ministry.

6

The Baptist Ministry

A basic consideration in determining the form of a church is the possession of appropriate officers. Among Baptists a church *completed* was traditionally defined as one having officers of God's appointment and the church's election. "A particular church," states the Philadelphia Baptist Confession, "gathered and completely organized according to the mind of Christ, consists of officers and members; and the officers appointed by Christ to be chosen and set apart by the church . . . are bishops, or elders, and deacons." These officers, they held, were essential to the *well-being* of the church but not to its very *being*. Having treated some aspects of the local church in preceding chapters, we now turn, in this chapter and the next, to the subject of officers essential to the church, as in their various roles they engage in ministry.

It is a basic principle among Baptists that all members of the church are, in a sense, ministers, carrying out the literal meaning of the word, which is "servant." There is, of course, a lay ministry and an ordained ministry, but all are engaged in serving Christ and ministering to fellow members as well as to all people everywhere. The ordained ministry includes many categories of persons who have been especially set apart to serve the churches in special ways, including pastors, chaplains, missionaries, seminary professors, regional and area ministers, certain types of denominational executives, and many others. The special nature of pastors in ministry, however, is defined by the literal meaning of that term, which is "shepherd." The pastor has the special ministerial responsibility of leading and caring for a local church or "flock."

Officers of a Local Church

The chief office-bearer in Baptist churches of an earlier day was the pastor (also called elder or bishop), who was to preach, teach, counsel, admonish, and administer. Deacons were to assist the pastor by looking after temporal affairs of the church, so that the pastor's attention need not be diverted from the main responsibilities. In some cases the church chose a ruling elder and/or teaching elder, following John Calvin's pattern of ministry. These latter offices, however, gradually disappeared from use by Baptists.

The New Testament Churches

When Baptist leaders of an earlier century customarily spoke of the offices of pastor and deacon as being "appointed by Christ," they were voicing a conviction that these were the specific and divinely prescribed offices essential to a church in every age. In principle, at least, Baptists were correct in this interpretation, although they did oversimplify the New Testament data. Since their time, biblical scholarship has demonstrated that the form of the ministry in the primitive churches was too varied to be reduced to a single pattern. Instead of a picture of uniformity of church officers, the New Testament records reveal variety. They reflect a situation in which institutional patterns were being established but had not yet become fixed. As the late Carl H. Morgan, a long-time Baptist New Testament scholar, wrote in a paper for a theological conference: "Since the church is a living organism, one simply cannot go back to the New Testament times for a complete description of church organization for today.... Perhaps the most important lesson to be learned from a study of the church of the apostolic age is that its organization was flexible; its form of worship adaptable; its vocabulary contemporary; and its methodology determined by its objectives." Officers, like other matters of polity, must be considered in relation to the nature and purpose of the church in a given context.

Perhaps one might expect to find more specific patterns of church offices in the New Testament, but examination of relevant passages shows that the writers gave little attention to such details. One cannot always distinguish between functions and offices. For example, in his first letter to Corinthians, Paul wrote: "And God has appointed in the church first apostles, second prophets, third teachers." He seemed to be listing particular offices in the church, but his list continues: "then deeds of power, then gifts of healing, forms of assistance, forms of leadership, various kinds of tongues" (1 Cor. 12:28). The latter categories refer to spiritual gifts and functions, but there is nothing in the statement to distinguish the first three terms from those which follow. It is also noticeable that no mention is made of pastors, bishops, elders, or evangelists in this list. Apparently the writer was thinking of spiritual gifts rather than offices in this context.

In Ephesians Paul wrote that Christ had given special ministerial gifts to his church: "The gifts he gave were that some would be apostles, some prophets, some evangelists, some pastors and teachers" (Eph. 4:11). It sounds as though these gifts are meant to be related to offices within the church. However, no further description of them is offered, and again we are left with questions as to his meaning. Are each of these terms intended to refer to distinct positions within the church? If so, were they to be temporary or permanent? Does the same person combine the work of pastor and teacher? If this is a list of church offices, why were not deacons included?

When the foregoing passages are compared with 1 Timothy, additional questions are introduced. In this letter there are definite references to particular offices. Nothing is said about evangelists, apostles, or prophets. In chapter 3, however, the qualifications of a bishop and of a deacon are stipulated. In the discussion of deacons, a reference is made to women (1 Tim. 3:11), but there is uncertainty about its meaning. Are they deaconesses, or are they wives of deacons?

Later (1 Tim. 5:3ff), there is a cryptic statement about widows, as though they may have occupied a special position in the church. Still farther along is the statement: "Let the elders who rule well be considered worthy of double honor, especially those who labor in preaching and teaching" (1 Tim. 5:17). Who is the elder? Is this a distinct office, or is this term synonymous with bishop and pastor? If the latter is the case, then why would only some of them labor in preaching and teaching? Elsewhere in the New Testament are references to a plurality of elders in a given congregation.

These allusions suggest that no uniform system of organization had been crystallized in the apostolic churches. The solution to the problems raised by the biblical data lies in recognizing the transitional character of this period. Only gradually did the Christian community see clearly that its identity was to become completely separated from Judaism. Consequently, it was slow in developing its own organizational forms; and when it did, it took over familiar patterns from the synagogue organization and adapted them to the new situation.

In the synagogue were boards of elders (presbyters), which served as governing bodies, and one of their number was the presiding officer ("the chief ruler of the synagogue"). As new Christian congregations were established, they appointed boards of elders to administer their affairs. Among the elders were individuals to whom special responsibilities were assigned, and perhaps some of them were called bishops (overseers). As the church was extended and the number of believers multiplied, there arose a need for a greater division of labor. Duties connected with worship, teaching, and ordination were assigned to bishops (or pastors), and distinctions began to be made between bishops and other elders (or priests).[1] With the rise of new needs, new offices were apparently created, as in the selection of seven men for administering the distribution of the common fund (Acts 6:1-6). The choice of the seven has traditionally been considered the beginning of the diaconate, but this inference is far from

---

[1]The Greek word for elder was *presbyter*, and *priest* is a shortened form of *presbyter*.

clear. By the end of the second century, a threefold ministry of bishops, priests, and deacons had developed in several centers.

It is a mistake then to expect to find in the New Testament an organizational structure that can be literally copied today. If the practice of early churches, as disclosed in the biblical records, was so varied, we may assume that it is unnecessary for us to duplicate any one pattern that was used in the primitive churches. The church is an organism, and its outward form may vary. Within certain limits, its organization is flexible, and adaptations may be made to meet changing conditions.

Guiding Principles for Determining Church Offices

Nevertheless, the absence of exact forms to be followed does not imply that there are no guidelines. To agree that the pattern of organization was developed in response to practical needs does not mean that it was a completely accidental or indiscriminate development. *The needs of the Christian community and its mission to the world supplied guiding principles which governed the development of specific offices.*

It may be useful at this point to take a backward look for a moment. In the second chapter, the church was portrayed as a people called by God to be the agency in and through which God is working out the redemptive purpose. As a nucleus of persons who had experienced the transforming power of God, they were to continue the ministry of Christ in the world. Restored to fellowship with God and brought into closer fellowship with other human beings, they were to be a redemptive community serving human need. The corporate nature of the Christian community is stressed in many figures of speech, and its ministry is shared by all its members.

The Ministry of the Laity

The characteristically Baptist belief that the ministry belongs to the church as a whole is expressed in the doctrine of the priesthood of all believers. Unfortunately, this doctrine has often been misunderstood, for its conventional interpretation is that it means no more than the right of everyone to approach God directly. It is true that Christ is our High Priest, and that his priestly work is unique and unrepeatable. We may indeed come to God in prayer and in humble confession of our sins without the intercession of a human advocate, but for that matter people under the Old Covenant could also do that! This interpretation is not what the doctrine of the priesthood of believers was originally intended to stress; it emphasized responsibilities more than rights. The idea of priesthood indicates something done on behalf of another; one cannot be a priest to oneself.

The concept of the priesthood of believers was formulated in the Reformation era, but its roots are in the New Testament. While the idea is implicit elsewhere, one of the few places where it is explicated is 1 Peter 2:9: "But you are a chosen race, a royal priesthood, a holy nation, God's own people, in order that you may proclaim the mighty acts of him who called you out of darkness into his marvelous light." The writer's obvious intent is to declare that, as God's people, the church has a priestly ministry. It means that all "Christians are called to bear witness to Christ, to testify to the forgiveness they have found, to pray for one another, and to give themselves in loving service to their neighbors."[2] The idea of the priesthood of believers, therefore, might be more aptly expressed as the *mutual ministry* of all believers.

With this idea in mind, Martin Luther announced that all baptized members of the church are responsible ministers of Christ. Nothing in the New Testament encourages the idea that a special clerical class was to be created that would be responsible for worship, witness, and teaching, while the great majority of members would be spectators. Nevertheless, now as in Luther's time, there is a subtle tendency toward clericalism, separating the status and functions of pastors and laity in a misleading way. The employment of the term "full-time service" to designate those who work in specialized church vocations has fostered the impression that people are serving God only when they are engaged in some activity of the institutional church. The implication

---

[2]W.S. Hudson, "The Ministry: Pastoral Call and Ordination," *Baptists in Transition* (Valley Forge: Judson Press, 1979), p. 73.

seems to be that the interests and occupations which take up the time of most church members are unrelated to the service of God. In order to correct false impressions about such service, we need to broaden our concept of the church's ministry.

First of all, the limited idea that the church exists and serves only when people are gathered for some formal church service needs to be dispelled. The church exists even when its members are dispersed in their homes and at their jobs, and its ministry is carried on through all the roles and relationships of individual Christians. Not everyone bears witness in the same way, but everyone is called to serve Christ in all of life.

Members serve God in a great variety of ways, and all of these are part of the ministry of the church to the world in the name of Christ. The ministry of church members is largely carried on in the home, factory, office, classroom, boardroom, legislative hall—wherever people live and work. Christians are missionaries on the frontiers between church and world, trying to influence the private and public institutions that condition their lives—advocating such causes as stewardship of natural resources, protection of the environment, respect for human rights, and the search for ways to peace and justice.

The Need for Leaders

There is another meaning of ministry in the New Testament, which is derivative and secondary. It is the one which we most commonly associate with the term, namely that of those who serve in pastoral office. Recognizing clearly the fundamental ministry of all members of the church, we need also to see the need for leadership within the churches. Although all members are ministers, not all are pastors. The distinction is one of role or function. There are diverse kinds of ministry, and among them is a ministry of leadership in the church whereby the entire fellowship is trained for its responsibilities. According to Paul, Christ's gifts to his church were "to equip the saints for the work of ministry"[3] and "for building up the body of Christ" (Eph. 4:12). Gifts of

---

[3]The comma after "saints" is properly omitted in the New Revised Standard Version and many other recent translations.

leadership are needed to enable the whole church to develop spiritual maturity so that it is prepared to fulfill the calling it has received from God.

It should be self-evident that churches need leaders in order to be faithful to their calling. This necessity is implied in Paul's enjoinder that things be done "decently and in order" (1 Cor. 14:40), and it is involved in the concept of the church as analogous to the human body. Declaring that Christians have diverse gifts, Paul compares them to different parts of the human body. It would not be good, he says, if the body were all eyes or ears; but each gift within the church supplements the other gifts, as varied parts contribute to the total functioning of a human life (Rom. 12:4-5; 1 Cor. 12:12-28). His point is obvious; namely, that all who make up the church contribute to the fulfillment of its task, each one according to the gifts God has bestowed.

The doctrine of the priesthood of all believers, therefore, does not eliminate the necessity for some division of labor within the church. Leadership is needed to help a group focus its efforts and achieve its purposes with a minimum of waste and confusion. Even in the primitive churches, there were some specialized leadership functions which required the establishment of particular offices, and the expansion of Christianity brought about further differentiation. It is fitting that the church recognize an ordained ministry alongside the mutual ministry of all Christians. The functions performed by an ordained ministry could be performed by other persons in most instances, but, for the sake of doing things decently and in order, it is better to delegate certain responsibilities to those who hold certain offices.

Those who serve in such offices act as representatives of the church. That is why Baptists insist that officers of a church be elected by the body. Since no one has a right to represent others without their approval, a congregation must approve the officers who are to act on its behalf. It is this principle which underlies the ordination of men and women to specialized ministries, as well as the election, or call, of the pastor and other officers. The rest of this chapter is devoted to a discussion of the office of the pastor, and the succeeding one deals with ministry through other offices of the church.

The Changing Nature of the Pastoral Office

What is the work of the pastoral ministry? There was a time when life was simpler and the role of pastors was clearer. They were leaders of the congregations, shepherds of the sheep (as the word "pastor" literally means), who were accountable to God for those placed in their care. Their duties included public worship of God, presiding at other meetings of the church, instructing the faithful from the pulpit, catechizing children, visiting in homes, baptizing converts, counseling the perplexed and distraught, performing weddings, and conducting funerals. One's schedule of activities was apt to be fairly simple, although by no means easy. Mornings were devoted to study so that the minister might properly instruct the people, afternoons were used for visitation, and evenings were spent with the family or at occasional church gatherings. Since members of the church lived within a convenient radius of the meeting-house, the pastor could know them intimately.

The present role of pastors is not so clear-cut. It includes most of the traditional duties, but many new demands have been added, which require increased knowledge, skills, and investment of time. Indeed, considerable effort has been expended in seeking an appropriate model or unifying concept of the ministry, which would integrate the numerous and diverse roles of the office. Some congregations are larger, and most are more scattered, reducing the opportunity for face-to-face relationships. The dispersed membership involves more hours in travel to meetings and for visiting; and calling on patients in two or three hospitals may fill a whole afternoon. Furthermore, organization is more complex and cumbersome with a multiplicity of boards, committees, and groups of different ages with different interests. These may involve heavy promotional and administrative responsibilities. Ministers are expected to represent the church in a variety of community activities and to attend many congregational and denominational meetings. An important task confronting churches in these days is that of restoring to the pastoral office a satisfactory image.

Roles of the Pastor

What, then, is a pastor? In the light of our concept of the church as a worshiping, teaching, witnessing, and ministering community, what ought the roles of pastors to be? What kind of leadership is called for? The pastor's role is primarily an inside job, namely "to equip the saints for the work of ministry, for building up the body of Christ" (Eph. 4:12). By "building up" the members, the pastor helps the church to be the church. In today's church this is accomplished mainly through worship, preaching, teaching, counseling, and administration.

Leader of Worship

Integral to the vitality of such communities of faith is the service of worship. Ordinarily, a church authorizes the pastor to lead its public worship. This authority is delegated to him or her both because good order demands it and because it is appropriate to appoint someone who is duly qualified for this responsibility. Likewise, baptism and the Lord's Supper, which are related to the church's worship, are acts of the church, which ought not to be performed without consent of the church. Such consent is expressed in ordination and the call to pastoral responsibility, and normally these acts are performed by the ordained minister, although the church may authorize laypersons to administer them when it seems desirable to do so.

The style of worship services varies greatly even within a denomination. Some Baptist services are rather formal, and others appear to be almost spontaneous. It is important to recognize that some orders of service may be more conducive to worship than are others, and appropriateness may vary with the nature of the congregation. Therefore, we need to make some judgments regarding forms that we use. This entails keeping sight of the purpose of public worship.

We recall Jesus' conversation with a woman at Samaria, as he said that it is not so important where one worshiped, but that "God is spirit, and those who worship him must worship in spirit and truth." (John 4:24). Although he did not explain further, these words would seem to require above all that there be sincerity of heart and willing obedience to God's will. In public worship the community of faith gathers to offer corporate praise, prayers of confession and intercession, and response to God's Word with repentance and deepened commitment.

Preacher

Preaching is certainly a high priority for the pastor, and it is a crucial part of the service of worship. The most basic and unchanging element of preaching is what the New Testament refers to as the "good news" (gospel) of God's love, manifested most fully in Jesus of Nazareth. Preaching as modeled in the New Testament is centered in Jesus—his birth, life and teachings, vicarious death, resurrection, abiding presence with us through the Holy Spirit, and the promised return to wrap up human history. The preacher's goal is to assure hearers of God's love and of human responsibility, so that hearts and minds are opened to insights from God's word, and consciences are quickened to faith and obedience to the divine will.

Teacher

In the New Testament preaching was often referred to as the *kerygma*, but alongside it was teaching *(didache)* as a part of the minister's responsibility. In today's church the pastor's teaching ministry is carried out both through the sermon and through leadership of Bible study groups or special courses. Teaching must go beyond the recital of the "old, old story of Jesus and his love" to interpret the significance of that story for the conduct of life in the contemporary world. In a broad sense it encourages spirituality, challenges consciences, and persuades people to courses of Christian action. Although some may complain when the preacher addresses contemporary issues, it is important that he/she illuminate the issues of our common life from a Christian perspective. Karl Barth's oft-quoted saying is pertinent—that we should read the Bible in one hand as we read the newspaper in the other. The God depicted in Scriptures is greatly concerned about justice in human affairs as well as personal piety. Indeed, Isaiah, Amos, and others of the prophets declared that God despises ritual worship by those who are indifferent to the poor and oppressed.

Counselor

Another essential aspect of pastoral ministry is response to individual members' special needs. In a small church the pastor can have close ties with all the members and share intimately all their joys and sorrows. In a larger church this sharing is more difficult, but a pastor still needs to be personally acquainted with all members of the congregation. This objective may be accomplished by a staff of more than one pastor. Also, it may be desirable to develop small fellowship groups within which individuals can experience the supportive concern that enables them to become mature and articulate Christians.

Much counseling time may be required to help some people deal with urgent personal problems. Modern living seems to produce an increasing number of anxieties for men, women, teenagers, and children whose lives are shattered by broken marriages, crippling and life-threatening illness, drug and alcohol abuse, financial stress, loneliness, and pressures of the home and job. Many are troubled by a sense of alienation from God, by feelings of personal inadequacy and lack of self-esteem, or by the perception that youth is slowly slipping away from them. All such situations, and countless others, need the healing word that can be brought by a wise and well prepared pastor. In additional to counseling, the pastor may help to develop support groups that offer a therapeutic effect in a fellowship of caring Christians. In dealing with the hurts of individuals, however, the pastor has a key personal role to play, in which no one else can adequately substitute.

Administrator

Pastors often consider administration as of less spiritual importance than preaching, teaching, counseling, or the conduct of worship. When rightly understood, however, effective administration is fundamental to leading a church in the development of a vital inner life and of outreach ministries. Through preaching, teaching, and worship, a pastor may articulate a vision of the church's ministry, but talking about mission is not to be confused with action.

A pastor is responsible to motivate and enlist members in support of the varied ministries of the local congregation and the wider mission of the denomination. Leadership involves skill in working with individuals, boards, committees, and other groups to facilitate the development of consensus about goals and programs so that participants will feel a sense of ownership. It is especially important in a congregational polity that members share with the pastor in designing the patterns of worship, witness, Christian education, and ministry that they are expected to support.

The Authority of a Pastor

Leadership implies some kind of authority, but what kind of authority does a pastor have? In some circles a pastoral authority is claimed which has the right to speak definitively about biblical and theological matters and to determine church policies and programs. Some churches stress the idea of "eldership" and the right of elders to rule in the church. In the Southern Baptist Convention, in the 1980s, this issue was heatedly debated. A well-known Texas pastor, W. A. Criswell, declared: "The pastor is the ruler of the church. There is no other thing than that in the Bible."[4] Subsequently, an annual meeting of the SBC passed a resolution, asserting that a doctrine of the priesthood of believers does not militate against the biblical injunction: "Obey your leaders and submit to them, for they are keeping watch over your souls and will give an account" (Heb. 13:17).[5] At least some ministers have taken this passage of Scripture to mean that pastors are above contradiction by anyone in their congregation.

In typical African American Baptist churches today, "the pastor is commander-in-chief by virtue of his call by God and the people, and often by virtue of his training. . . . The 'humble' pastor in past years often found the reins of leader-

---

[4]Cited in Nancy Ammerman, *Baptist Battles* (New Brunswick: Rutgers University Press, 1990), p. 87.
[5]*Ibid.*, p. 88.

ship removed from him.... The traditional black pastor was used to *giving orders* and seldom took orders. To take orders tends to be considered a sign of weakness."⁶ There is some movement away from such autocratic leadership today, but strong leadership is still expected in many congregations.

For many years the most common image of the minister among Baptists was that of the pastoral ruler. Andrew Fuller, one of the most influential Baptist ministers in the early nineteenth century, portrayed the typical Baptist minister of his time, saying: "There must be a *rule* in the church of Christ, as well as in other societies."⁷ Members, he said, ought to submit to the pastor's authority on three grounds: First, because the congregation had chosen their pastor after examining his qualifications; second, because he must urge upon them only what Christ wills; and third, he must urge only "things which . . . are equally binding upon himself."

Whatever may be the practice in some churches, and whatever may have been the case in the past, autocratic pastoral leadership is inconsistent with Jesus' teachings about leadership and conflicts with a Baptist polity that takes seriously the concept of the priesthood of believers. The authority of a minister is not the kind that can pull rank or issue orders (1 Peter 5:3). It is an authority *in* the church, but not *over* the church. A pastor's authority is only that which is granted by a church to act as its representative in preaching the Word, teaching, baptizing, presiding at the Lord's table, comforting those who are troubled, and challenging all to faithfulness and obedience. This is an unusual kind of authority, for it essentially depends upon being a servant to others.

A *Policy Statement on the Ministry,* adopted by American Baptist Churches in 1989, states: "All authority in the church is modeled on the example of Christ who 'came not to be served, but to serve,' and who taught that among Gen-

---

⁶Floyd Massey, Jr. and Samuel B. McKinney, *Church Administration in the Black Perspective* (Valley Forge: Judson Press, 1976), p. 35.

⁷Cited in N. H. Maring, "Andrew Fuller's Doctrine of the Church," in W. S. Hudson, ed., *Baptist Concepts of the Church* (Valley Forge: Judson Press, 1959), p. 90.

tiles 'their great men exercise authority over them. It shall not be so among you; but whoever would be great among you must be your servant' (Matt. 20:25-26, 28). For ordained ministers this means that ultimately authority depends upon a servant style of leadership, which is manifest in genuine care for others, a willingness to work in partnership with others, a readiness to place the gospel before personal ambitions, an openness to evaluation and growth."[8]

Of course, there is a kind of authority given by the church as it delegates responsibilities, and there is also a kind of authority involved in having expertise in biblical study and theology, but in the church these qualifications do not allow one to impose opinions or decisions upon the church body or other individuals. The authority to influence others must be won by patient, wise, and loving service.

Qualifications of a Pastor

Obviously, the pastor needs leadership gifts, including an aptitude for study, balanced judgment, and an ability to communicate clearly and persuasively. In addition, one needs a profound concern for people and a sensitivity to their feelings. This kind of interest will spring from a deep experience of the reality of God's redeeming love in the pastor's own life.

Baptists have always held that the most basic qualifications for the pastoral ministry are moral and spiritual. Once they couched these in such biblical terms as unblamable, not covetous, patient, humble, sober, apt to teach, etc. In modern times some clergy have reacted to unrealistic expectations and, to demonstrate their humanity and personhood, have rebelled against the notion that pastors should behave any differently from other members of their congregations. Contrary to other professions, however, character and personal qualities are even more important than proficiency in the pastorate.

It is impossible to quantify and measure personal qualities such as character, dedication to the Christian ministry, and

---

[8]Published by the Commission on the Ministry, American Baptist Churches, P. O. Box 851, Valley Forge, PA 19482-0851.

spirituality. The American Baptist Ministers' Council has developed a *Code of Ethics* to set standards acceptable to the ministers themselves, highlighting some considerations governing the character and behavior of ministers. The importance of such expectations is attested by an extensive survey of Protestant churches conducted by the American Association of Theological Schools, which sampled opinions of laypersons, clergy, and seminary professors. The three expectations which were clearly most important had to do with the character and spirit of the minister. Admittedly, it is difficult to make rules about such matters without falling into legalism, but it is important to affirm the need for ministers to exhibit integrity, humility, self-control, and a commitment to moral and spiritual values. "It is a false humility," writes a well-known Christian ethicist, "that would encourage them to refuse to accept the fact that they will be and are made morally different by being a minister."[9] This subject ought to claim the attention of those who aspire to the ordained ministry and those engaged in theological education.

Educational Preparation

Of capital importance also is educational preparation of a high quality. A broad knowledge of the world in which we live and an understanding of human behavior are important for the pastor, and graduation from a liberal arts college is essential to an adequate preparation for the Christian ministry. This is followed by a more specialized theological education on the graduate level in a seminary or divinity school. A thorough acquaintance with the Scriptures—the "sourcebook of the Christian community"—is a foundation for all other studies. Courses in church history, theology, and Christian ethics provide perspectives and understandings that give the minister a frame of reference for dealing with people and issues. Courses in Christian education can lead to understanding the processes by which people learn and form attitudes. Training in counseling, as well as clinical pastoral education, has value both for self-understanding and for

---

[9] Stanley Hauerwas, "Clerical Character" in *Christian Existence Today* (Durham, N.C.: Labyrinth Press, 1988), p. 145, note 1.

helping others deal with their personal and family problems. A study of liturgies and worship can help the minister develop orders of service which will be more creative and effective than simply following old ruts. In short, the whole range of theological studies is needed to prepare those who would become effective pastoral leaders.

When we speak of pastoral ministry as a learned profession, we mean that pastors should be learned both in the Christian faith and in the ways of the world, and that they should have the skills and knowledge to help people develop a mature Christian faith. Of course, education alone will not make one a competent minister without the prior possession of "natural" and "spiritual" gifts. It is equally true, though, that such gifts are inadequate without careful and disciplined educational preparation for this calling.

The Call to the Ministry

The term "call to the ministry" may be misleading, for, as has already been stated, all Christians are called to be ministers. Most are called to serve in ordinary occupations in a manner similar to the way that some are called to engage in ordained ministries of the church. Many people seem to think that a calling to the pastoral ministry is purely a private matter between an individual and God. Some people declare that no one has a right to question another's sense of call to such a ministry, no matter how unsuited that person may appear to be. Such an individualistic interpretation of the call of God, however, is not in line with Baptist thought prior to the middle of the nineteenth century. Since the pastor preaches, teaches, and ministers in a representative capacity, the call of God involves an *external call* which comes through the church. There is also an *internal call*, which is an inner assurance on the part of the individual that it is God's will that she/he should become useful in the role to which the church has summoned. Such an inner call finds expression in a willing response to the external call of the church.

Today, when it is common to regard a call to the ministry as strictly a private matter, it is well to remember the importance Baptists have placed upon the church's role in a call.

If the ministry belongs ultimately to the whole church of Christ, then it is the responsibility of the particular church to select qualified and gifted persons to act as its representatives in the broader ministry of the whole church. Early Baptist churches were frequently reminded to seek out those among their members whose "gifts" and aptitude for learning suggested they might have the capacity for pastoral leadership. The initial call of the church to them might be a word spoken to someone by a pastor, a deacon, a Sunday church school teacher, or some other member. If the individual responded affirmatively and the entire congregation was convinced of the genuineness of the "gifts," the procedure was to issue a license to preach. This was the signal that the person called might exhibit "gifts" as opportunity arose and pursue the necessary studies to prepare for the ordained ministry.

Before the ordination, a council composed of representatives of neighboring churches reviewed a statement of the candidate's call, Christian experience, and educational preparation, and made a decision as to the candidate's suitability for the pastoral ministry. Ordination, therefore, became a public affirmation by the church that an individual's qualifications had been tested and that approval had been given for setting the person apart to the gospel ministry.

It is important to state that women, as well as men, may be called to the ordained ministry. Women were leaders in at least some of the New Testament churches, and women today experience the call of God to the ordained ministry as men do. It is a mistake to allow our prejudices to deny them access to the pastoral office. Certain passages of Scripture, which probably applied to local or cultural conditions, should not be allowed to overshadow the more important declaration that in Christ "there is no longer Jew or Greek, there is no longer slave or free, there is no longer male or female; for all of you are one in Christ Jesus" (Gal. 3:28). It took centuries for the Christian conscience to see the implications of that statement for human bondage, and it has taken even longer to understand its meaning for women in ministry. It is high time for churches to recognize that God calls women as well as men to ordained ministries.

Ordination

Few today question that a pastor needs an education, although people may differ as to the kind and amount of education that is necessary. There are also many who strongly oppose the requirement that formal education be a criterion for ordination. Many Baptists have no such requirement, but since 1965 American Baptist Churches as a denomination has had ordination standards that include four years of college and three years of seminary in order to be fully recognized.[10] In most of the denomination these standards are adhered to, but allowance may be made for special circumstances so that the requirements may be modified in some areas.

The Procedure for Ordination

As in the past, the usual procedure leading to ordination begins with licensing by a local church and the regional department of ministry. This license signifies that a local church believes a person possesses the abilities, emotional stability, and spiritual sensitivities necessary for ministry, and that he/she is enrolled in an educational program. The licensee is taken under joint "watchcare" and will be counseled periodically by the pastor, a church committee, and/or the regional department of ministry. This procedure is in keeping with the historic understanding of licensing as a step toward ordination. There are instances where licensing is used as the authorization of lay preachers, but such is not the generally accepted use of the practice.

When the licensee has become adequately prepared, the local church then presents him or her as a candidate for ordination. In keeping with the associational principle, however, other churches are invited to share in the ordaining process. After the standing committee of the association or region has examined the candidate's credentials and found

---

[10]*Recommended Procedures for Ordination, Commissioning, and Recognition for the Christian Ministry in the American Baptist Churches,* Commission on the Ministry and the Minister's Council, 1986.

them in order, the church is notified that it may proceed to call for an ordination council. This council inquires into the candidate's Christian experience, call to the ministry, statement of doctrine, and any other matters considered pertinent. After the questioning period is completed, the candidate is excused from the room while the council votes to approve (or disapprove) her/his qualifications, and if the vote is affirmative recommends to the originating church that it proceed to hold an ordination service.

When a church is notified of a favorable action by the ordination council, it proceeds to plan the ordination service. Representatives of the church's broader fellowship in the association, cluster, or region are invited to participate in the service. The central act of ordination is the ordination prayer, in which God's blessing is invoked upon the ordinand's ministry, and which is accompanied by the laying-on-of-hands by the ordained ministers present. In this practice, they follow biblical examples, such as the commissioning of Paul and Barnabas by the church at Antioch (Acts 13:3) and a reference in 1 Tim. 4:14. This ceremony has never signified for Baptists a belief in apostolic succession or the conveying of a special power or elevation to a superior status. Rather it is a symbolic act of prayer for God's blessing upon the ordinand's ministry and for the guidance of the Holy Spirit.

Sometimes, and appropriately, one or two deacons of the ordaining church also take part in the laying on of hands. Prior to the prayer, the recommendation of the council is read, an appropriate sermon is delivered, a charge is given to the candidate, and the candidate responds by affirming vows of ordination. The ordinand is seated in the congregation until requested to stand for the charge and then comes forward for the ordination prayer. Following the prayer, it is customary for a welcome into the ministry to be extended to the newly-ordained person, who then pronounces the benediction as the first act of pastoral office.

The fact that representatives of other churches and of the regional and/or associational body have shared in the service indicates that the ordination is of interest to the denomination as a whole. Following the affirmation and validation by the ordination council and the ordination service in which denominational representatives have shared, the newly ordained minister is given appropriate recognition by the denomination.

As noted above, there are situations in which the full educational standards of the denomination must be modified. There are often circumstances in which congregations are unable to support a full-time pastor, but where a bi-vocational minister with some theological training but not enough to meet the full requirements for national recognition is available to serve. Regions, therefore may find it necessary to modify the national standards to fit particular situations, and it is possible to have an ordination which is *regionally* recognized though not *nationally* recognized. There is also the possibility that a church may ordain someone who has not been approved by anyone other than the local church itself, and such ordination is recognized as applicable only to that church.

The reference to bi-vocational ministers should not be taken as synonymous with lack of credentials for full national recognition. Recognition is based on qualifications, not on sources of income. Bi-vocational ministers have always been a part of the Baptist ministry. That is, there have been persons who have earned a livelihood in full or in part by some occupation other than a pastoral ministry. Indeed, at one time the typical Baptist minister was bi-vocational. There are still many persons devoted to serving in the inner city or in other places where churches cannot financially support a full-time ministry. Such bi-vocational ministers are likely to meet the full educational requirements for national recognition, but simply feel God's call to minister in these places.

Other Ordained Ministries

The discussion of ordination so far has centered upon the pastoral office, but ordination is not limited exclusively to pastoral ministry. In early times the pastor of a congregation was the typical minister, and descriptions of ministry were couched in language pertinent to this form. Gradually, however, ordination was extended to missionaries, evangelists, seminary professors, and denominational administrators. Included today are associate pastors, chaplains, pastoral counselors, and editors of religious publications. With regard to ministers of Christian education, youth work, or music, there has often been uncertainty whether they should be ordained. There are general principles on which such questions can be decided.

With good reason ordination was extended beyond pastors of local churches, for there are many who serve in ways that require qualifications similar to those of a pastor, but who are not, strictly speaking, pastors. For example, executive and area ministers, evangelists, institutional chaplains, pastoral counselors, administrators, and professors in theological seminaries and religion departments of colleges are all outside of the actual pastoral ministry as such. Yet they serve churches in ways similar to the duties of the pastoral office, and most of them engage to some extent in preaching and teaching. When such persons share the pastoral ministry in its broad sense and have the appropriate educational credentials they should be ordained. This same principle would apply to ministers of Christian education, youth, or music.

In general, ordination is appropriate for those who have special responsibility as bearers of the Christian tradition and of their own Baptist heritage, transmitting and applying the gospel in their ministry of the Word, administering the ordinances, and overseeing the churches. Implicit in such criteria is the requirement that those who are ordained have a specific place of service and suitable qualifications for that particular ministry.

Withdrawal of Recognition

In view of the fact that Christian ordination signifies the approval of the church for a woman or a man to serve in a specialized church calling, there needs to be some way to reverse the process. In some cases ministers have ceased to serve in any form of specialized ministry, and they are engaged in an occupation for which ordination has no relevance. Sometimes, indeed, scandalous behavior has forced their withdrawal from leadership in the church. In the American Baptist Churches, it is possible for the recognition of ordination to be withdrawn by the regional department of ministry. This is done after written notice has been given, followed by personal consultation with the regional or executive minister and any appeal to the appropriate body has been heard. It is also possible for one who is no longer functioning as a minister in the ABC to be placed on an inactive list in the Registry of Professional Leaders of the American Baptist Churches in the U.S.A. If after five years, the person is still unrelated to the structure and function of the denomination, the name is dropped from that inactive list.

Lay Preachers

In some places the category of lay preacher has been restored. It is not necessary that public preaching be limited to ordained persons, but it is important that no church member engage in preaching without the approval of the church. As the Philadelphia Confession puts it: "Although it be incumbent on the bishops or pastors of the churches to be instant in preaching the Word, by way of office; yet the work of preaching the Word is not so peculiarly confined to them but that others also gifted and fitted by the Holy Spirit for it, and approved and called by the church, may and ought to perform it." Notice especially the words, "approved and called by the church." Those so approved and called were lay preachers. There were and are many ways in which a lay preacher may be of service—for example, when a neighboring church is without a minister or when a neighboring pastor is ill. Ordination is not necessary for such a person to render acceptable service by public preaching and teaching when the need arises. Even a lay preacher, however, is a representative of the church and should not preach publicly without the approval of the church. Nor should such approval be given unless the person has the ability to perform these tasks in a creditable way. Too often persons with nothing to commend them but fluency of speech have been prevailed upon to fill pulpits in cases of necessity. Such a relationship lacks the support and approval of the church and demeans the office of pastor.

Occasionally, the license to preach, which represents a step toward ordination, has been misused for the purpose of giving some type of certification to the lay preacher. Instead of misusing the license, and instead of proceeding irregularly in allowing anyone to preach who might be asked to do so by an individual, it is suggested that churches would act more wisely to identify those in their congregation who are capable of preaching effectively. Churches could commission or certify such persons as lay preachers, available to fill the pulpits of neighboring churches as occasion demands.

7

Other Officers of the Local Church

Few churches today are organized so simply as to require no officers other than pastor and deacons. The complexity of the organization of local churches varies so much that it is difficult to offer a model which would fit the needs of every church. In some cases, a church may have a staff of several persons with professional training, each of whom shares in the pastoral responsibilities, whereas the typical congregation usually can support only one full-time person in the pastoral ministry. Yet even a small church needs a number of officers to carry on its programs. Considerable room should be allowed for flexibility, therefore, so that adaptations can be made to local situations.

Drafting a Constitution and Bylaws

It is occasionally suggested that a church does not need a constitution, and churches have sometimes tried to get along without one. The Bible, they say, is all they need to guide them in the conduct of church affairs. Although the motive is to rely solely on the direction of the Holy Spirit and Scriptures, the notion that such a method is a sign of superior spirituality is erroneous. Many churches have learned, to their great regret, that a lack of clear definitions of authority and accountability invites conflicts over the exercise of power and the use of power by individuals to dominate a church.

In any kind of organization, including a church, power is essential to making decisions and settling disputes. When power is exercised by authority of a church, it is legitimate, but when there is no such authorization, power is used arbitrarily. A constitution and bylaws will make clear where authority is vested and will make clear the procedures for establishing and executing policies. These documents will also provide a means for adjudicating misunderstandings and conflicts which may arise. Even a small church needs a constitution and bylaws, stating that authority resides in the full congregation, defines the mission, lists the officers and organizations, describes their responsibilities, and makes clear the lines of accountability. A church which has no such basic documents is more likely to experience unspiritual controversies than one with well-designed constitution and bylaws.

An examination of several constitutions in use by Baptist churches will reveal some basic similarities, which flow from functions inherent in the central mission of Christ's church. There will also be considerable variety in specific details, since no two situations are alike. A church ought not to adopt completely a ready-made constitution, but should tailor it to carry out the vision set forth in its statement of purpose in its own locale. Some important considerations are to be found in the following summary of guidelines listed in *Guidelines for Developing a Constitution and By-Laws for a Local Congregation.*[1]

1. The organization should be kept as simple as possible, so that it can function efficiently, trying to allocate human resources wisely by forming committees which are not too large for the congregation but large enough to allow for a democratic process.

2. Make clear distinctions between policy decisions and implementation of policies. Policies are made, or ratified,

---

[1] This document was prepared by the Office of Program Operations of the Board of National Ministries of the American Baptist Churches.

by the congregation. Boards and committees of the church are implementing groups.

3. Organizational structure should provide for the coordination of all groups and subgroups, so that all will contribute to the common purpose and goals of the congregation. In a multiboard system, a small coordinating group is needed to avoid duplication and conflicting activity and for sharing ideas. Such a group is often called the Advisory Council, but many prefer Church Council or Executive Committee. In churches which have a single-board system, there is a built-in coordinating body to which all subgroups are responsible.

4. In establishing boards and committees, it is important to have clear lines of accountability from subgroups through the coordinating council to the congregation. The number of major boards (commissions, departments) should be from three to six, and these are responsible to the coordinating group and ultimately to the congregation. Standing committees usually report to the coordinating group. In some cases, however, committees are subunits of major boards (commissions or departments) and are accountable to them.

5. Care needs to be taken to keep the size of committees commensurate with available leadership within the church and with the duties assigned. A committee ought not to have so many members that some will feel unnecessary. On the other hand, it should be large enough that members will not be overloaded with responsibilities.

6. A proper allocation of personnel resources should provide balance among (1) administrative functions for decisions and planning, (2) looking after internal church programs, and (3) service and outreach beyond the congregation's internal life. The tendency of churches is to attend to their own internal needs, leaving service and outreach as a kind of afterthought. Such outreach to the community is not to be left solely to individual initiatives, but should be an integral part of the corporate life of the church.

Additional information on the constitution and bylaws may be found in chapter 4 of this book, in connection with the organization of new churches. Also, sample documents are provided in Appendix 3. Note that the constitution is a basic document which should be subject to amendment only after very serious consideration and action by more than a simple majority vote. Bylaws, on the other hand, relate to structural and operational matters of the church and may be more easily amended.

General Officers of the Church

The Moderator. The option to have the pastor serve as moderator or to choose someone from the congregation for this office has already been described in chapter 4. Whoever serves in this capacity presides at the congregational meetings and is usually the chairperson of the Church Council. She/he is also an *ex officio* member of all boards and committees.

The Church Clerk. A church clerk is essential even in the smallest congregation. Someone must keep the records. Obviously the qualifications for such an office include carefulness as to details, a sense of responsibility, and the ability to keep accurate records in legible form. Since a clerk must also carry on correspondence in the name of the church, care should be taken to select a person capable of expressing ideas in grammatically correct language. The chief duties of this office are to keep minutes of all congregational and Church Council meetings, to maintain an accurate roll of the membership, and to carry on correspondence (including letters of dismission to other churches). It is also the clerk's responsibility to furnish statistical reports and other data required by the local Baptist association as well as regional and national organizations. The clerk is elected by the congregation. Since there is special value in having continuity in this work, the office probably need not be rotated. Unless the incumbent is incompetent, there is no reason why someone should not continue in this position indefinitely.

The Treasurer. The treasurer is expected to provide for the safekeeping and the disbursement of funds in accord with the instructions of the church. Here again accuracy and dependability are of great importance. In view of the fact that not everyone has the ability to keep careful financial records, suitable training or experience should be a factor in electing a person to take charge of this work. The records should be kept in such form that they can be easily examined by an auditing committee prior to the annual meeting of the church.

The Financial Secretary. It is usual for a financial secretary to receive and count all moneys and to deposit the receipts in the proper bank accounts. He/she then turns over to the treasurer a statement of such deposits. This officer keeps a record of the contributions of individual members given through envelopes provided by the church. Periodically each contributor should receive an accurate statement of his or her giving.

The Church School Superintendent. The general superintendent serves as the administrative head of the Sunday church school, in cooperation with the Board of Christian Education. In some churches, where there is a director of Christian education, it may be considered advisable for that person to do the work of the superintendent. The director is related to the entire educational program of the church, including vacation church school, weekday Christian education, Sunday evening programs, Sunday church school, and all other educational activities. When the superintendency is a separate office, this person is concerned solely with the Sunday church school, including all its departments. Too often in the past the Sunday school has acted almost independently of the church itself, choosing its own officers and having its own budget. More recently there is general recognition that this school has meaning only as an arm of the church, and acknowledgment of that fact is made when we refer to it as a Sunday *church* school. The superintendent is therefore either elected by the church or appointed by the Board of Christian Education. By providing for the needs of the school through the regular church budget, the church can direct the school's affairs in a way that will best serve to fulfill its teaching ministry. When the officers and teachers of the Sunday church school are ready to assume their duties, a public installation service is appropriate to recognize that they are sharing in the teaching work of the church.

Boards of the Church

Reference has already been made to the choice between multiple-board organization and a single-board system. Most churches operate on the former plan, but the latter is growing in favor. Each has its advantages and disadvantages. In what follows, the multiple board system is assumed, but a brief description of the working of a single-board structure will be given later in this chapter.

The Board of Deacons (Diaconate)

Whether or not the choosing of the seven to handle the common fund and serve the tables, as described in Acts 6, was the beginning of the office of deacon is a moot question. There is good reason to believe, however, that the biblical account was given for the purpose of explaining the beginning of the Diaconate. In the situation depicted there, those who administered the Word (the Twelve) were being compelled to neglect their preeminent responsibility by becoming too involved in routine matters. Consequently, seven men were chosen from the congregation to relieve the apostles of these other duties. This step did not indicate that "serving tables" was unimportant. Indeed, the dispute which they were appointed to resolve was shattering the unity of the church. What it did mean was that those who had the special responsibility for ministering the Word should be freed to give full attention to that service for which they were best equipped. The pastoral officers should be relieved of direct management of the temporal concerns of the church which can be handled by other members.

The work of the deacons in the early church is not made very clear, although the requirements specified in 1 Timothy 3 offer some clues to their duties. They apparently were expected to have oversight over the administration of finances, and particularly to supervise the distribution of relief to the poor. In general they took charge of the temporal affairs of the churches. It is not necessary, of course, to find a pattern of activity for this office and to imitate it slavishly, but again we find guiding principles in the functions they performed.

In the United States, Baptists have generally viewed the Diaconate as intended to assist the pastor, but at various times other roles have been emphasized. Evidence gleaned from confessions of faith and other sources indicates that in the seventeenth and eighteenth centuries it was common to describe their duties as "table servers": (a) serving the Lord's table by providing the necessary elements for the Lord's Supper and admonishing those who neglected this ordinance; (b) serving the table of the poor by collecting and distributing funds for the needy; and (c) serving the table of the pastor by gathering funds for his (or possibly her) support. They also shared with the pastor the disciplining of church members.

By the middle of the nineteenth century the emphasis shifted to the role of the deacon as manager of the temporal affairs of the church. This trend was given strong impetus by a book entitled *The Deaconship,* by R.B.C. Howell, a minister in Nashville, Tenn., published by the American Baptist Publication Society in 1846. The book, which had wide influence, stated his view that "they are a board of directors, and have charge of all the secular affairs in the kingdom of Christ."[2]

In the early twentieth century, it was increasingly stressed that the main responsibility of deacons was evangelism, and greater emphasis was placed upon the Diaconate's assisting the pastor by personal witness, occasional preaching, and visitation of church families. Especially among northern Baptist churches there was a tendency to assign spiritual duties to the deacons and temporal concerns to trustees, with a concomitant implication often drawn that deacons must have spiritual qualifications while these were not so important in selecting trustees. Historically, the qualifications for a deacon have been spiritual insight, trustworthiness, familiarity with the Scriptures, and administrative ability. In American Baptist churches today deacons generally provide for the Lord's Supper, distribute the Deacons' Fund (Fellowship Fund), visit members, care for the sick and needy in the church, consider applicants for mem-

---

[2]John F. Loftis, "The Emerging Identity of Deacons, 1800–1950," in *Baptist History and Heritage,* XXV (April 1990), p. 16.

bership, and take charge of some services in the pastor's absence. When the pastoral office is vacant, they provide direction for the church.

With the multiplication of boards and committees to carry on the expanded programs of churches, a trend began among Baptists in the North to diminish the area of responsibility of the deacons. Oversight of finances and property was gradually shifted to trustees, and special committees often were developed to look after evangelism and pulpit supply. Some churches, on the other hand, have adopted a single-board plan and made the Diaconate the central board of the church. (In some churches, however, the single board is composed of elected managers or stewards instead of a Diaconate as such.)

In the Southern Baptist Convention it is still typical for the Board of Deacons to be responsible for general oversight of all concerns of the church. In the National Baptist Conventions, the Board of Deacons is usually "the power board," although a Board of Trustees may also have considerable influence.[3]

The number of deacons necessary for a church depends upon the size of the congregation and the duties assigned the Diaconate. In a small church, two or three may be enough, whereas a larger church would need many more. There should be enough so that the responsibilities will not fall unevenly upon a few individuals, and enough so that they can keep in touch with the entire membership.

A deacon used to be commonly elected for life, and some churches follow this practice still. During the twentieth century, however, a rotating system has come to be widely adopted. This allows a deacon to be reelected until he/she has served a specified number of terms. Then it is necessary to retire and to wait until the lapse of a year before becoming eligible again for reelection. On the whole, results have indicated that the rotation system is superior to life tenure.

Should deacons be ordained? Such was formerly the uni-

---

[3]Floyd Massey, Jr. and Samuel B. McKinney, *Church Administration in the Black Perspective* (Valley Forge: Judson Press, 1976), p. 40.

versal practice, but there has been a tendency in many churches to discard it. Many American Baptist churches still ordain deacons, but many do not. It is still customary in Southern Baptist churches, National Baptist churches, and probably among most other Baptists. It is difficult, however, to justify the ordination of deacons any more than trustees, church school superintendents, and other officers. There should be, at least, a service of recognition to install deacons as well as those elected to other offices.

Women as well as men should be elected to the Board of Deacons. Although there is evidence that Baptists had women deacons in the past, it seems that they were usually thought of as in a category different from male deacons, usually not being ordained. In the twentieth century the election of women to this office has become more common— again, with Baptists in the North taking the lead. It is still more the exception than the rule among Southern Baptists to elect women as deacons. While some churches have accepted the practice, there is strong opposition in some areas of the South.

The long hesitancy to allow women to speak in church services and the general cultural factors pertaining to roles of men and women militated against their serving in this capacity. The absence of clear data in the New Testament was another hindrance to changing the practice. Although there is a reference in the instance of Phoebe (Rom. 16:1) and a passage where it is uncertain whether it refers to deaconesses or the wives of deacons (1 Tim. 3:11), the meanings of these references are inconclusive. Restricting this office, as well as that of pastor, to males, however, is based upon erroneous ideas. Not only is the present emphasis upon equality of the sexes in society a reason for electing women as deacons, but a renewed interest in biblical study of the roles of sexes provides support for so doing. The Pauline objection to women speaking in churches probably was culturally conditioned and not consonant with God's intention in creation. Women were important in the ministry of Jesus, and they have served as deaconesses in early church history. Moreover they can bring their special gifts to the ministry of deacons. Finally, Paul's statement in Galatians 3:28 should remove any biblical grounds for objection.[4]

The Board of Trustees

Qualifications for the position of trustee in a Baptist church should be similar to those for the Diaconate, and there is no warrant for the prevalent notion that spiritual discernment is less important for trustees than for deacons. In many states, a Board of Trustees is required by law, in order that property may be vested in their names if the church is incorporated. In some instances, as in the single-board plan, deacons may be designated as trustees.

Until legislation was enacted by the states regarding incorporation of churches, there was no office of trustee. At first the trustees were merely figureheads, in whose names title to property was held, but gradually their responsibilities were broadened, especially among churches in the North. It was natural to delegate to them responsibility for maintaining or improving church property, and ultimately many churches relegated all financial matters to this board. Not only real estate, but securities, cash, and other church assets were placed under their jurisdiction.

In many churches the Board of Trustees must be consulted in all matters involving money and salaries, and in some instances they have assumed the prerogative of determining the minister's salary without action by the congregation. No doubt there must be delegation of responsibility in some of these cases, but the scope of the authority of the trustees should be clearly defined so as to ensure that the authority of the congregation is not bypassed.

The church constitution or bylaws should indicate the duties and the authority of the Board of Trustees as of other offices, and it should make clear that the decisions made by trustees, as of other committees and boards, are always subject to ratification, veto, or modification by the congregation. It is therefore important that the Board of Trustees should

---

[4] Bill Stancil, "Recent Patterns and Contemporary Trends in Deacon Life," *Baptist History and Heritage,* XXV (April 1990) 2, pp. 24–26.

make complete, accurate, and regular reports to the church. Most decisions will be made within the framework of a budget adopted by the church. (See also the section on the Finance Committee.) Matters not covered by budgetary provisions should be referred to a congregational meeting for the expression of its will.

The Board of Christian Education

Most American Baptist churches have a Board of Christian Education,[5] designed to correlate learning, sharing, and growing as Christians. This board does not confine its interests to the Sunday church school, but includes in the scope of its activities all phases of Christian education. Among these are the youth fellowship, vacation church school, and leadership training. Many churches have day-care centers and/or preschool programs, which benefit children and working parents and also utilize buildings throughout the week. These programs are a part of community outreach, but they are essentially educational in nature and are properly administered by the Board of Christian Education.

The Board of Christian Education will supervise and administer the entire education program in the church. The following list summarizes most of the specific duties to be assumed by this board:

Establish the objectives of the program
Study the needs
Determine the program
Enlist and support educational leaders
Coordinate activities and projects
Prepare job descriptions
Prepare and administer the education budget
Provide adequate rooms and equipment
Evaluate the program
Interpret the educational program to the congregation

The size of the board will vary according to the membership of the congregation, but there should be enough persons

---

[5]Kenneth D. Blazier, ed., *The Teaching Church at Work* (Valley Forge: Judson Press, 1980).

so that attention can be given to all aspects of the educational work. For example, three may be enough in a church with fewer than 100 members, but six would be more suitable for a congregation of 100 to 500 members; and for over 500 the board should have at least nine members. All members of the board need to be elected by the church, taking into consideration the specific responsibilities they are to exercise on the board, since they are called to do a work in which they represent the church in its teaching ministry. If there is a director of Christian education, this officer works in close cooperation with this board. All funds for the educational program should be provided in the church budget, and all regular offerings from the various organizations should go into the church treasury.

Whatever the size of a church there is a continuing need for better prepared leaders and teachers. A chief handicap of many churches is the inadequate supply of persons who can give leadership in its diversified programs. It is possible to strengthen its leadership, however, if training is systematically provided to equip teachers and other leaders. No person ought to be chosen for a position who is not willing to give time and effort to become competent in the work associated with the office. It is the responsibility of the Board of Christian Education to see that opportunities are afforded for teachers and workers of the church to receive help that will enable them to perform their services more efficiently.

Local church programs of leadership education may deal with the content of the Christian faith, with teaching methods, or with relating Christian convictions to contemporary problems of social and personal ethics. Specialized leadership courses can often best be done cooperatively on an association, area, or community basis, bringing in persons with special expertise in the field involved.

Therefore the association, area, or region should wherever possible serve as a unit for planning and conducting leadership training courses each year. In addition to the instruction offered locally, laboratory schools are held under denominational auspices in most regions and at the national assembly. Churches should encourage their teachers to take advantage of opportunities to improve their knowledge and skills, and they should underwrite the expenses for at least one person to attend a laboratory school each year.

Committees of the Church

Numerous committees are needed for specific purposes, but their number and kind will vary with the size and needs of each church. Needless multiplication of organizations should be avoided, but there are aspects of the church's life which need the emphasis which a committee can give to them. The duties of each committee need to be clearly defined, and its purpose should be integral to the main mission of the church. Described here are some of the areas in the life of most churches that call for attention which a committee can give them. It is recognized, of course, that not every church has sufficient available leadership to have all the committees described, and in many cases responsibilities will have to be combined.

Before proceeding to specific committee functions, something needs to be said about the *concept of mission* which underlies evangelism, missions, and social concerns. The term "missions" has been so commonly associated with something done beyond our own country, or at least beyond our immediate locale, that many now prefer the singular form "mission," which includes a wide range of ministries. Mission comprehends many important functions, and there are sharp differences among Baptists and other Christians today concerning what the proper mission of the church is. All agree that God has called the church into being in order to "send" it into the world for some purpose. Many see this as a call to support institutions and agencies committed to social welfare or social change—even to working for legislative reforms. Others, however, would restrict mission to ministries which are "spiritual" in a narrowly defined sense. They do not believe that the church is responsible to become involved in efforts to effect changes in society, to support or oppose legislation, or to take positions on public issues.

This divided opinion is not just between "evangelicals" and "liberals," as some charge. Many who are conservative in theology are persuaded that Christians ought to be actively engaged in efforts to change society. Speaking to this point, Arthur F. Glasser wrote: "They [evangelicals] contend that the development of individual and inward faith must be accompanied by a corporate and outward obedience to the cultural mandate broadly detailed in Holy Scripture. The world is to be served, not avoided. Social justice is to be furthered, and the issues of war, racism, poverty, and economic imbalance must become the active, participatory concern of those who follow Jesus Christ. It is not enough that the Christian mission be redemptive; it must be prophetic as well."[6] The organization "Evangelicals for Social Action" illustrates his point, and there are other such individuals and organizations.

Nevertheless, there is sharp disagreement regarding what issues are appropriate for church involvement, ways of dealing with public issues, and stances with respect to specific matters. The reason is not always doctrinal. Many churches are preoccupied with their own internal programs and apathetic toward problems of society. Certainly worship, nurture, pastoral care, evangelism, youth work, and finances are essential concerns, but there is also a mandate to continue the ministry of Jesus in feeding the hungry, healing the sick, liberating the oppressed, and challenging complacent consciences. Not many non-Christians are persuaded that God cares when they see churches that do not seem to care about human needs and problems. The church's mission includes Christ's Great Commandment as well as his Great Commission—both an evangelistic witness to the unsaved and a ministry to those whose problems are caused by unjust conditions rooted in social structures.

There is no more critical item on the church's agenda than getting Christians to accept the New Testament vision of its task. This vision embraces both winning others to accept the gospel and reaching out in love to victims of prejudice, discrimination, and injustice. The church has been called an evangelizing army on the march and an oasis for rest and refreshing only when in need of fresh instructions and

---

[6]Arthur F. Glasser, "Evangelicals and the Contemporary Debate," *Evangelical Dictionary of Theology* (Grand Rapids: Baker Book House, 1984), p. 726.

renewal of spiritual energies. We are bidden to put on the whole armor of God, in order to engage in warfare against principalities and powers which oppress people. It is legitimate for Christians to want comfort and assurance, but there is also a need for challenge to action in the arenas of life.

Evangelism and Missions Committee

Evangelism is closely linked with all that the church does, but the task of winning men and women to faith in Jesus Christ as Savior and Lord needs to be kept before the church by a specific committee. Through this committee the church is kept reminded that its mission of proclamation to the world is central to its whole life. Working with other committees, boards, and organizations, this particular committee can help members to become witnesses in all of their lives by word and deed.

Evangelism is not intended as a device for churches that feel the need to get more members only to help meet the budget. The goal of numerical growth is based on a much deeper imperative of faith, love, and divine mandate. A church should be intentional about reaching men and women with a message of God's forgiveness and acceptance and the divine offer of abundant life now and in the life to come. Biblically grounded denominational programs are usually available, such as the "Grow By Caring"[7] approach to evangelism developed by the American Baptist Churches in the 1980s to win people to the Christian faith in a natural way.

Evangelism and missions are essentially the same, but the latter term stresses the fact that some of the members of the church are commissioned to represent it in proclaiming the gospel beyond its own locality. "Missionary" means one who is sent, and the word conveys to our minds the thought of those who go overseas to other lands, or to classes of people

---

[7]*Church Growth—ABC Style,* Emmett V. Johnson (Evangelism Staff of National Ministries, ABCUSA, n.d.); also, the *American Baptist Quarterly* VIII (Sept. 1989) 3 is devoted to discussion of this program.

with special needs or problems in our own country. Whether at home or abroad, the emphasis should be upon ministries by which we serve others. That is why American Baptists renamed their national boards "Board of National Ministries" and "Board of International Ministries," instead of Home and Foreign Mission Boards. As William Carey, pioneer Baptist missionary to India, soon recognized, ministry to non-Christian people involves more than verbal proclamation. It calls also for feeding the poor, ministering to the sick, educating those without access to institutions of learning, and working to achieve more humane conditions. American Baptists have also learned that it means accepting nationals of other countries as equal partners and preparing such indigenous leadership to take over responsibilities for all phases of their church life.

Mission is a concern of the whole church, and both women and men should be informed about this work. In the ABC-USA, American Baptist Women's Ministries and American Baptist Men are organizations in which members may become better informed about opportunities for service through denominational agencies. Through schools of missions, women's societies, men's fellowships, and adult study groups such instruction can be offered. All members need to become acquainted with the theology of missions, the particular problems and needs of modern missions, and the work of specific ministries. The evangelism and missions committee will see that study opportunities are scheduled, that special events are publicized, and that missionaries are scheduled to speak in the church on occasion.

Community Outreach and Public Mission Committee

As the mission of the church begins at its own doorstep, it is fitting to have a committee that keeps the congregation posted on needs and opportunities in the community. In every place there are conditions calling for service, which may go unnoticed by the church. To bring these needs to the attention of the congregation and to find ways to organize interest and support for them is a responsibility of this committee. Often ministries in the immediate area are beyond the means of a single church and may well be undertaken by cooperating churches through an interfaith council. There may be need for financial assistance and volunteers to provide shelter for the homeless, food and clothing for the needy, day-care and preschool programs, help in building homes through Habitat for Humanity, meals and other services to senior adults through Meals on Wheels and backing for efforts to ameliorate world hunger through Bread for the World and the annual CROP Walk sponsored by Church World Service. Besides enlisting volunteers and encouraging financial gifts, there is need for the committee to arrange study courses and workshops to increase awareness of opportunities for Christian ministry in the community.

If Christians are to be witnesses in all their roles and relationships, they need to be able to relate their faith to social as well as personal issues. The church program should provide information, encouragement, and channels through which the lordship of Christ may be acknowledged in family, community, nation, and world. Racial tensions, poverty, education, drug and alcohol abuse, abortion, environmental issues, and religious liberty are typical of the problems which the Christian citizen faces. Although problems are so numerous and so complex that they overwhelm us, the Christian community needs to make its voice heard in the public square. All of us are so largely conditioned by the culture that the church often reflects its values instead of questioning them from a biblical viewpoint. If we are not simply to mirror the assumptions of our society, we must learn to make informed moral and ethical decisions as Christians. It is therefore necessary to study issues of our day critically from a Christian perspective.

The church needs the benefit of a committee responsible to see that significant issues are brought to the congregation and that places are made in the church program where discussion can take place. Pertinent literature and knowledgeable resource people need to be made available to the members. Information can be supplied by the Issue Development section of the Board of National Ministries. Also, every two years American Baptist Churches selects certain issues as potential "Statements of Concern" for study by the churches in preparation for a vote on them at the next biennial meeting. Materials to inform churches on these proposed statements are available for study groups. Books on current issues, illuminated by theological and biblical reflection, can become the basis for elective courses in Sunday church school. Also the Baptist Joint Committee on Public Affairs[8] publishes a monthly periodical, *Report from the Capital,* as well as material pertaining to legislation dealing with church-state issues and other matters of conscience.

Pastoral Relations Committee

Mutual trust and open communications are essential to a healthy relationship between pastor and people. Since this relationship is fraught with possibilities of misunderstandings and tensions, it is important to have a Pastoral Relations Committee[9] which will be a liaison between pastor and congregation. This committee should have three to five judicious and discreet members, at least some of whom should have served on the pulpit committee which discussed mutual expectations of congregation and minister in candidate interviews prior to the extending of a call.

At an early stage it is wise to draw up a set of expectations agreeable to pastor and Board of Deacons, and these can become the basis for an annual performance review. The committee should meet on a regular basis, not just when conflict arises. It is better to try to maintain good relationships and prevent conflict than to wait until a conflict gets out of hand. Meetings will be used partly to provide in-service training for members as they discuss reading assignments intended to make them more familiar with the work of pastoral ministry, sources of frequent conflict in churches, systems of dealing with conflict, and ways of evaluating performance. At the meeting there can be a sharing of perceptions, reporting of praise or criticism, and dealing with any incipient problem.

It will be the duty of the committee to conduct the annual performance review and to report and interpret it to the

---

[8]200 Maryland Ave., N.E., Washington, D.C. 20002.
[9]Emmett V. Johnson, *Work of the Pastoral Relations Committee,* (Valley Forge: Judson Press, 1983).

Board of Deacons. The annual review of compensation will also be a responsibility of this committee, which will report and make recommendations to the Finance Committee. It is well also to review with the pastor plans for continuing education which will contribute to his/her personal development and to particular needs of the congregation. This committee should also encourage young men and women who have suitable gifts to consider whether they are called to the ordained ministry.

Nominating Committee

This committee should be appointed at the annual meeting or by the Church Council for the ensuing church year, since the choice of leaders is a matter which requires careful planning. It should be a standing committee, so that it will be able to make plans well in advance of the election of officers, and also to make recommendations for filling vacancies created between the annual elections. In making recommendations for any office, the Nominating Committee works closely with the Church Council or Board of Deacons (whichever serves as the central leadership of the church).

Worship and Music Committee

This committee may well be a subunit of the Board of Deacons. In conjunction with the pastor it will have general oversight of the public worship services of the church. It will also have responsibility for the entire musical program. This includes the children's and youth choirs, as well as the regular choir. The appointment and supervision of the organist, choir director, and other music staff members comes under this committee's jurisdiction.

Ushering Committee

An Ushering Committee should be a subunit of the Board of Deacons. It sees that ushers are provided for the regular services of worship and any other occasions when they are needed. It is the responsibility of this committee to see that ushers are properly instructed in their duties.

Finance Committee

The Finance Committee may be a subunit of the Board of Trustees. Its duty is to prepare the annual budget to be submitted to the church, and it should work in cooperation with the Church Council. In addition to preparing a budget, it plans and directs the every-member canvass. The Finance Committee also has responsibility for oversight of the disbursements during the year. Under such circumstances it is expected to see that expenditures stay within the budget, to check income to ascertain whether or not it is in line with estimates on which the budget is based, and to make arrangements for emergency situations which may arise. Some churches prefer to assign these functions directly to the Board of Trustees rather than to a separate Finance Committee.

Auditing Committee

The work of this committee is to make a check upon the financial records of the church at least once a year and report its findings to the congregational meeting. It is composed of persons other than the treasurer, financial secretary, and the Board of Trustees.

Pulpit or Search Committee

When the pastoral office becomes vacant for any reason, a committee should be elected by the congregation or appointed by the Church Council to search for a successor. The size of the committee will vary with the size of the membership, but it should be large enough to afford representation of the various age groups and departments of the church life. The method of selecting such a representative committee differs considerably in Baptist churches, but the individual church should provide a clear-cut system in its bylaws. Instructions for the guidance of a Pulpit Committee are usually available from denominational book stores or regional offices.

Communications Committee

Essential to a healthy church life is a good system of communications. If members are to keep informed and in close touch with each other, good channels of communication are necessary. The weekly bulletin can disseminate some information about scheduled meetings and special events, but a weekly or monthly newsletter will be able to cover a wide range of reports and information about people and events of interest to the congregation. Such a newsletter may be typed, duplicated, and distributed by a church secretary, but it is helpful to have a volunteer editor to collect and edit the news. Members of the church should be encouraged to report to the church office any items that should be included in the newsletter. This publication can help to promote special occasions and may serve to inform people about denominational matters (association, area, region, or national). The committee should also help to interpret the purpose of the church to the community by means of radio, television, newspaper, and other media, projecting an image of the church and its purpose and activities to the general public.

Other Committees

Additional committees or special organizations may be needed for the fulfillment of a church's goals and responsibilities, but unnecessary duplication of agencies should be avoided. Every organization within the church should have its objectives carefully reviewed periodically to see its place in the overall purpose of the church. When societies or special organizations have outlived their usefulness, they should not be perpetuated. Those that continue to make a significant contribution to the ministry of the church should be encouraged, but any that no longer serve a real purpose should be discontinued. There are too many demands on time and energy to keep alive agencies that are irrelevant to, or at cross purposes with, the aims of the church.

Auxiliary Organizations

Besides the church school, other organizations play important roles in the nurture and training of church members.

Among these are the Woman's Society, the Men's Fellowship, and the Baptist Youth Fellowship. All church members should be considered members of these groups, and efforts should be made to enlist active interest and participation of everyone in their activities.[10]

The Church Council

Such a profusion of boards, committees, and other organizations may result either in disorder or in a smoothly operating church organization by which the gifts of the Spirit are channeled to serve the whole body. A central unit is needed to coordinate the diverse interests into a harmonious church program. Some churches attempt to provide such coordination by means of the Church Council (or Advisory Council). Such a body is composed of representatives from key boards, committees, and other organizations plus two or three at-large representatives from the congregation. A single-board church may use the Diaconate for this coordinating function.

To this representative group is entrusted the responsibility for overseeing the total life of the church. It sees that the many interests and responsibilities of a church are adequately provided for in the program, and it works the varied objectives into a coherent plan. The council arranges a schedule of activities for the year, and long-range studies of the ministry and needs of the church come under its surveillance. In the interval between church business meetings the Council may act on behalf of the church; however, the Council is fully responsible to the church, which may review its decisions and affirm or veto them.

A Single-Board Plan

A growing number of churches have adopted the single-board plan of organization. It has special value for small

---

[10]Information on the purpose and operation of each of these organizations may be had by writing to the corresponding national office: American Baptist Women's Ministries, American Baptist Men, and Department of Discipleship Education, BEM—all located at American Baptist Churches, USA, P.O. Box 851, Valley Forge, PA 19482-0851.

churches, where the number of persons available for leadership responsibilities is limited, but it may also be advantageous in midsize or large churches. The Church Council or the Board of Deacons may serve as the central board, although some churches have a Board of Managers (or stewards) and make the Diaconate a committee of the central board.

When the Diaconate is the single board, the deacons are restored to their earlier role of sharing with the pastor the general oversight of the life of the church. The greatest benefit, though, is that the single board is a coordinating body which supervises the work of all departments and subgroups. Some have objected that it concentrates too much authority in the hands of a few individuals. Such need not be the case, however, where a clear distinction is made between policy decisions and implementation, with the congregation clearly responsible for making policy, having final authority over all church matters.

The Board of Deacons (assuming that it is used for the single board) is thus responsible for general oversight of all spiritual and temporal concerns of the church. All subunits are accountable to it, and all matters pertaining to the life and implementation of church policies are subject to its supervision. In order to cover all the church's goals and programs, the board creates several departments (or commissions, or standing committees), such as Evangelism and Missions, Christian Education, Worship and Music (preparing for the Lord's Supper, ushering, flowers, etc.), Property and Finance, Community Outreach, Personnel, and Pastoral Relations. Each department, standing committee, or commission will need to establish subcommittees to attend to specific responsibilities. The number of departments or standing committees and their subunits can be increased or decreased to fit the needs of the situation.

The number of elected members of the Church Council or Board of Deacons in this plan will be from six to twelve, being divided into three classes, one-third of whom will be elected each year. Members should not serve more than two consecutive terms. The pastor will be an *ex officio* member, and it may be desirable to have certain other officers share this *ex officio* status. The chairperson of the board will be the moderator of the church, unless the church prefers to have the pastor in this office, and three members of the board will be designated as trustees. The other members will be assigned to various departments, with one of the deacons serving as chairperson of each department. Additional members of the departments will be needed, and these may be nominated by a nominating committee, elected by the board, and ratified by the church. Each department and its subunits will report at the monthly meeting of the board.

Of course, there are many variations of such a plan, but the above description furnishes a general outline of this system. It may be preferable to have the Pastoral Relations Committee, Nominating Committee, and Personnel Committee directly elected by the congregation and immediately accountable to it. There are few hard-and-fast rules to govern such decisions, but general principles of effective organization and administration should be considered in making these choices. The fundamental purpose of the church and the resources at hand to accomplish the goals need to be kept constantly in view at every stage in designing the structure.

8

Baptism and the Lord's Supper

Since the apostolic age, baptism and the Lord's Supper have been recognized as practices mandated by Jesus. Some call them *ordinances,* while others prefer the term *sacraments*. Before proceeding to a consideration of baptism and the Lord's Supper, it may be useful to discuss briefly these terms. Neither of them has the advantage of biblical sanction, for none of the scriptural writers employed them to refer to either of the two rites. Our judgment about these words will depend mainly upon the way in which they are defined, but the overtones that the words carry in popular thought may make us prefer one above the other.

Ordinance or Sacrament?

Baptists in general seem to prefer to speak of ordinances rather than sacraments. There was a time when they were less hesitant to call the Lord's Supper a sacrament, and that term is still more common among British Baptists. Opposition to the latter word arose from the fact that to many it seemed to imply an almost magical concept of the bestowal of divine power.

For centuries a sacrament has been commonly defined as "an outward and visible sign of an inward and spiritual grace." In such a definition there is nothing inherently offensive to Baptist doctrine. Usage of the term, however, conveys to some an impression that goes beyond this definition. It suggests that a sacrament is the means by which some change is brought about in an almost mechanical way. This understanding, though not necessarily confirmed by official theologies, seems to minimize the need for faith on the part of a recipient. Thus actual practice has often magnified the degree of institutional control over God's grace and minimized human response. As has already been noted, broad agreement has been reached on two points: the necessity of faith on the part of the recipient of baptism and the fact that "baptism is both God's gift and our human response to that gift."

Should a word which is easily misunderstood be avoided? If a more suitable word were available, perhaps it should. But the word "ordinance" is also open to misunderstanding. To call baptism an ordinance is to say that it is something ordered, or instituted by Christ. Obedience to a command of the Lord is the primary emphasis in this term, but accounts of baptism in the New Testament lead us to believe that there is more to it than that. Of course, emphasizing the point that baptism is mandated does not preclude the possibility that something more than obedience occurs in baptism, but the tendency is not to go beyond that point. In both baptism and the Lord's Supper, God's grace and the human response of faith are closely related, and we need terms which will help us to keep aware of these two poles. "Ordinance" does not seem altogether adequate for this purpose.

Before we decide about the use of these words, we may want to consider other views. For instance, George Beasley-Murray, a New Testament scholar, favors a sacramental view of baptism. His credentials as a Baptist and an evangelical, having been the principal of Spurgeon's College in London and for many years a professor at Southern Baptist Theological Seminary in the United States, warrant our giving him a hearing. He writes: "The idea that baptism is a purely symbolic rite must be pronounced not alone unsatisfactory, but out of harmony with the New Testament itself. ... The Apostolic writers make free use of symbolism of the baptismal action; but they go further and view the act as a symbol with power, that is, a sacrament."[1] He says further: "In baptism the Gospel proclamation and the hearing of faith become united in one indissoluble act, at one and the same time an act of grace and faith, an act of God and man."[2] By detailed biblical exegesis he shows that, in the New Testament, baptism ordinarily is linked to receiving the Holy Spirit.

An opposite view is offered by Markus Barth, who would not use the term "sacrament" in connection with either baptism or the Lord's Supper.[3] Although not a Baptist, he is a Reformed New Testament scholar who was closely associated with Baptists while he taught in Chicago. Not only is "sacrament" not a biblical term, he says, but the concept of sacrament has misleading connotations. He does not deny that baptism may be related to reception of the Holy Spirit, but he thinks that many churches have used this rite in a way that seems to attribute divine power to baptism itself, implying a guarantee that one who is baptized will receive the Spirit. When the impression is given that God's action is tied to a ceremony of the church, it appears that the church controls God's grace. But God has not granted such power to human beings, and "sacrament" is a word too misleading to be useful, says Barth.

We may finally decide simply to speak of baptism and the Lord's Supper without resorting to any word that comprehends them both. It is important that we understand their meanings so that our observance of these rites will speak to us.

---

[1] George Beasley-Murray, *Baptism in the New Testament* (New York: Macmillan, 1962) p. 263.

[2] *Ibid.*, p. 272.

[3] Markus Barth, *Die Taufe: Ein Sakrament?* (Zollikon-Zurich: Evangelischer Verlag, 1951). Not translated, but see review article by N. H. Maring, in *Foundations,* Jan. 1960, pp. 74–83. See also M. Barth, *Rediscovering the Lord's Supper* (Louisville: John Knox Press, 1988), pp. 100–102, regarding the Lord's Supper and sacrament.

Understanding Religious Symbols

There is a tendency among Baptists to minimize the importance of signs and symbols, and that attitude is reflected in our approach to the two sacred observances we are considering. If a thing is only *symbolic* of reality, we say, why not take what is real and discard what is symbolic? Thus we may speak of baptism and the Lord's Supper as "mere symbols," and the adjective shows our low evaluation of symbols.

This disparagement of symbols indicates a lack of understanding of their value in human communication. A sign or symbol not only points to some reality, but it may also be the means of communicating ideas and awakening responses. A symbol rings a bell, as it were, which calls to mind a whole cluster of associated events and meanings. Not only does it speak to the mind, but it calls forth emotions and may lead to decisions and actions.

Symbols as Means of Communication

Symbols are of many kinds, and they are used in all spheres of human life. We know how the American flag, under certain circumstances, may arouse deep feelings of pride, joy, patriotism, and exultation. It can do so because it brings to mind a whole series of thoughts and meanings, and thus has power to awaken a response in our feelings and actions.

Not only do symbols stir our memories and emotions, but they may be the means of transmitting something from one person to another. A handshake, for instance, is nothing more than a casual custom by which we greet acquaintances or friends. A handshake on occasion, however, communicates feelings too deep for words. When a friend has been bereaved of a loved one, and we hardly know what to say, we may grasp a hand, and in that handclasp we express unuttered thoughts and feelings. Thus a handshake communicates something of ourselves. A mother's kiss is also a symbolic act. But it is an act which conveys her affection and concern, and by it a child is reassured and made to feel secure. Surely we should not treat symbols carelessly, for they communicate and may even participate in the reality which they represent.

What is true in ordinary human affairs is true in the realm of religion. Here, too, are symbols through which intangible and unseen realities are communicated to us. The power of God is mediated through symbols, and through such signs we apprehend something of deep mystery, which goes beyond our ability to explain in words. It is of such things that our Baptist forebears spoke when they talked of "the means of grace." The reading of the Scriptures, prayer, preaching, the singing of hymns, family devotion—all were regarded as means by which grace was communicated.

Baptism and the Lord's Supper as Symbols

Included among the means of grace were baptism and the Lord's Supper. These were symbols, but Baptists did not disparage them by speaking of them as "mere symbols." The same God who had condescended to act in human history, to bring the Incarnate Son of God to birth in a stable, had ordained that other elements of our common life should be means of divine action. Through immersion in water and through the eating of simple bread and wine, human beings could be made more aware of God's presence and power.

It is not necessary to think of these acts as channels through which God *automatically* communicates with those who take part in them. Baptists have always been sure that it is possible for a person to be baptized without being affected by the experience. It is equally possible that some persons may eat and drink at the Lord's table without being changed in any way by their act. On the other hand, these vividly symbolic actions may be the means through which the Holy Spirit speaks and acts. Therefore, they have been ordained by our Lord as special ritual observances. "By the administration of baptism and the Lord's Supper, prayer, and other means appointed of God, faith is increased and strengthened," says the Philadelphia Baptist Confession. In other words, God works through these signs. Since the same article also states that faith is wrought by the Spirit, it seems evident that baptism and the Lord's Supper were regarded as means of grace.

Although these symbols go beyond the intellect in reaching the inner depths of one's being, they do have a certain cognitive content. An appreciation of their meaning may help us to participate in them more fully. There is constant danger on the one hand that these events may be reduced to empty ceremonies; and on the other hand that they may be exalted beyond their true significance. Hence we should seek to understand their purpose.

A Theology of Baptism Needed

Before proceeding further, we must note that Baptists have often been remiss about undergirding their baptismal practice with a theology of baptism. In their polemic against infant baptizers, they have concentrated attention almost exclusively upon finding New Testament data pertaining to the subjects and the mode of baptism. In general they have considered the case closed when they have demonstrated that Christ bade his disciples to baptize, that the Greek word for "baptize" means "immerse," and that the New Testament evidence favors believers' baptism rather than infant baptism. They have made worthwhile contributions in such studies, and happily today there is a wide agreement on these points. As noted in chapter 5, the *Baptism, Eucharist, and Ministry* document of the World Council of Churches acknowledges that "baptism upon personal profession of faith is the most clearly attested pattern in the New Testament."

There is more to understanding baptism, however, than resolving questions regarding the subjects and mode. *The most crucial issue is whether God does something in baptism or not.* If so, what happens? How is baptism related to the forgiveness of sins, regeneration, and the reception of the Holy Spirit? Is this a rite of initiation into the body of Christ, and what is its connection with membership in a local congregation? When one has accepted the fact that baptism is administered only upon a profession of faith, there are still important questions regarding the status of children in the church. When should they be baptized? Does baptism have the same meaning for children as for mature adults? How are they to be nurtured in the years prior to and following baptism? Baptists have had weak answers. These questions and others can be answered only by a theology of baptism. At this point, Baptists have been negligent.

In view of their historic emphasis, one might expect Baptists to have produced more serious studies on baptism. Even Karl Barth's landmark lectures on baptism in 1943[4] elicited little response from Baptists in the United States, where most Baptist reside. Barth came out strongly in those lectures in opposition to infant baptism, contending that New Testament baptism required persons to come to the rite only upon a personal profession of faith. He also supported immersion as the appropriate mode. His lectures caused consternation in all the major Protestant traditions in Europe, provoking a spate of books in reply to his arguments.

In the ensuing discussions, British Baptists published several significant works on the subject, but not many noteworthy contributions emanated from Baptists in America. In one of the more substantial responses, Warren Carr, a Southern Baptist pastor, raised some searching questions regarding baptismal practices, basing them on in-depth biblical and theological study.[5] Dale Moody, a professor of theology at Southern Baptist Theological Seminary, published a very impressive study of contemporary theology and practice of baptism among all major Christian denominations. This survey, *Baptism: Foundation for Christian Unity,* is a most informative book, which should have aroused greater interest among Baptists in the United States. Moody's wry comment regarding Southern Baptist slowness to become interested in baptismal theology would apply to other Baptists as well: "Part of it is due to preoccupation with practical concerns such as the raising of money for their institutions and the recruitment of members for the local congregations. All too often there has been the unexamined assumption that their beliefs and practices are all based on the Bible."[6]

Formulating a theology of baptism is not a simple task. It requires not only making a careful exegetical study of the New Testament, but also placing baptism in the context of

---

[4]Karl Barth, *The Teaching of the Church Regarding Baptism,* tr. by E. A. Payne (London: SCM Press, 1948).

[5]Warren Carr, *Baptism: Conscience and Clue for the Church* (New York: Holt, Rinehart and Winston, Inc., 1964)

[6]Dale Moody, *Baptism: Foundation for Christian Unity* (Philadelphia: Westminster Press, 1967), p. 258.

a broader biblical theology. No doubt, it is the difficulty of the subject, plus the feeling that not many are interested in the results of such study, that hinders Baptist pastors and theologians from more serious study. Nevertheless, the lack of material in such an important area of concern is a serious gap. It is sorely needed for reflection upon our baptismal practice and its significance for Christian discipleship.

Baptism

The act of baptism has been interpreted in a variety of ways in the history of the church. In general, two tendencies characterize the diverse interpretations. On the one hand are those that emphasize the ceremony as a means by which God does something to a passive human being. On the other are those that stress the human role in responding through the baptismal act. Within the former group there is wide diversity. These viewpoints range from a belief that sins are actually washed away by this act, to the conviction that it is a sign and seal of God's covenant whereby God reassures us of the truth of the Word. Those who stress baptism as primarily a human action also offer several explanations. They see it as a testimony to the world, a confession to God, a means of stirring those baptized to more vivid reflection upon God's dealings with them, or a simple act of obedience to a specific command. At one extreme are persons who believe that without baptism one is lost eternally, while at the other extreme are those who think that the act of baptism is completely unnecessary.

Baptist Concept of Baptism

While Baptists have sought to keep in sight both God's grace and human response, the primary tendency has been to emphasize baptism as an act of obedience in which we respond to God. But even when so understood, baptism is a recognition of what God has done in Christ. What we say and do in baptism rests upon God's gracious act in Jesus Christ, and signifies our identification with him in his death on our behalf. In this way baptism recapitulates the whole Christian story and thus may become a means of grace.

Andrew Fuller, once an influential Baptist theologian, described baptism as "an act by which we declare before God, Angels, and men, that we yield ourselves to be the Lord's; that we are dead to the world . . . and risen again to 'newness of life.' " Calling baptism the "initiatory ordinance of Christianity," he likened it to a soldier's oath of allegiance and to a military uniform. The analogy of an oath is a reminder that in baptism we are saying something to God, while the idea of a uniform suggests that our confession to God is made before others. By an oath a soldier pledges his loyal service to a nation, and wearing a uniform identifies him as one committed to such special service. Likewise, baptism is a means in which we yield ourselves to God, and the fact that it is done publicly makes it a sign to the world that we are members of Christ's church. Both of these aspects of baptism are essential to our understanding of it.

Thus, Baptists are numbered among those who think of baptism as primarily a human response. In baptism a person signifies repentance toward God, trust in God's mercy, and surrender to God's will. As the baptism of Jesus was a public acknowledgment of submission to the Creator's will, so the Christian's baptism is a public acknowledgment of submission to the judgment and will of God. This repentance and faith are expressed to God, but the act takes place in the presence of the church and the world. While baptism is a human response, it is closely related to the grace of God. The fact that it is a response implies that God's grace is prior to baptism, for only because God has acted in Christ is there a basis for our responding. It should be remembered also that baptism is the act which Christ designated as the appropriate means by which such public confession to God should be made.

The baptism which is a confession *to God before others* is more than a private affair of an individual with God. It is administered in the context of the church by whose representative the candidate is baptized. Those who have borne witness to this person and have led the new convert to accept Christ as Savior and Lord are now administering baptism in Christ's name. Thus the visible church is involved as a witness both to the grace of God and to the repentance and faith of the person baptized. The one who has accepted Christ's offer is initiated into the body of Christ and usually at the same time admitted into the visible church in the place where the baptism occurs.

At this point the question is left open as to whether some actual change is effected in a person in baptism. On this point Baptists are divided. The acknowledgment of God's prevenient (or anticipatory) grace to which a response is made does not settle the question of whether God also acts in the baptismal event. Does something happen to the person in baptism? Is he or she regenerated in the waters of baptism? Is the Holy Spirit bestowed at that particular time? Many, probably most, Baptists believe that the baptized person has already become regenerate by the work of the Spirit prior to the baptism, and that baptism is just a public acknowledgement of that fact. Having already repented and confessed faith in Christ, the convert has been received by Christ into his church. Now in baptism there is a public confession of what has already been done in private.

Other Baptists, however, find this view of the matter deficient. We have already seen that George Beasley-Murray thinks the New Testament teaches that in baptism one actually receives the Holy Spirit. Neville Clark, a British Baptist minister, has written in similar vein: "Baptism . . . implies, embodies, and effects forgiveness of sin, initiation into the church, and gift of the Holy Spirit"[7] On the other hand, the late Ernest A. Payne, an outstanding British Baptist church historian, wrote: "The case for the subject of baptism being a believer is overwhelming, and this is generally admitted by scholars. The exact relation of the rite to the experience of the Spirit and the member of the church is not so clear"[8]

As one reads the book of Acts, it is difficult to avoid the conclusion that in the minds of early Christians, God's action upon the believer was ordinarily related to baptism. In Acts 2 it is reported that those who listened to Peter's preaching at Pentecost were "cut to the heart," and asked what they

---

[7] Alec Gilmore, ed., *Christian Baptism* (Valley Forge: Judson Press, 1959), p. 308.

[8] Ernest A. Payne, *The Fellowship of the Believers* (London: Carey Kingsgate Press, 1952), p. 89.

should do. Peter replied: "Repent, and be baptized every one of you in the name of Jesus Christ so that your sins may be forgiven, and you will receive the gift of the Holy Spirit" (Acts 2:38). Elsewhere in Acts, at baptism persons usually received an inner power which they perceived as the reception of the Spirit (e.g., 8:14-17; 9:17-19; 19:5-6). In at least one instance (10:44-48), however, people were baptized *after* receiving the Holy Spirit. Therefore, one should not link such reception inseparably to a human act administered by the church. That is to say, baptism is not inevitably accompanied by some purifying or renewing power of God. The church cannot guarantee that the performance of baptism will be followed by the imparting of divine grace. God's grace, or divine power, is not within the control of the institutional church, and it cannot be manipulated by its representatives.

Does it follow that nothing significant takes place in baptism? Not necessarily! In the act of baptism, sins may or may not be washed away, regeneration may or may not be effected, and the Holy Spirit may or may not be bestowed. The evidence is not entirely conclusive, but it does seem at least that water baptism is always fulfilled in relation to baptism of the Spirit, *whether for its reception* or *as a recognition of its prior reception* with a concomitant forgiveness and transforming power.

In any case, it seems that baptism may and ought to be an experience of rich, spiritual blessing. When, in accord with God's ordinance, we come to the appointed means of signifying our response, it is a prayer of confession of sin, expression of trust, and submission of our lives to holy obedience. Our lives are more open to God's activity, and we should have a heightened assurance of God's presence and power. However, God's Spirit acts freely and is not bound to the baptismal act. To regard baptism in this light keeps grace and faith in a dynamic relationship. God's grace takes the initiative, and human beings respond. When one responds in repentance and faith and is receptive to God's will, there is an openness for the Spirit of God to work more freely in that life.

Baptism is a human act, but it is God's appointed means;

and we must not so strongly emphasize the human aspect of baptism as to lose sight of God's activity. Following this tendency, Baptists have sometimes treated baptism too casually, neglecting to prepare people for a meaningful experience. In reacting against the claims of other people, they have often been so busy declaring what baptism is not, that they have neglected to make clear what it is meant to be. We will do well to invest the ceremony with the fullness of its New Testament significance, so that it will have meaning for those who are baptized.

Baptism, then, may be thought of as a rite ordained by Christ through which his disciples are to express the humble confession, the faith, and the willing obedience required of them. Jesus himself experienced baptism as a public testimony of his submission to the will of God, and thus instituted it as a ceremony for his church. In his final instructions to his disciples, he included "baptize" among their responsibilities, and the church understood this baptismal act to be a binding obligation upon all Christians.

The Subjects of Baptism

Inasmuch as baptism is related to repentance and faith, Baptists have normally practiced believers' baptism rather than infant baptism. They have held that New Testament examples, as well as theological significance, favors the restriction of the rite to persons capable of making a conscious commitment. Nevertheless, during the course of history the baptism of infants became an accepted practice among Christians of other denominations, so that today the great majority of Christians have been so baptized. Therefore, Baptists have had to face the question as to whether they will give a limited approval to infant baptism. Some have taken a position that it may be defended on theological grounds as an unsatisfactory but valid form of baptism.

Instead of baptizing infants, Baptists often dedicate such children to God. In such a service, parents and congregation publicly express their acceptance of the responsibility to offer every help and encouragement to their children, seeking to lead them to become committed Christians in later years. There is value in such a special ceremony, which impresses upon home and church alike the importance of cooperation in providing Christian nurture. Nevertheless, since the dedication service involves an acknowledgment of responsibility by parents, it should be held only if at least one of the parents is known to be living a responsible Christian life. To dedicate children indiscriminately, regardless of the faith and life of the parents, would rob the service of meaning.

The Mode of Baptism

Baptists are also on firm ground when they insist upon immersion as the most appropriate form of baptism. That it was the usual way in which the primitive churches baptized is clearly indicated both by the use of the Greek word *baptizo* (meaning "to dip or submerge") and by the context of statements about the performance of baptism in specific cases.

Also, as a symbol it is a pictorial and dramatic representation of what is taking place. Coming before God acknowledging that we are sinners, helpless to save ourselves, we cast ourselves upon God's mercy. When we are baptized, we are not just saying that we have resolved to change our way of living. Rather, we are recognizing that our hope is in Christ. Being identified with him in his death and burial, we hope to share in the resurrection of which he was the firstfruits. It is because of Christ that we have the boldness to seek God's forgiveness and the gift of new life. Thus baptism both points to the grace of God, which precedes all human action, and declares our response to God's mercy. Besides expressing our repentance and faith, baptism also signalizes our obedience to Christ as Lord; for obedience in this act symbolizes our surrender of our total lives to follow his will.

Pointing to the central facts of the incarnation, immersion pictorially expresses our own identification with Christ in his death, burial, and resurrection. It signifies the radical change which has been wrought by God, whereby we have become dead to sin and alive to Christ. For such a decisive event, immersion is a more expressive and appropriate form than either pouring or sprinkling. The latter methods become symbols of a symbol, and are inadequate signs of that to which they point.

Although immersion is indeed defensible as the most suitable means of baptizing, we need to be cautious not to overemphasize the amount of water used in baptism. A great deal more imagination is required to make either pouring or sprinkling symbolize an identification with Christ in his death and resurrection, but even a poor symbol may be used to express that which baptism signifies. There are undoubtedly cases where persons who are aged or infirm ought not to be immersed, and they should not be denied the opportunity to make a public confession in baptism. In such cases, pouring may be an acceptable substitute. Since the reality that is symbolized is the most important thing, and since a poor symbol may be used to express that reality, we ought not to stress the form so much as to make us lose our perspective. In our ordinary practice, however, immersion ought always to be employed.

If immersion is to be a high point of Christian experience, two things are necessary. First, there must be sufficient instruction prior to the act, so that persons know what they are doing. Second, baptism should be performed with decency and care so that the experience may not be marred by awkward incidents.

Baptism should be preceded by sufficient instruction to ensure that the persons baptized understand the nature and implications of the commitment which they have made. The amount of such teaching will vary according to the background of the persons involved. Usually, more time must be given to children than to adults; and more attention will be necessary for people in other cultures than for those who have been reared in the church and a Christian family. Always, however, there should be a pastor's or discipleship class for the instruction of converts. The extensiveness of the training will be determined by the needs of the situation.

The Role of the Church in Baptism

Who should be the administrator of baptism? Baptists have assigned such responsibility to ordained ministers as a part of the pastoral office. For the same reason that certain other functions are delegated to such leaders, baptism ought ordinarily to be performed by those who hold special pastoral office. This requirement does not imply that the pastor has any special power to effect something which others could not. It is a matter of doing things in an orderly fashion. To permit persons to baptize indiscriminately would lead to carelessness and confusion, which would be injurious to the practice of baptism. There may be instances where a pastor is not available, but such cases would be infrequent. If such should be the case, a church may appoint a deacon to baptize, or could seek the help of a neighboring pastor. Care should be taken lest such a precedent open the way to careless practices which could be unwholesome for the life of the church.

A question that is sometimes raised is whether a person should be baptized when there is no intention of affiliating with a local church. It is hard to conceive of a case in which such baptism would be proper. Since baptism represents public affirmation of repentance and faith, and surrender of life to God, signifying identification with Christ, it means that one is incorporated into the body of Christ. It is inconceivable that one who is becoming a member of Christ's church should not wish to become a member of a visible church. Indifference toward the visible church reflects a serious lack of understanding of the nature of Christian commitment and of the place of the church in God's economy. Where such misunderstanding exists, further instruction is needed before baptism is administered. Baptism is Christian initiation and it signifies an identification with Christ which is equivalent to incorporation into his body, the church. Although a distinction needs to be made between baptism as initiation into the body of Christ and becoming a member of a particular local church, such baptism should lead to identification with a visible church. It is in and through the churches that God's Spirit works especially for the redemption of humankind.

It has sometimes happened that a member who was baptized as a child on profession of faith requests to be rebaptized on the ground that the early baptism had little meaning. Occasionally, a pastor has acceded to such a request. In recent years, however, such requests have become so common in some Baptist circles as to become a problem. It has been reported, for example, that in 1987, some 26,000 church members were rebaptized in Southern Baptist churches.[9] Historically, Baptists have not advocated this sort of practice, and they have always protested against the charge that they were rebaptizers.

Such rebaptism is of dubious validity and ought to be discouraged. It is normal for adults to grow to deeper levels of Christian understanding and assurance, and their earlier experience may then seem vague and deficient in meaning. It would be a mistake, however, to allow every experience of spiritual renewal to become an occasion to ask for a rebaptism. So rarely has this kind of problem occurred in Baptist history that one can scarcely find reference to it in the voluminous literature on the subject. It is too easy for an adult to forget the intensity of childhood experiences and to dismiss them as having no significance. Usually a child baptized at an early age did have a sincere intention at the level of his or her capacity at the time. It is better to advise such a person to accept the early baptism and to renew the sincere commitment made as a child, only now with more mature understanding and responsibility.

This problem of rebaptizing church members already baptized upon a profession of their faith underscores the advisability of administering baptism only to persons who have reached an age at which they are capable of making a responsible decision to commit their life to the lordship of Jesus Christ. One of the reasons why Southern Baptists have this problem is that they have in the past few decades baptized so many very young children. Bill Leonard states that "several thousand preschoolers are baptized each year into the believers' churches of the SBC."[10] At the same time they failed to develop a theology of conversion appropriate for children and different from the conversion of mature adults.

The possibility that such a problem can arise can be attributed in part to the need for Baptists to develop a more adequate theology of the child in relation to the church and

---

[9] Bill J. Leonard, *God's Last and Best Hope* (Grand Rapids: Wm. B. Eerdmans Publishing Co., 1990), p. 90.

[10] Ibid, p. 89.

for greater care in preparing persons for baptism. Believers' baptism calls for repentance and faith which are more appropriate for those who are mature enough to make responsible decisions regarding lifelong commitments. To expect such decisions of children is psychologically wrong, and until the twentieth century most Baptists received baptism no earlier than adolescence, and most commonly in older youth. Nevertheless, this waiting period leaves the status of the child in the church lacking clear definition. The nurture of children in a Christian context, with an understanding that they can trust a loving God and encouragement to manifest that trust in various ways, is the responsibility of the church through its church school and other organizations for children. The matter of commitment to a life of Christian discipleship and membership in the church can wait until adolescence or youth. To baptize preschoolers, or even preadolescents, is in effect to practice the equivalent of infant baptism. It is a practice inconsistent with the Baptist emphasis upon churches made up of committed, informed, and disciplined Christians.

The Lord's Supper

The other ordinance, or sacrament, of the church is the Lord's Supper. Baptism is a decisive, once-for-all event, marking the entrance into a new life in Christ. The Lord's Supper is intended to be repeated frequently, and symbolizes the sustaining of that life by Christ. The former denotes the beginning of a new relationship, and the latter the maintaining of a vital relationship between Christ and the church.

As in the case of baptism, the passage of time since New Testament days has brought a bewildering diversity of views among Christians concerning the meaning of the Lord's Supper. Some believe that the bread and wine change into the actual flesh and blood of the Savior, and that the actual body of Christ is eaten. This doctrine is known as transubstantiation. At the other extreme are those who emphasize that the elements are simply signs reminding us of past events. Some, therefore, expect something of an almost magical nature to happen in the ritual; others do not expect anything to happen in the eating of the bread and drinking the wine.

What does the rite really signify? Although there may be many facets of meaning, some one idea must be central. Only a few passages of the New Testament directly refer to this supper, several of which are parallel accounts in the different Gospels. In three or four other places, indirect reference is made. On the basis of very scant statements concerning this ritual, theories have been formed to interpret the rite which Jesus Christ instituted on the night of his betrayal.

Baptist Understanding of the Lord's Supper

Baptists have usually stressed the fact that the Lord's Supper is a memorial meal, relying on Paul's account of the tradition he had received, in which Jesus said before both the bread and the cup, "Do this in remembrance *(anamnesis)* of me." Sometimes we have been inclined to say that it is a "mere memorial," as though it has little value for the church. To be sure, the casual way in which it is sometimes observed indicates the low regard in which it is often held. There is no reason, however, to use the disparaging word "mere" in connection with it.

Very close to the center of its meaning is the significant fact that the Supper is intended as a memorial. To make this statement, though, does not mean simply that it points backward to ancient history. The memorial is not just a sign pointing to a historical event, as does the Fourth of July celebration. The Fourth is set apart to remind a nation of its roots; its celebration recalls a declaration of principles of freedom. The intent of such an occasion is to inspire its celebrants to similar courage and high-mindedness. Something more than that is involved in the Lord's Supper.

The Lord's Supper is more nearly analogous to the Passover feast of the Jews. That ritual meal, which was observed each year, also pointed to the past. When a family sat about the table, the head of the household reminded the others of the reason for the annual observance, saying in effect that this meal is a reminder of the time when the Lord God delivered their forebears out of the land of Egypt. However, this recital of past events was not made just in order to arouse their heroism and loyalty. Reminded of what God had once done, they were to remember that the God of their ancestors was also the God of the children: "The God of Isaac

BAPTISM AND THE LORD'S SUPPER

and Jacob is our God." This meal was a means of helping them to maintain their identity and continuity as the covenant people of God.

In a similar way the Lord's Supper is intended to remind the church of the foundation upon which it rests, for in this ritual we see depicted the mighty acts of God in Christ. The elements of bread and wine point to the body and blood of Christ. As visible symbols that reinforce the gospel preached in words, they remind Christians of the incarnation, of which the high points were death, burial, resurrection, and exaltation. These events signify God's deliverance of humanity from bondage to sin, and they recall to the church that Christ is the reason for their existence. In looking back to the origins from which Christians have sprung, they remember that Christ is still their living Lord. They are encouraged to remember what God has done, in order to be more vividly aware of what God continues to do and has promised yet to do.

Recalling the past in order to be reminded of the existing situation is therefore more than a "mere memorial." The backward look leads immediately to the present and future. It is an important means of aiding the church to remember its identity as the people of God, and Christ's promise to be with them to the end of the age. The remembrance of what God has done is thus a preparatory step to a fresh encounter with the living God, who is in their midst working out the divine purposes in and through them. It reminds them of their dependence upon the Lord Jesus Christ, who is the Bread of Life by which its life must be sustained daily.

Close to the center of the meaning of this memorial rite are four related ideas: covenant, church, Christ, and communion. Pointing to the work of the incarnate Christ, Christians speak of the New Covenant sealed with his blood. "This cup is the new covenant in my blood" (1 Cor. 11:25), Jesus is reported to have said to his disciples, as he bade them drink of it. This covenant, like that with Israel, is not a contract between equals, but an offer made by God to human beings who could not save themselves. It was an offer of pardon and power which could be freely received by those willing to accept it with gratitude and faith.

The mention of the covenant immediately suggests those

who are the covenant people of God, the church. As Israel was constituted through the Old Covenant, so the church is the people whose existence rests upon the New. When the people of the church gather around the Lord's table, therefore, they partake of a covenant meal, by which they are reminded of their identity as a people God has called—God's purchased possession, an instrument for God's purpose.

At the head of this church, or covenant people, is Jesus Christ the Lord. He who once lived among men and women in visible form is now in the midst of his people wherever they are gathered. In the prayer of invocation we call upon the Holy Spirit, who makes Christ contemporary to each gathered congregation in every generation. To meet together and be reminded of their identity as a covenant people is to recognize the real presence of Christ in their midst; it is to remember that God always stands over against them in judgment and mercy.

The church so gathered and so engaged is in communion with Christ and with one another. Partaking of the meal is a reminder that they are participants in the new life in Christ, that they are not isolated individuals each in search of God in his/her own way, but sharers in the fellowship of the Spirit. "The cup of blessing that we bless," wrote Paul, "is it not a sharing in the blood of Christ? The bread that we break, is it not a sharing in the body of Christ? Because there is one bread, we who are many are one body, for we all partake of the one bread" (1 Cor. 10:16-17).

In this service, as in baptism, God's grace and human faith are in close union. The elements of the supper depict in vivid fashion the redemptive action of God in Christ. By them we are reminded of the incarnation—the life, death, resurrection, exaltation and promised return of Jesus Christ. These events have become a part of our own history, for we have accepted the forgiveness of God and have responded to the invitation to become God's people. United with Christ and with one another, we are not a loose collection of individuals but a fellowship of believers who have a corporate existence as the church of Jesus Christ.

Another point close to the central meaning of the Lord's Supper is the eschatological dimension which Paul includes:

"For as often as you eat this bread and drink the cup, you proclaim the Lord's death until he comes" (1 Cor. 11:26). These words are not in the Synoptic reports of the institution of the Lord's Supper, but in each of them, with only slight variations, the future look is referred to: "I will never again drink of the fruit of the vine until that day when I drink it new in the kingdom of God (Mark 14:25; see also Matt. 26:29 and Lk. 22:16). In this promise is caught up all the anticipation and hopes expressed again and again in the Old and New Testaments. This meal, which looks backward to what God has done, also looks forward to the consummation of God's kingdom, when Christ is united with his church to share his glory and the joyous life envisioned by Isaiah (2:1-5, 11:1-9) and by John (Rev. 21:1-7).

To see in this supper, then, a memorial rite is not to rob it of meaning. A service which helps the church to a realization of its own identity and reminds it of its call to live responsibly before Christ has significance. Although the Lord's Supper is primarily a memorial symbol emphasizing covenant, church, Christ, communion, and anticipation of the fullness of the kingdom of God, other derivative ideas are associated with it. Surely it is an occasion for rejoicing and for thanksgiving, and hence a eucharist. Although it is not a reenactment of the sacrifice of Christ, but rather a reminder of the sacrifice offered by him once for all, it does become a time when we offer ourselves anew to God. While not primarily an occasion for seeking forgiveness of sins, it does invite self-examination and repentance.

When the Lord's Supper is observed as it should be, it leads to fresh encounter between Christ and his people. No more than in baptism can we manipulate or dispense God's grace, for God's divine power is beyond our control. Nevertheless, in the moment of our remembering who we are as the church of God, our spirits are quickened. As we remember what God has done, continues to do, and will do, our consciousness of the divine presence is strengthened. If God thus vouchsafes to us the assurance of holy presence and power, this service becomes for us a means of grace.

Early Baptists had a concept of the Lord's Supper which made its character as a memorial preeminent, but they also believed that Christ was truly present to the believers in that meal. The Particular Baptists expressed their view of the Lord's Supper as something more than a look back to past events. In the supper, they averred:

> Worthy receivers, outwardly partaking of the visible elements in this ordinance, do then also inwardly by faith, really and indeed, yet not carnally and corporally but spiritually, receive and feed upon Christ crucified and all the benefits of his death—the Body and Blood of *Christ,* being then not corporally or carnally but spiritually, present to the faith of believers in that ordinance, as the elements themselves are to their outward senses.[11]

Here is the backward look, but its purpose is to remind us of present relationships and responsibility. Participation in the Lord's Supper rekindles faith and results in a fresh meeting between Christ and his church.

Some Practical Questions Regarding the Lord's Supper

A number of practical questions relative to the observance of the Lord's Supper frequently arise. How often should it be celebrated? Is it to be confined to the use of a local congregation, or can it be held in larger gatherings? Should the elements be taken to private homes for observance of the rite? Should this ordinance be administered only by ordained persons? Is open or closed communion more consistent with our Baptist doctrine?

The Lord's Supper is a church ordinance, and we must be careful to see that its observance is consistent with its meaning and purpose. However, Christ gave little or no instruction about the way in which it should be conducted. Therefore, we must make our deductions about this service from our understanding of the church and of the nature of this ceremony.

Above all, the connection of this Supper with the church should be kept in sight. As the Passover feast was linked to

---

[11] W.L. Lumpkin, *Baptist Confessions of Faith* (Valley Forge: Judson Press, 1959), page 293.

the Israel of the Old Covenant, so the Lord's Supper is closely associated with the church as God's covenant people. This rite signifies the New Covenant ratified by Christ's vicarious death, and its observance should always be such that it will emphasize the presence of Christ in his covenant community. As these central factors are kept clear, the covenant meal will contribute to the deepening of the fellowship within the Christian community, as the members look to Christ the head of the church.

The Lord's Supper ought always to be an integral part of the worship service and should be accompanied by the preached word. The bread and the cup are visible signs which represent the same thing as the preached gospel, and the visual elements and the actions serve to reinforce the preaching. To separate the Supper from the sermon is to invite a superstitious attitude toward the rite, for history has demonstrated the ease with which people can give an almost magical meaning to it. It is not a sacred mystery in which some divine power is imparted by the very eating and drinking. No attempt should be made to create an atmosphere of deep solemnity, which would invest this occasion with some dignity different from that of other worship services. There should be a quiet reverence in any meeting where a congregation gathers to worship the Lord, but no extra solemnity should characterize the Lord's Supper. Indeed, it is a joyous celebration and a time of thanksgiving, when God's people join in a meal reminding them of their origins and purpose.

There is no rule about the frequency with which the Supper should be observed. Baptist practice has varied from holding it every week to holding it once each quarter of the year. There are good reasons for observing it each week, but considerations of time make that frequency difficult. Also, there is the risk that something repeated too often may lose its power to speak to us. Probably once each month is a suitable practice. The important thing is that it should be held regularly and that careful attention be given to interpret its meaning to a congregation.

Should the Lord's Supper be confined to the local church? There are some Baptists who would so limit it, mainly those who have been influenced by Landmarkism, which restricted the definition of the church to the local congregation. This notion is based upon a false assumption. The church is larger than the local congregation, and representatives of churches gathered in meeting also have an ecclesial character. At meetings of associations, regions, or national conventions, it is appropriate to celebrate the Lord's Supper.

Nevertheless, when we have agreed that there are other places where the Lord's Supper may be held, the question will be raised as to where the lines are to be drawn. Should a pastor administer the Supper to parishioners in the hospital and in homes? Should Communion be observed by small fellowship groups of the church, led by one of the laypersons?

After considerable study, a group of British Baptists concluded that "occasional Communion" is appropriate under certain circumstances other than in local churches. They formulated some principles to guide them in determining when such a service would be appropriate. The first requirement, they concluded, is that the gathering should be very clearly held for such Christian purposes as indicate the churchly character of their meeting. Second, the meeting should be of a kind where it is fitting that those present should profess their Christian faith and obedience in an act of corporate worship at the Lord's table. Third, the situation should be such that the observance can be carried on reverently.

Accordingly, an associational meeting would be a very appropriate place for holding the Lord's Supper; so might a regional or national gathering, although the difficulties of having a reverent service in a crowd of several thousand persons might present a problem. Whether men's or women's organizations should meet for Communion breakfasts is a question to be decided on the basis of the tests listed above. Hard-and-fast rules cannot be made for such matters. However, it is not easy to justify such an observance for a wedding party.

There still remains the question of taking Communion to those who are ill at home or in the hospital. Is such a practice appropriate? If this is an ordinance intended to deepen the church's experience of Christ's presence and to strengthen its sense of identity as the church, then the pastor should not serve Communion on a one-to-one basis to individuals. Not only does such a practice convey a false idea of the church; it also tends to encourage a superstitious reverence for the Lord's Supper, obscuring its real intent.

However, there are undoubtedly persons who by circumstances beyond their control are deprived of an opportunity to participate in the services of the church. Some provision is necessary to extend the fellowship of the church to them beyond the walls of the meeting house. Therefore, it is proper for the Lord's Supper to be served in the home of a shut-in, or in a hospital or other setting, if care is taken to make this a service of the church. The pastor ought not to go to such occasions alone, but should take one or more deacons or other members along to represent the congregation. In connection with the service, there should be a prayer, a Scripture lesson, and a brief message to interpret and prepare for the memorial meal. When thus safeguarded, the Lord's Supper is kept in line with its intent.

Whether there should be an ordained minister officiating at such a private service is another practical question. Historically, Baptists have usually insisted that an ordained person preside at the Communion service. Indeed, there have been instances in which Baptist churches went a year or two without such an observance because no pastor could conveniently be with them for the occasion. Such a circumstance would not be likely today, and they probably carried this rule too far. Laypersons may administer the Lord's Supper, although they should do so with the authorization of the congregation, inasmuch as they are representing the church at this time.

The reason for insisting upon ordination as a requisite for administering the Lord's Supper is to keep it from being treated carelessly. Baptists have felt that allowing other persons to preside at such a service could set a precedent that would open the way to anyone to do so. However, it does not seem necessary to be so strict that no exceptions can be made to a general rule. The church is responsible to see that due seriousness and reverence are shown toward the observance, and it carries out that responsibility in part by delegating the leadership of the service to the pastor. In certain cases a church may vote to authorize a deacon, a theological student not yet ordained, or another selected church member to administer Communion. Care should be taken to choose persons fitted in spirit, character, and ability to lead in this kind of service.

The question of open or closed Communion once agitated Baptist churches deeply. Until the twentieth century most Baptist churches practiced closed Communion. That is, they would allow only those who had been immersed upon profession of faith to take Communion with them. They reasoned that baptism ought to precede participation in the Lord's Supper; all churches, they said, hold that unbaptized persons must not take Communion. However, as Baptists saw the matter, infant baptism was not genuine baptism. Moreover, many churches of other denominations had interpretations of the Lord's Supper different from theirs. Therefore, the churches felt that they had no alternative but to refuse to join with Christians of other denominations at the Lord's table.

This refusal was often a matter of regret and of embarrassment to Baptists. They were troubled about their practice of closed Communion, for they regarded as Christian many brothers and sisters whom they could not admit to their Communion services. Sometimes, even a minister of another denomination who supplied their pulpit was unable to share in the Communion service.

Gradually there came a reversal, as the obligation to recognize fellow Christians was felt more strongly. There is, obviously, a discrepancy when one accepts others as fellow Christians, but refuses to sit with them at the Lord's table. The practice of open Communion is now almost universal among Baptists in the United States, although in some parts of the South closed Communion still persists.

The Lord's Supper in the BEM Document

Reference was made in chapter 5 and earlier in this chapter to the Faith and Order document, *Baptism, Eucharist, and Ministry,* in connection with baptism, and there may be value in noting its affirmations on the Lord's Supper. When one considers how very divided the churches since the Reformation have been over this ritual meal, it can be understood why a Lutheran commentator called this document a breakthrough, which "offers a quantum leap in reversing a millennium or more of the splitting of the Christian Church."[12] There is indeed a remarkable convergence on the part of major Christian traditions on central points of significance in the Lord's Supper: thanksgiving to the Creator, memorial of Christ, invocation of the Spirit, communion of the faithful, meal of the kingdom.

Although complete agreement is not reached on some of the most controversial issues, such as the meaning of "sacrifice" and the nature of the "real presence" of Christ, these have been put in contexts which contribute to better understanding and have removed some of the bitter conflict which once attached to these differences. The problem remains for many as to the term "sacrament" in this connection and what it implies. Does the Lord's Supper itself have the power to effect a change in persons? This issue is raised by American Baptists in their response to the document.

In the American Baptist Churches' response, strong appreciation was expressed "for the rich exposition of the meanings of the Lord's Supper," and for the treatment of "sacrifice" in the "Eucharist" section (par. 3). It acknowledged that there is biblical validity in emphasizing the element of thanksgiving and hence use of the term "Eucharist," which is derived from the Greek word for gratitude. However, the response asserted that Baptists prefer the title "Lord's Supper" and favor placing the most stress on the memorial character of the rite. Appreciation was expressed for that part of the document dealing with the Supper as a memorial of Christ, with an emphasis upon *anamnesis* (remembrance), which leads away from a "very thin" notion of that element.

In spite of the positive reaction to the document in general, there were some points at which a difference was registered. "Most Baptists," says the American Baptist response,

---

[12]Kenneth E. Christopherson, "Putting Humpty Dumpty Together Again: the *Baptism, Eucharist, and Ministry* Document," in *American Baptist Quarterly,* Dec. 1985, p. 365.

"would have reservations about the suggestion that Christians receive 'the gift of salvation' through Communion (par. 2), or that the Eucharist 'transforms Christians into the image of Christ' (par. 26)." It adds: "One of the reasons that Baptists have tended to avoid the terminology 'sacrament' is that they have wished to avoid any suggestion that rites in themselves convey grace, while at the same time affirming that they may be occasions and means of grace (though not of salvation). Thus, a 'sacrament' does not transform us, but the grace of God does."

The American Baptist response has more detailed comments explaining Baptist practice, affirming what is stated in the BEM document, and welcoming the more cordial relationships and understandings which the document has achieved. The comments above, however, are among the most important parts of the response. Regarding the Lord's Supper, there has been a significant movement toward Christian consensus, as this document indicates.

Conclusion

Thus Baptists have their own traditional views of the two ordinances, or sacraments. While they are not sacramentalists, their interpretations do allow room for considering baptism and the Lord's Supper, under proper circumstances, as means of grace. The use of the term "ordinance" emphasizes that these two observances are based upon commands of Christ. However, God's grace and persons' faith are closely related in both of these rites; and, when properly observed, either occasion should bring a heightened experience of God's presence and power. Therefore they may be called sacraments, provided that this word is properly defined. In order to avoid misunderstandings which grow out of the associations connected with the terms "ordinance" and "sacrament," one may simply speak of baptism and the Lord's Supper by their own names, and ignore both of the other designations. It should always be kept in mind that both rites are intimately related to the life of the church. They are to be performed only within the context of its fellowship and by its authorized representatives.

9

The Associational Principle of Baptists

There is a natural tension between commitment to the wider church and loyalty to the local congregation. Early Baptists tried to give a visible form to this dual relationship by their "associational principle," but the tension will always be there. Too often the emphasis upon the local church has been allowed to weaken a sense of responsibility to the larger fellowship.

Baptists have maintained first of all that "the holy catholic church" becomes most visible in particular local churches. According to their understanding, each congregation of professing Christians is an outcropping of the larger church, a local expression of the body of Christ. By attempting to maintain regenerate church membership, they sought to make the composition of the particular churches approximate that of the church as it is known to God. To each such local church, they said, Christ has given all power necessary for ordering its life under his headship. Yet they believed that the Christian church as a whole is greater than any local church, and that local congregations have mutual responsibilities.

Origins of the Associational Principle

A further step had to be taken, therefore, to make plain the relationship between the universal church and the particular churches. Some safeguard was needed to prevent an excessive stress upon local independence from obscuring the unity of the body of Christ. Local churches did not regard themselves as isolated units, but rather as integral members of the total church which is the household of God. The earliest London Baptist Confession of 1644 pointedly expresses a sense of interrelatedness: "Though we be distinct in respect of particular bodies . . . yet are all one in communion, holding Jesus Christ to be our head and Lord." Other statements in the various confessions supported this concept of unity which those Baptists held.

More than verbal assent was needed, however, to the idea of unity among the churches. As a visible means of expressing the interdependence and mutual concerns of the particular churches, they devised the association. The term "association" did not come into use as a common designation for the formal cooperative life for a few years. However, both General and Particular Baptists had begun the development of an associational life by 1660.

The associational principle was strong in Baptist life both in England and America. Associations met practical needs and were rooted in their view of the church. In 1652 the Berkshire Baptists stated their associational principle as follows: "There is the same relationship betwixt particular churches each towards other, as there is betwixt particular members of one church, for the churches of Christ do all make up but one body or church in general under Christ their head."[1] In England these organizations served as means of distributing benevolences, constituting new churches, resolving disciplinary problems, settling questions of theology and polity, and eventually of supervising ordina-

---

[1] E. A. Payne, *The Baptists of Berkshire Through Three Centuries,* Appendix I, pp. 147ff. (London: Carey Kingsgate Press, 1951). Cited by Hugh Wamble, "The Beginnings of Associationalism Among English Baptists," *Review and Expositor,* Oct. 1957, p. 547.

tion. Both General and Particular Baptists aspired to have national organizations in the seventeenth century, calling them General Assemblies.

The Philadelphia Baptist Association

The theology and practice of associations was also accepted by Baptists in America. A look at the formation and activities of the Philadelphia Baptist Association affords a view of the way in which such an organization was conceived.[2] Organized in 1707, it was the parent stem from which all the major cooperative Baptist bodies in America have sprung. The fact that it did not begin until that date has led some to the mistaken conclusion that the associational idea was something that independent churches developed only gradually. Actually, however, the General Baptists seem to have formed an association, or yearly meeting, in New England by 1670. Most of the few Baptist churches in New England then were of the General persuasion and belonged to that body.

Prior to 1690 the Particular Baptist churches in America were too few and scattered to have an associational life. At that date there were four Particular Baptist churches in the middle colonies, and they had begun informal meetings together. In 1688, the Pennepack Baptist Church in Pennsylvania had come into existence, and shortly thereafter there were three others in neighboring New Jersey: Middletown (1688), Piscataway (1689), and Cohansey (1690). These churches held joint meetings for fellowship, administering baptism, observing the Lord's Supper, and ordaining ministers. A few years later the Welsh Tract Baptists formed a church. In 1707 these five Particular Baptist churches organized the Philadelphia Baptist Association.

Until the second half of the century this was the only association of Particular Baptists in America, and it came to include some churches from other colonies. Under the impact of the Great Awakening, Baptists began to increase,

---

[2] W. S. Hudson, "The Associational Principle Among Baptists," *Foundations*, 1(Jan. 1958)1; also in *Baptists in Transition* (Valley Forge: Judson Press, 1979), pp. 37–51.

and they formed more associations. When the Charleston Baptist Association was organized in 1751, it followed the pattern of the Philadelphia association; and numerous others did the same before long.

The Role of the Philadelphia Baptist Association

How did this early association conceive its nature and function? It is difficult for Baptists today to realize the strong corporate sense of the Baptists in that day. Accustomed to more individualistic ideas, we may too easily read into the earlier terms "independence" or "particular churches" some modern ideas of "the autonomy of the local church."

In their theory of the association, Baptists tried to steer a course between the extremes of overemphasizing or underemphasizing the place of the local church. While acknowledging their belief in "the catholic or universal church," they also stressed the importance of the local congregation. Particular churches, they maintained, represented the larger church and had all the powers belonging to the larger Christian fellowship. On the other hand, along with this recognition of the significance of particular churches, there was an equal insistence upon their interdependence. Such churches, declares a manual of discipline issued in 1743 by the Philadelphia Baptist Association, "may and ought to maintain communion together in many duties which may tend to the mutual benefit and edification of the whole." Thus, their thinking about the association simply reiterated that of the English Baptists in the seventeenth century.

We may learn more about their viewpoint from "An Essay on the Power and Duty of an Association," which was approved by the Philadelphia Association in 1749. Beginning with the assertion that "an association is not a superior judicature," this document proceeds to assert the powers which belong to the local church under Christ. However, the statement also adds: "Yet we are of opinion that an association of the delegates of associate churches have a very considerable power in their hands, respecting those churches in their confederation." What they regarded as independence of the churches was balanced by a strong sense of interdependence.

Although the association had no legal control over the churches, the representative body had an authority of its own. Admittedly, an association could not interfere directly in the affairs of a congregation. It could not, for example, discipline a member in one of the churches. If a member of a particular church needed to be disciplined, however, the association could recommend that the delinquent individual be dealt with in a disciplinary way. The church was then expected to heed that advice, and if it refused to do so it might be excluded from the association. The relationship of the association toward its member churches was explained in the "Essay" as analogous to that of a church to its members: "But in the capacity of a congregational church, dealing with her own members, an association, then, of the delegates of associate churches, may exclude and withdraw from defective and unsound or disorderly churches."

Thus the association could not dictate to the churches what they were to do, but churches were expected to seek the counsel of the association in difficulties and to respect the judgment of the delegates. Although that body had only limited powers of enforcement, the power to expel uncooperative members constituted an important authority. Since the Baptist doctrine of the church constrained a congregation to be associated with other churches, it was important to keep the associational connections intact. To be forced out of the larger fellowship would deprive it of needed encouragement and help, and to live in isolation was a virtual denial of its doctrine concerning the unity of the church.

Examination of the records will reveal that these early Baptist churches felt an obligation to hold fellowship with one another. They united in associations where they could cooperate in matters of mutual interest and in the furtherance of the gospel. There was no thought of living in isolation, for each church was representative of a larger whole.

A look at the activities of the Philadelphia Baptist Association shows how diverse and broad were its concerns. In general terms its aims were "to consult about such things as were wanting in the churches, and to set them in order." Whatever touched the lives of individual churches or affected their common witness came within the scope of its interest.

In keeping with the aim of having an informed membership in the churches, this association considered the edification of the churches as one of its major aims. It was to that end that several sermons were preached at the regular meetings. Circular letters were sent out to the churches from the association, dealing with points of doctrine or practice. The association also served as a forum where doctrinal or practical questions might be discussed. In order to encourage the development of an informed constituency, the association published printed materials such as its confession of faith, the *Treatise of Discipline,* a catechism for children, and a hymnal.

A second important purpose was the provision of a suitable ministry for the churches. Churches which were "destitute" of a minister would be provided with supply preachers, and arrangements were made for them to observe the Lord's Supper. To guard churches against unqualified persons who claimed to be Baptist ministers, the Philadelphia Association asserted the right to examine and certify "all gifted brethren and ministers that might come in here from other places." It also urged churches to seek out young men with promising talents for the ministry, and then took steps to make it possible for such persons to receive a proper education. This interest in education ranged from the use of educational funds to the establishment of a college.

Third among the general aims of the Philadelphia Association was the maintenance of peace among the churches. From the beginning it claimed the right to hear appeals from aggrieved members of churches, and to give advice in the settling of disputes. Initiative could be taken where churches seemed to be in distress, as illustrated by this entry from the *Minutes* of 1731:

> The associated brethren seeing no messengers from Piscataqua as usual, and hearing by some of our brethren of the sad and distracted condition of that congregation, they thought proper to write to them, and to appoint Mr. Jenkin Jones and Mr. Joseph Eaton to give them a visit before winter, which by the blessing of God, proved a means to reduce that church to peace and order.

It should not be necessary to add that the association could not coerce a church or impose a decision upon it; it could, however, determine and declare its convictions. When the association has expressed itself, says the *Treatise of Discipline,* "the churches will do well to receive, own, and observe such determinations."

Another aspect of its work had to do with the forming of new churches. Representatives of the association were sent to the South on more than one occasion. Later in the century, support was raised for missions to the Indians. After the establishment of William Carey's mission in India, the association encouraged an interest in foreign missions.

As the number of churches increased, it became necessary to form other associations. The first of these was the Charleston Baptist Association, in South Carolina, established in 1751, when there were four Baptist churches in that vicinity. Before long there were associations in Virginia and in New England. The new associations were modeled after the Philadelphia pattern. Part of the intention was that the associations themselves should be affiliated with one another in order to maintain unity among the Baptist churches. With the rapid Baptist growth after the Revolutionary War, however, it was difficult to maintain this relationship, and greater diversity in practice and doctrine began to develop.

Early Visions of a National Denomination

It is interesting to observe that as early as 1770, while the number of churches and associations was still small, proposals were made looking forward to the development of a national organization. A Philadelphia pastor, Morgan Edwards, suggested the outlines for such a body. He described its advantages as follows: "It introduces into the visible church what are called joints and bands whereby the whole body is knit together and compacted for increase by that which every part supplieth. And therefore it is that I am so anxious to render the same combination of Baptist Churches universal upon this continent."[3]

---

[3]Quoted by W. W. Barnes, *The Southern Baptist Convention, 1845–1953* (Nashville: Broadman Press, 1954), p. 9.

Even earlier, another Baptist had written to James Manning, the president of Rhode Island College, in a similar vein. Written on the occasion of the founding of the Warren Association in Rhode Island, the letter stated:

> For, as particular members are collected together and united in one body, which we call a particular church, to answer those ends and purposes which could not be accomplished by any single member, so a collection and union of churches into one associational body may easily be conceived capable of answering those still greater purposes which any particular church could not be equal to. And, by the same reason, a union of associations will still increase the body in weight and strength, and make it good that a three-fold cord is not easily broken.[4]

The foregoing quotations are samples of a widespread sentiment which contemplated the expansion of the associational principle embodied in the Philadelphia Baptist Association. The missionary and educational movements, however, had not yet arisen to make the churches feel the urgency of completing a national organization. By the time that the necessity did become apparent, other influences were at work which shifted the development to a new direction.

The Challenge of the Society Method

Early in the nineteenth century a series of new movements affected the course of Baptist growth and development. A fresh awareness of the missionary and evangelistic responsibility of the church called forth new forms of cooperation among churches and among denominations. This interest, which included home and foreign missions, Christian education, evangelism and the dissemination of Bibles and Christian literature, elicited new methods of raising funds to meet the great opportunities.

This rising tide of concern for missions gave impetus to Baptist interest in some additional organizations. When the Judsons and Luther Rice changed their denominational loy-

---

[4]*Ibid.*, p. 2.

alty from Congregationalist to Baptist, there arose an urgent need for some means of supporting them as missionaries in Burma. Luther Rice returned to America to seek the support of Baptists, and in conjunction with Baptist leaders of Boston and Philadelphia he spearheaded a move to awaken the interest of the churches in organizing to support foreign missions. At about the same time there was a growing desire to extend the work of home missions and to establish educational institutions, each of which gave a further impetus to the development of a national organization.

At this juncture, it was not clear what forms of organization the Baptists would adopt in order to participate in these new movements. The early pattern of the Philadelphia Baptist Association offered a basis for the development of an associational life on the national level. The natural line of development would have been to expand the associations into state and national organizations, and there was strong sentiment in favor of such a plan. State and national conventions would be organized and related to the local churches through the associations. Through such an organization the Baptists could meet the challenges of missions, education, evangelism, and publications.

In opposition to the natural expansion of the associational principle, however, were an individualistic spirit and vested local interests. Many people feared any tendency toward centralization of authority, and they favored the formation of separate voluntary societies to sponsor each particular missionary and educational concern. Such societies were not composed of churches but of assorted individuals or groups interested in the project represented by that particular society. Membership, being voluntary, was based upon payment of dues. Forgetting the theology which had undergirded the associational principle, the advocates of this viewpoint wished to bypass the older design in favor of the "society method" of cooperative work. Between 1814 and 1826, though there was a divided opinion, the strong desire for an integrated denomination seemed likely to win the contest. By the latter date, however, the individualistic spirit had triumphed, and the decentralized pattern represented by the societies was adopted.

The Triennial Convention

In 1814, it was the hope of Luther Rice to see the development of a unified national body of Baptists. It was his plan to lead in the formation of a national organization made up of representatives of state conventions, and these in turn would be composed of delegates from associations and local societies. Dr. Thomas Baldwin, of Boston, also envisioned a similar close-knit denominational body, as did many other ministers. There were other influential leaders, however, who wished to avoid any tendencies toward a strong ecclesiastical organization. Under the pressure of time, the leaders formed a Baptist Missionary Convention which had for its one purpose the support of foreign missions. It was expected by some that this "Triennial Convention," as it was commonly called, could be developed into a more comprehensive body later, and various attempts were made to expand and strengthen it.

The first step toward extending the purpose of the Triennial Convention came in 1817 when the constitution was amended. A need was felt for a national Baptist college to prepare ministers, and there was a desire to combine home and foreign missions in the work of this agency. By changing the constitution, power was given to the Board authorizing it "to appropriate a portion of the funds to domestic missionary purposes." The Board was also authorized, when funds should become adequate, "to institute a classical and theological seminary, for the purpose of aiding young men" of promise for the ministry. The purpose of the missionary convention was further expanded in 1820 when the name was changed to state its objectives broadly as "foreign missions and other important objects relating to the Redeemer's kingdom."

With these constitutional revisions the foundation had been established for a comprehensive denominational life, but the machinery to implement this dream was yet to be completed. Membership in the Triennial Convention was based upon the payment of a sum of money by a local society. Therefore, it was not really a denominational body representing the churches, but rather a voluntary society composed of dues-paying members. However, at that point in its development, the Triennial Convention was intended by some to be only a stopgap until a denominational organization could be effected.

State Conventions as a Necessary Link

A necessary step in the process of completing the national body was the formation of state conventions, which could be joined into a general convention. Local churches would then be represented by delegates to the association, and associations would send delegates to the state convention. The latter would in turn choose representatives to attend the General Convention. In this way the churches would be united in a nationwide denominational organization of a representative type.

The first state convention was formed in South Carolina in 1821. Favoring an integrated denominational body, William B. Johnson, leader of the movement to establish this organization, framed it so that it would coordinate Baptist work in the state. The associations were united into a state convention, and the aims stated in its constitution included missions and education. Before long, a college had been started, which was owned and controlled by the state organization. Home and foreign missions were also promoted under state auspices. It was ready to become a link between churches and a national convention.

The Massachusetts convention, formed in 1824, anticipated the time when it would become a constituent of a national body. Its constitution stated that "whenever a General Convention formed from State Conventions shall be formed or designed, it shall be in the power of this Convention to send delegates to meet in such Convention."[5]

Most of the other state conventions, however, were essentially missionary organizations, often based on payment of dues rather than comprising churches of a state. Their primary focus was on raising funds for overseas missions and for support of evangelists to plant churches in their own

---

[5] W. S. Hudson, "Stumbling into Disorder," *Foundations,* April 1958, p. 47; also in *Baptists in Transition,* p. 85.

region. They did not have the objective of becoming links in a national denomination.

The Triumph of the Society Method

It had been anticipated that by 1826 the dream would be realized of having a national denominational organization. Before that date arrived, however, certain strong local interests had thwarted the whole movement. In New York the new state convention sought to bring missionary and educational interests together under the auspices of the single Baptist body. However, the educational society that controlled the new college, unwilling to relinquish this control, remained independent. Moreover, the Hamilton Missionary Society did not wish to lose its identity. Instead of merging the mission society with the state convention, therefore, the reverse procedure took place, and the state organization became the Baptist Missionary Convention. Hence, instead of a truly representative Baptist convention emerging in New York, the state body became a missionary society based upon contributions from interested people. Individualism and particularism were winning the day.

At the meeting of the Triennial Convention in 1826, the influence of the New York State delegation, coupled with that of influential men from Boston, prevented the anticipated fulfillment of the hope for a national convention. Instead of moving toward a more unified and representative organization, the Triennial Convention voted in 1826 to restrict its interests to foreign missions, and its money basis for individual membership was retained. Separate societies directed the work of publication and home missions, and each educational institution was operated by an independent society. At last the decentralized pattern had won, and Baptist organization became atomistic. The same spirit that had led to frustration of the associational principle now fostered an increasing trend toward local autonomy, which removed the idea of independence from the context of the lordship of Christ over his church. The tendencies toward independence and localism and the triumph of the society method divorced missionary and educational agencies from accountability to the churches and hampered the development of a coherent and efficient denominational organization in the United States. The society method had won out over the associational principle. Thereafter, associations were further eroded as their functions were increasingly preempted by other organizations.

Further Erosion of the Associations

American Baptist Home Mission Society

In 1832, to meet the needs of a rapidly growing western population, Baptists organized the American Baptist Home Mission Society. John Mason Peck was their first missionary to the western frontier, sent to evangelize settlers, start new churches, and organize Sunday schools; and Isaac McCoy was sent at the same time to minister to Native Americans. This society was responsible for supporting many home missionaries in the following decades. They won converts, established churches, started Sunday schools, erected buildings, formed associations, constituted state conventions, and founded colleges. A great many of today's churches in the Midwest and West, as well as other institutions, exist as testimony to the sacrificial labors of hundreds of pioneer preachers employed by the Home Mission Society.

City Societies

As cities began to burgeon with the influx of immigrants and migration from rural to urban areas, a need was felt for new organizations to minister to immigrants, to evangelize, and to plant new churches. Instead of turning to local associations, enterprising individuals formed city mission societies to raise money to employ full-time workers who would concentrate on city ministries.

Church Councils

Another device for handling certain kinds of activities was the council. Councils were *ad hoc* bodies, each called to meet a particular situation, and they were dissolved when the task was completed. Originally councils were instruments used by associations, but later they were often convenient extra-associational gatherings, held when distance made it difficult to convene a special meeting of the association to deal with an urgent matter demanding attention. Councils were thus sometimes instruments of the association and sometimes unrelated to an association. The unintended effect of councils was to make the character of the association more ambiguous and contribute to its dwindling importance.

Councils were used to examine candidates for ordination, formerly the function of the association. The need to have representatives of other churches to share in ordination continued to be an expectation, but it was sometimes more convenient to invite a few churches located nearby than to go through the association in calling for the council. A similar process affected the procedures for forming new churches, as *ad hoc* councils met to ascertain qualifications of persons presenting themselves for charter membership and to examine the doctrinal standards and covenant of the proposed church.

One other kind of situation in which councils were useful was the settlement of disputes. Initially, the association appointed committees for this purpose. Many cases are on record where internal strife attracted the attention of other churches and a council was called for the purpose of mediation. Usually the council was called at the request of the church involved, but sometimes the association took the initiative. On other occasions, an aggrieved member brought his/her case to the attention of the association, and sometimes a council was called to deal with a church which had received into its fellowship someone who had been "excluded" by another church. Eventually, extra-association councils took over the functions of mediating disputes and administering discipline, but (like the exercise of discipline in the churches themselves) these practices became almost obsolete by the twentieth century.

The significant decision of the Triennial Convention in 1826, adopting a society method instead of extending the associational principle to develop a coherent national denomination, determined the organization pattern of Baptists in the North for the rest of the century and beyond. No doubt there were good practical reasons for developing societies independent of a more churchly structure. The accomplishments of the numerous societies were of great importance and their contributions should be recognized. At the same time it must be noted that the society method had negative as well as positive results. Direct responsibility for mission outreach was removed from the churches bit by bit, as societies composed of dues-paying members took over the work of missions, publication, Christian education, and other functions. The associational route would have likely kept alive a vision of the wider church, acted as a check to an exaggerated autonomy of local churches, and involved churches more directly in mission.

There had been no deliberate intention to weaken associations, but a desire for efficiency seemed to favor the society plan. Associations did not lose their importance all at once, but they were greatly weakened as they lost important functions to societies. As Delavan Dewolf, New Jersey Baptist superintendent of missions, observed in 1898: "Evidently, whatever the association was in the days of our Fathers, it is not that to the churches today, and has not the hold it once had."[6]

Defects of the Society Method Recognized

Baptists in the North utilized the society method of supporting missions until its weaknesses became so apparent that a better plan of organization was sought. Instead of agencies integrated into a national denomination, a series of independent corporations operated by self-perpetuating boards of managers had developed. The American Baptist Foreign Mission Society, the Woman's American Baptist Foreign Mission Society, the American Baptist Home Mission Society, the Woman's American Baptist Home Mission Society, the American Baptist Historical Society, the American Baptist Education Society, and the American Baptist Publication Society were all legally incorporated institutions responsible to constituencies determined by their payment of membership dues. Even state conventions, at first, were essentially missionary societies. Theological seminar-

---

[6]Quoted in N. H. Maring, *Baptists in New Jersey* (Valley Forge: Judson Press, 1964), pp. 248–249.

ies and colleges were administered by self-perpetuating boards of trustees, instead of being under the control of the denomination. Although some attempts were made to coordinate the work of separate agencies, and each society was effective for a long while, eventually the competition for funds and the wasteful duplication of efforts became a problem.

With the passing of years the need for a more unified plan was felt, but the road to reorganization was blocked. The society method had promoted a spirit of independence stronger than the will to cooperate. Vested interests in the independent societies were reluctant to surrender their autonomy for the good of the larger Baptist work until the twentieth century.

Moreover, the nineteenth century saw a substantial erosion of the older theology of the church and the associational principle, which might have provided the basis for a better structure. Under the impact of individualism and revivalism, Baptists of the nineteenth century had undergone subtle changes that gave them a new self-image. By the late nineteenth century, the strict Calvinism that had characterized earlier Baptists had virtually dissolved, although the process had been largely unconscious. In place of the early bonds that had united Baptists in association, a new emphasis on independence came into vogue, denying that there was such a thing as the "interdependence" of Baptist churches. The spread of this concept was aided and abetted by the publication of E.S. Hiscox's popular manual entitled *Baptist Church Directory* in 1859.[7]

The idea of the universal church tended to drop out of

---

[7] Two later books by Hiscox, based on his earlier volume, continued to propagate his ideas among thousands of churches: *The Standard Manual for Baptist Churches* (1890) and *The New Directory for Baptist Churches* (1894). In 1964, with the approval of the Hiscox family, these were merged by Frank T. Hoadley (then book editor of Judson Press) into a single volume entitled *The Hiscox Guide for Baptist Churches,* in which the strong emphasis on local church independence was eliminated, a new section headed "The Wider Fellowship of Baptists" was added, and much of Hiscox's archaic practical advice to churches was revised.

common use, and Landmarkist influence led many to deny that the New Testament recognized any other meaning of "church" besides that of the local church. The New Hampshire Confession, which superseded the older Philadelphia Baptist Confession in popular usage after about 1850, did not even mention the church universal. Oblivious of their origins from English Dissenters, some Baptist even denied that they were Protestants. Earlier adherence to confessional statements gave way to the notion that Baptists had never had confessions or creeds except the New Testament. Furthermore the theory that Baptist churches cannot be represented came to be accepted as a traditional Baptist principle.

In 1907 the Northern Baptist Convention was organized to bring about more cooperation among the societies, but the new plan did not embrace associations or build on the associational principle. Another, more thorough reorganization, resulting in a more coherent structure, did take account of the associational principle. Nevertheless it did not make any provision for associations themselves, and consequently in some regions there are no longer any associations. By the 1990s, however, there were some attempts to find ways to revive associations, although there was considerable disagreement as to whether such renewal was necessary, desirable, or possible.

The Revival of the Associational Principle

It has long been debated whether associations can be, or should be, revived. In theory it seems plausible that the association could again have an important place in denominational life, forming a bridge between local churches and the regional and national organizations. Comprising a number of churches, each association makes available a combination of strength and wisdom that can supplement the resources of a local church. Through consultation and cooperation, each congregation might be strengthened and mutual tasks undertaken more efficiently. Moreover, efficiency is not the only benefit that might accrue from more participation at the grass-roots level. A stronger associational life might well contribute to the kind of solidarity of the denomination which many feel is needed.

There seems to be a lack of closeness and identity of purpose between the local churches and the regional and national bodies. The requisite sense of partnership among local churches, regions, and national boards is not easy to achieve. Regional and national organizations may appear efficient, but efficient bureaucratic organization is no substitute for personal relationships at the local level. In a system where policies and programs are developed by regional and national bodies and passed down to the churches, it is not easy for those at the local level to feel a sense of ownership. There are many who believe that better means are needed that will allow for greater participation of local churches with the denomination in making decisions and determining policies and programs.

Local church participation through an association might result in more realistic denominational planning and more effective results. The association can serve as a means of disseminating information and providing inspiration. Evangelism, church planting, missions, and community action can be strengthened, leadership training workshops conducted, and public ministries supported. Ordination may be supervised in cooperation with regional and national bodies to assure that ordination standards are maintained. In many ways the recovery of a wholesome associational life in coordination with regional and national bodies could result in greater effectiveness, while the increased level of participation might result in a stronger sense of corporate identity as a denomination.

This stronger sense of commonality and mutual trust could in turn open the way for a church's neighbors to be available to give advice and counsel in church problems or disputes upon request. It is neither desirable nor feasible, of course, for an outside body to impose decisions upon a Baptist congregation. However, in a day when church conflicts are frequent and sometimes lead to litigation, it would be a healthy step for a church voluntarily to seek help from an associational body, as was commonly done in the past. There is value in being able to turn to a body of Christian brothers and sisters for mediation, rather than to appeal to civil courts to settle differences about church issues. Indeed, the apostle Paul scolded members of the church at Corinth because "a believer goes to court against a believer—and before unbelievers at that," and he urged that Christians settle disputes among themselves (1 Cor. 6:1-6). The association may be better suited to this purpose than a regional or national body.

While such a revival of associational life may sound plausible and attractive in principle, repeated efforts so far have not met with much success. Even if important functions are given to associations again, it is virtually impossible to sustain programs and continuity over long periods of time without permanent full-time staff members. No matter how willing and capable are volunteer workers, nevertheless unexpected problems (even church leaders moving away from the area) interfere with their commitments. Associations seem to work better in the Southern Baptist Convention, where directors of missions are available to all of them. In the American Baptist Churches, associations function most effectively where they have merged with city societies, enabling them to have endowments and permanent staff.

Although associations can continue to be valued for fellowship and inspiration, many do not believe they are capable of undertaking major mission responsibilities again. There are those who contend, however, that the associational principle may be retained even when associations themselves cease to exist. They maintain that in the American Baptist Churches today, the region carries out the purposes which once belonged to associations.

One executive minister has argued that "the purposes of regions today are consistent with those which characterized Baptist associations in the past: fellowship, discipline, advice, missions, evangelism, education, and religious liberty."[8] His position is explicated by assertions that even "the principal function of fellowship . . . which has always been the historical strength of the associations, has been taken over by the regions." Furthermore, he states, "Regions have

---

[8]George D. Younger, "The Associational Principle and Regions of the American Baptist Churches in the U.S.A.," *American Baptist Quarterly*, VIII (March 1990) 1, pp. 6-23.

the budget and staff, a clearer purpose, a fuller program and a more direct connection to the national denomination. In fact, regions are in the position of trying to foster or strengthen associations, areas, or clusters, rather than drawing their own strength from the activity of those areas." He adds that "the region is the organizing agent and the source of day-to-day supervision for most of the mission that is conducted in its geographical area." Moreover, "the role of consultation with local churches that was taken by associations in Baptist beginnings . . . is today being principally fulfilled by region staff members, especially those with the title of area ministers."

There are many who share this view of the region as the liaison between churches and the national organization and as a legitimate successor to the old associations. Believing that associations *per se* are obsolete, they hold that the region is our best hope of recovering the equivalent of associational life.

This point of view, though widely shared, is by no means unanimous. Many others hold that associations were once the heart of Baptist life and that the failure to include them in the restructuring plans was a mistake. They contend that the lack of strong church life at the associational level has contributed to the apathy of local churches towards regions and national organizations and to feelings of alienation that cause church members to think of wider organizations as "they" rather than as an extension of themselves. Consequently, in some regions there have been attempts to find ways to revive associational life.

One area minister who advocates the renewal of associations is convinced that they are a missing link that could bring strength and vitality to the reorganized denomination. As he sees it, the new structure which was intended to make the churches a more integral part of the denomination actually moved them to the periphery of denominational life. The heart of the problem, he thinks, is that no clear provision was made in the representative system to give churches enough opportunity to participate in decision making and planning. As a result they have had little sense of ownership of policies and programs. The tendency to develop programs at a national level, promote them through the regions, and expect churches to support them became the prevailing mode. This "trickle-down" approach to programming often failed to win support from local churches, when programs did not coincide with their interests. Conversely, he argued, "associations allow for grass root participation among churches, enabling a 'perking-up,' rather than a 'trickling-down' concept of ministry and mission."[9]

He therefore recommends that associations generate interchurch fellowship groups and coordinating committees which would develop cooperative projects related to their special needs and interests. He reports that in tests this approach has increased the churches' associational participation through their "ownership" of projects they have developed as against those handed down by national and regional offices. Although much more time and wider testing would be needed to validate the viability of such an approach, there is some basis for thinking that associations have a potential for increased value to Baptist life. To succeed would require counsel and support from regional executives and area ministers as they encourage grass-roots involvement. Regions might well provide the context in which personal relationships, planning and working together at the associational/cluster level, and building a sense of community can take place. This would represent a somewhat different style of leadership from that which is most common today.

It appears that the 1990s will be a time of testing for the associational principle. Some regions have been reconsidering their earlier negative judgments on the association and its potential for effective ministry and for the development of a corporate sense of denominational identity and unity.

---

[9]Malcolm G. Shotwell, *Renewing the Baptist Principle of Associations* (Ann Arbor: University Microfilms International, 1990), pp. 230-249. This D.Min. thesis examines associations in historical, theological, and sociological perspective, describes the new model and its testing in five associations, and furnishes a constitution for the new model of the association. In his new role as Executive Minister in the Great Rivers Region, the author is testing out these ideas in a larger arena.

There are values in associational life which seem worth recovering, but it remains to be seen whether some combination of old and new forms will actually lead to their recovery.

10

Regional and National Organizations

Baptists have had difficulty in establishing effective structures for cooperation in mission, especially since the nineteenth century, when their associational principle became eroded and their consciousness of the wider church was weakened. As national organizations expanded in more recent times to meet changing circumstances, it was difficult to develop the sense of solidarity between local churches and national agencies that had once been possible. This condition persists, partly because each group is preoccupied with its respective area of responsibility and views things from its own perspective. It is difficult to maintain personal relationships and communications, and a lack of structures to provide for effective participation of the grass-roots constituency in decisions on policies and programs contributes to misunderstanding and breakdown of trust. The alienation is increased when there are different perceptions of what is legitimately included in Christian mission.

This sort of tension is not peculiar to Baptists, but a denomination with a congregational polity is apt to have special problems. As noted earlier, a societal method supplanted the associational principle in the nineteenth century. Associations, which were churchly bodies with a confessional basis, had previously generated cooperation among churches in common tasks. When a host of new challenges arose, however, additional single-purpose voluntary societies seemed a convenient way to support new mission enterprises, and associations were bypassed. Since then, most regional and national organizations among Baptists have been established largely on pragmatic grounds, with little consideration for biblical or theological principles of ecclesiology. The inherent balance between local independence and the wider fellowship became weakened, giving way to a one-sided emphasis upon local autonomy. Nevertheless, *a compelling sense of need to engage in mission tasks* too large for an individual church *made necessary some kind of cooperative organization.* The nineteenth and twentieth centuries have seen numerous attempts to develop organizations with the *twofold aim of enabling churches to work together without making commitments that would threaten local independence.*

As long as the mission of the church was narrowly conceived, a loose-knit federation of churches was adequate to accomplish objectives that required cooperation. Of course, even in those times when organization was simpler, there was friction. Even when associations were the only form of organization beyond local churches, there were sometimes conflicts over the boundaries of associational authority. On the whole, however, associations did serve almost universally to enable churches to maintain doctrinal unity, provide fellowship, supply a ministry, and work together in a few common undertakings. The potential for conflict increased as churches multiplied, memberships grew, Baptists became more scattered, the concept of the church's purpose grew, and the need for additional organization increased.

In the nineteenth century, Baptist churches that had heretofore thought of themselves as of "like faith and order" became fragmented into many separate Baptist organizations. In some cases, such as the Primitive and Landmark Baptists, divisions resulted from tensions between their insistence on local autonomy and the claims of societies and conventions produced by the mission impulse. Other breaches came about over slavery, the desire of freedmen to have their own church organizations, the inclination of ethnic groups to maintain their identities, controversies over doctrine, and personal clashes over leadership and power. As a consequence of repeated schisms, a recent *Yearbook of American and Canadian Churches* listed twenty-four Baptist bodies, and there are numerous others which do not appear in that volume.

Sharing a common heritage of doctrine and practice, Baptist groups have adhered to some basic principles of polity with regard to local churches and associations. Associations were a familiar part of Baptist life almost from their beginnings, and are similar enough to be recognizable in whatever group of Baptists they are observed. When new challenges called for wider organizations, however, there were no good precedents to follow. Impelled by commitment to missions, local churches tried to devise regional and national organizations that would enable the churches to cooperate in mission and at the same time would safeguard local independence. At these wider levels, therefore, diversities in Baptist polity are striking. Only a few examples can be described briefly to illustrate the diversity.

Varied Ways of Organizing for Mission

A general idea of how a denomination works can be gained by reading its constitution, but this does not always give the full picture. To understand the actual operation, it is of the utmost importance to locate the centers of power for decision making. Informal power structures are often more significant than constitutions and organizational charts. Unintended results often flow from constitutions, and what appear on paper to be democratic structures can become in practice oligarchies or autocracies.

Southern Baptist Convention

The Southern Baptist Convention is the largest Protestant denomination in the United States, and its impressive growth, despite a loose formal connection between churches and national organization, has puzzled many observers. It has been common to attribute its success to the fact that it developed a "convention method" rather than the "society method" when it organized in 1845. That theory is only partially correct.

It is true that William B. Johnson, the principal designer

of the constitution of the Southern Baptist Convention, favored an organization capable of "eliciting, combining, and directing the energies of the whole denomination." Accordingly, the constitution provided for a convention with boards of foreign and home missions and others as needed, and they were supposed to be under control of the convention. The rest of the constitution, however, failed to provide an organization consistent with that aim. It followed the society pattern of the Triennial Convention, of which Johnson had been a long-time member and was its president immediately before the southern withdrawal. Instead of a convention composed of churches, the SBC membership was based upon payment of money by individuals, churches, or other interested groups. Therefore, the Southern Baptist Convention was only *potentially* an integrated and efficient denomination, and for about seventy-five years it operated very much like a society.[1]

The SBC as an entity actually existed only during the few days of its annual (at first triennial or biennial) meetings. The boards each had treasuries, but no provision was made for funding—not even for paying the printing bills of the convention itself. In the interim between meetings there was no means of correlating the activities of its boards, which functioned as quasi-autonomous bodies, competing with each other in raising funds. For decades there was little denominational consciousness or loyalty. By the early twentieth century, there were still no standing committees, no commissions, no general secretary, and no headquarters. Not until 1931 was the basis of membership modified to provide that the convention would be made up of messengers from churches that cooperated with and contributed to the work of the SBC.

A major step toward realizing its potential as an integrated denomination was taken with the appointment of an

---

[1] R. A. Baker, *The Southern Baptist Convention and Its People, 1845–1972* (Nashville: Broadman Press, 1974), pp. 164-176, 308-318, 400-406; and H. Leon McBeth, *The Baptist Heritage: Four Centuries of Baptist Witness* (Nashville: Broadman Press, 1988), pp. 388-391, 609-623.

executive committee in 1917, providing for the first time a way to direct mission boards, schools, and the publication house other than by boards of the agencies themselves. In 1925 the Cooperative Program was established, creating a common treasury for all denominational purposes. Two years later the functions of the Executive Committee were expanded, and, utilizing the Cooperative Program and the support of the Sunday School Board, the SBC was on the way to a stronger denominational organization.

Messengers to annual conventions elect officers and board members, adopt a budget, pass resolutions, and vote on policies. They elect trustees for the boards, commissions, and agencies, but nominations are made by committees appointed by the president. For the rest of the year the Executive Committee acts for the convention and oversees all the agencies of the SBC. Thus a great deal of power is concentrated in the hands of a few individuals, who direct a large bureaucracy. Aggressive evangelistic and missions programs and intense denominational loyalty, symbolized by the Cooperative Program, led to a phenomenal growth from about 1940 to 1990, increasing membership from a little more than five million to nearly fifteen million members. Sociological factors, a predominantly conservative theology, capable administrative leadership, and efficient organization all contributed to this advance. It must not be overlooked, however, that denominational unity in missions succeeded because of what one Southern Baptist calls the "Grand Compromise," viz. a tacit agreement to tolerate diversities in theology and social values in the interest of cooperative missions.[2]

The acceptance of pluralism, which had been subordinated to mission for years, finally broke down. In 1979, a concerted effort was launched by a consciously conservative group to win control of the Executive Committee, mission boards, seminaries, and other commissions and agencies. This takeover movement was possible because the constitution allowed the president to appoint a committee which

---

[2]Bill Leonard, *God's Last and Best Hope: the Fragmentation of the SBC* (Nashville: Broadman Press, 1990), pp. 38-39.

appointed another committee that nominated all trustees to educational, mission, and other boards and commissions. By electing a succession of presidents year after year sympathetic to their aims, a well-organized political movement succeeded in filling the boards with like-minded supporters. The process had been virtually completed as of 1990, leaving moderates with the dilemma of accepting a regime that would impose a "biblical inerrancy" test on board members, missionaries, and seminary professors, or of withdrawing from the convention. Thus, a flawed constitution, which had envisioned a coherent and democratic denomination but failed to provide structures adequate for that purpose, left open a door to centralization of power and imposition of doctrinal tests contrary to historic Baptist doctrine.

The Conservative Baptist Movement

Another pattern is represented by the Conservative Baptists, who withdrew from the American Baptist Churches (then the Northern Baptist Convention) in 1947. A major factor in their leaving was apprehension about what they perceived as threats to the independence of local churches. The first organization they formed was the Conservative Baptist Foreign Mission Society. Then came the Conservative Baptist Association, the Conservative Baptist Home Mission Society, and seminaries.

In the desire to protect local autonomy, the CBA had no organic relation to its cooperating mission societies and seminaries. It has no unified budget to assist these agencies, and they "prefer to speak of their *movement* rather than their denomination, because the CBA creates only a loose affiliation for its churches."[3] Conservative Baptists have grown to about 1,200 churches with around 200,000 members, and they support nearly 1,000 career and short-term missionaries through their foreign and home mission societies.

---

[3]Bruce Shelley, *Dictionary of Christianity in America* (Downers Grove: InterVarsity Press, 1990), pp. 313-314.

The National Baptist Conventions[4]

Two of the black Baptist organizations also have rather looseknit structures, while a third has adopted a more ordered system of government. Together these three report a membership of over 12,000,000. The National Baptist Convention, Inc. came into being in 1895, with the merging of three previously existing bodies: a foreign mission, a home mission, and an educational organization. An offshoot from it, in 1915, was the National Baptist Convention of America. Both of these have organizations for home and foreign missions, education, and publications. Reading their constitutions would lead one to expect to find democratic governments operating in these conventions. Delegates from churches, mostly clergy, attend annual conventions, and the constitutions give them power to elect officers, decide policy issues, and to have authority over the boards. The boards, however, have often acted independently. As these conventions do not have executive secretaries, presidents are more than ceremonial figures. Most of them have had long tenures in office and have developed a great deal of power. Supported by executive committees, they have been able, in large measure, to control agendas, defeat opposition, and shape policies and programs. In effect, governance tends to be more oligarchical than democratic.

Joseph H. Jackson, president of the National Baptist Convention, Inc., from 1953 to 1982, was the most outstanding and most controversial head of this convention. Opposing all efforts to limit the tenure of presidents, he was elected to successive terms in spite of a growing demand for a change of leadership. He managed to dominate the convention by means which many considered autocratic and manipulative. The desire for a new leadership was enhanced by his support of gradualism in the civil rights movement in opposition to many who favored a more aggressive approach to overcoming political, economic, and social discrimination.

Failure to unseat him from office led to a call for a meeting

---

[4] Leroy Fitts, *A History of Black Baptists* (Nashville: Broadman Press, 1985), pp. 79-106 and *passim*.

in 1961 to discuss "How to Build a Democratic Convention Dedicated to Christian Objects." The desire to limit tenure in office and the differences over gradualism in regard to civil rights were major factors in the founding of the Progressive National Baptist Convention. An executive secretary was elected, and the Foreign Mission Bureau was adopted as the foreign missions arm. In 1962, the Women's Auxiliary was organized, as was the Congress of Christian Education. As a later general secretary has written:

> For the first time in the history of Black Baptists in America, we have a National Baptist Convention, which is incorporated, observes tenure, has a full time Executive Secretary with a headquarters, and strives to operate on a unified budget. The Progressive National Baptist Convention is a full service Convention. We are interested in and contribute to all areas of life—missions, education, civil rights and human freedom. Our slogan is "Fellowship, Progress, and Peace."[5]

Baptist Conferences

There are other types of national organization, but reference to three other groups which call themselves "conferences" will suffice to illustrate the point. Two groups of Baptists previously affiliated with the Northern Baptist Convention (now ABCUSA), are the Baptist General Conference and the North American Baptist Conference.[6] Owing much of their origins as Baptists to the American Baptist Foreign and Home Mission Societies, these bodies became independent in the 1940s, partly to maintain their ethnic identities (Swedish and German, respectively) and partly to maintain a conservative theology. The former has over

---

[5] Brochure compiled by Sloan S. Hodges, General Secretary, and distributed by the Progressive National Baptist Convention, Inc., 3907 Georgia Ave., N.W., Washington, D.C. 20011.

[6] Frank H. Woyke, *Heritage and Ministry of the North American Baptist Conference* (Oakbrook Terrace: North American Baptist Conference, 1979); Adolph Olson, *A Centenary History Related to the Baptist General Conference of America* (Chicago: Baptist Conference Press, 1952).

100,000 members and the latter around 60,000.

The third originated in the seventeenth century and was represented in America at that time. It was distinguished from other Baptists primarily by adherence to the Seventh Day (Saturday) as the biblically prescribed day of worship. Although somewhat more numerous abroad than in the United States, the Seventh Day Baptist General Conference represents about 68 churches in this country with around 5,000 members.

Each of these three conferences has mission and educational organizations and at least one educational institution (two of them have seminaries). Because of their relatively small size, they can maintain intimate relationships among churches, seminaries, and denominational officers. With a network of personal ties, they have a high degree of unity and coordination of purpose and program through their institutions. Having executive heads, as well as owning their own seminaries and providing support and direction of missionaries, the conferences combine formal and informal patterns of power and authority to form a close-knit-family type of denomination.

American Baptist Churches in the U.S.A.

ABCUSA, the acronym by which the denomination is familiarly known today, differs from any of the above bodies. The rest of this chapter will focus upon the process by which this denomination has taken shape and a description of its present form. It has passed through periods of development marked by changes of name. Called the Northern Baptist Convention in 1907, and renamed American Baptist Convention in 1950, this denomination adopted the name "American Baptist Churches in the U.S.A." in 1972. Over these years it has developed a more cohesive pattern of organizations than any other Baptist group in the United States. For nearly two centuries Baptists of this group have proceeded by trial and error to find a *suitable way to achieve both freedom and order,* both a system which can *speak and act on behalf of local churches* and one which will *not deprive these churches of their freedom.* This process has moved from local church to national organization. Beginning with a very loose collection of associations, state conventions, and societies for missions, education, publication, and evangelism, it has moved to a system of relationships among the various parts with well-defined lines of authority and accountability. This outcome is the result of a desire for a polity that would adapt the associational principle to new conditions and facilitate the churches' fulfillment of their vocation as part of the body of Christ.

Remodeling the organization did not take place suddenly. Churches and societies long accustomed to acting independently, often with little regard for the needs of the larger fellowship, had to develop a new consciousness of corporate identity and purpose before radical changes could be effected. To persons who associate local autonomy with Baptist orthodoxy, any move to infringe upon that autonomy has been viewed with suspicion. There is a fine line between freedom and order, between autonomy and commitment to common mission and purpose. The ideal system has not been fully achieved, but the denomination continues to change as weaknesses are identified. There is reason to think that the current organizational plan represents an improvement over the past, combining a regard both for the nature and mission of the church and for principles inherent in Baptist theory and practice.

Drawing the Churches Together: The Northern Baptist Convention

The first step in remedying the problems of the societal method of Baptist churches in the North was the organization of the Northern Baptist Convention in 1907. As the defects of a very decentralized denomination forced consideration of a better system, it was difficult to rally support for anything more than modest changes. The independent societies and the local churches were jealous of their autonomy, and any move to interfere with it was quickly checked. In 1907, after the failure of other plans of cooperation, the Northern Baptist Convention was constituted to coordinate the financing and work of the various societies, but it was an awkward compromise between the "convention" and "society" methods. Instead of merging the several organizations into a single entity, the Act of Incorporation and By-Laws provided for a loose federation of societies and churches. From the outset there was continuing tension between preserving the independence of churches and societies and achieving effective, united action.

Relationship to Societies

The constituent societies were designated as *cooperating organizations,* but each one remained legally separate, and the relationship with the convention could be terminated upon a year's notice. Operation was coordinated by holding the annual meetings of the societies simultaneously with the Northern Baptist Convention and by allowing the delegates to the convention to be considered voting members of the separate societies. As a coordinating agency, an executive committee was to include the officers of the convention, its past presidents, and thirty other members. The prime objective of the convention was cooperation in raising funds, and each society agreed to regulate its spending in accord with a budget prepared by a finance committee and approved by the convention. However, even this limited purpose was often frustrated by lack of coordination among denominational agencies.

Relationship to State Conventions and City Societies

Also related to the convention were the state conventions and city societies, which were called *affiliating organizations.* Having been conceived originally as links in the chain between local churches and a national body, the state conventions gradually extended their functions: They added new departments and activities, fostering Christian education, youth work, and campus ministries; assisting churches in finding pastors; and promoting national programs.

For years there was poor correlation among state conventions, city societies, and national organizations. Although the former played an important part in promoting policies and programs of national agencies and in making up budgets, the roles and relationships of state and national organizations were poorly defined. Much of the interaction between these two levels rested upon custom.

Moving Toward Community:
The American Baptist Convention

By the middle of the twentieth century the convention had become conscious of the inadequacies of its loosely federated system, and there was a growing desire for greater unity and efficiency. In 1950 it symbolically changed its name to American Baptist Convention. In so doing it identified more closely with the societies, each of which used the word "American" rather than "Northern" in its title. The name change also responded to the dropping of territorial limits by Southern Baptists, who since World War II had been establishing churches in the North, and it signified reciprocally that churches in the South were welcome to affiliate with the American Baptist Convention if they wished to do so.

Having experienced theological tensions, large-scale defections, stagnation in the large cities, and a weakened evangelistic thrust, the convention now began some serious self-examination. Dissatisfaction with itself was prompted especially by the fact that the denomination was not sharing the degree of religious interest others were experiencing after World War II. The American Baptist rate of growth compared unfavorably with that of most other major denominational bodies.

Although American Baptist problems could not be attributed to a single cause, many felt that the lack of a cohesive organization was a hindrance to concerted action. Organizational structures may have been part of the problem, for adequate forms are important means of accomplishing goals. If institutions are to be effective, however, there must be people with a vision who are unified by a common purpose. Before restructuring the denomination, there was need for a renewal of spirit and a fresh vision of the purpose of the church and the gospel.

Laying Foundations for Restructuring the Denomination

Before the structure of the denomination could be reformed, a renewal of purpose and a greater unity were needed. Reorganization was preceded by a series of emphases intended to provide a sounder basis for denominational life by projecting a *more biblical vision of the church,* an *enlarged concept of mission, openness to diversity,* and *better structures for fulfilling the mission.*

During the 1950s important steps were taken. Special emphasis was placed upon studying Baptist history and a theology of the church. A series of theological conferences dealt with a broad range of subjects, including ecclesiology and Christology. Pastors, college and seminary professors, and denominational leaders (many of whom had been aligned with opposing theological parties for years) became acquainted and found that they had much more in common than expected. Out of the discussions came a broad consensus and an increased sense of denominational unity. A new journal *(Foundations: A Baptist Journal of History and Theology,* later renamed *American Baptist Quarterly)* was founded; an Advisory Board for Theological Studies was established; and a new *History of the Baptists* was written by Robert G. Torbet.

Articles illuminating Baptist history and examining the past in the light of biblical and theological views of the church were published. A book entitled *Baptist Concepts of the Church,* edited by Winthrop S. Hudson, contained studies of Baptist thought and practice which contributed to the insight that wider-than-local bodies may have an ecclesial character. Significant also was the influence of Jitsuo Morikawa, head of the evangelism division, who helped the churches to see that evangelism must be linked with involvement in mission, including social action, and that the church's mission embraces ministries to the poor, to racial minorities, and to all powerless victims of oppression. A call to accept Christ as Savior, he asserted, is a call to service under the lordship of Christ. The church is the agent of God's kingdom in the world, he proclaimed, and it is to exemplify God's concern for social justice and peace. His vision of evangelism thus combined traditional appeals with compassionate service and a militant confrontation of entrenched evils. Not everyone was convinced by his eloquent appeals, rooted in a biblical theology though they were, but his message made a lasting impression upon the churches of the American Baptist Convention.

Creating a Unified Denomination: ABCUSA

The journey to the present structure was a long one. To develop an appropriate organization for churches with a congregational polity presented special problems. How can efficiency in mission be achieved at a national level without infringing the independence of local churches? How can churches on the local level and ecclesial bodies at the regional and national levels come to share a similar vision, enabling them to have a united witness? How can wider church groups make policies and adopt resolutions that truly speak for constituent churches? Such an undertaking is no easy task.

Since the formation of the Northern Baptist Convention in 1907, numerous committees had been appointed to suggest ways to improve the organization. Changes of a pragmatic nature were proposed, without taking account of a biblical theology of the church or of the association principle. Twice, comprehensive studies were made by outside agencies, as a result of which drastic alterations were recommended, but they did not win wide support. In ensuing years, successive modifications were made in piecemeal fashion, and there was continuing tension between aims expressed in the incorporating documents. On the one hand, "the independence of the local church" was to be protected; but the convention was to "promote denominational unity and efficiency." For the first time, it was decided that an administrative officer was needed to head the denomination, and Reuben E. Nelson was appointed as the first general secretary. With the name change to the American Baptist Convention, the General Council also recommended sweeping changes. Since 1950, a steady movement toward achieving a coherent and more efficient denominational organization can be traced.

Two Important Steps

Symbolic of the mood to bring national agencies into more harmonious relationships was the vote in 1958 at Cincinnati, to move the agencies from various locations in New York and Philadelphia to a central headquarters at Valley Forge, Pa. The Home and Foreign Mission Societies and the Board of Education and Publication moved to the Valley Forge site, along with the Office of the General Secretary. The main offices of the Ministers and Missionaries Benefit Board remained in New York City, and the main collection of historical records of the Historical Society remained in Rochester, N.Y., although that society's headquarters and the collection of denominational archives are located at Valley Forge.

In 1961, at Portland, Oregon, an important reorganizational step was taken. The General Council was expanded to ninety-six, more than doubling its former size. With forty-six voting members and fifty nonvoting members from the incorporated boards, the cooperating societies, and the affiliating organizations, the intention was to bring all state secretaries, heads of other agencies, and a number of staff persons into the General Council. At the same time, members of the Council were to have representatives on all the boards and divisions. Thus, communication among various departments of denominational life would be facilitated, and those responsible for interpreting policies and programs in the state conventions and city societies would share in making decisions. The administrative heads of the program boards became associate general secretaries of the American Baptist Convention. Uniform educational standards for ordination were soon adopted, and a study was begun to eventuate in a more effective support system for ministers, including a central repository of personnel files kept on computers and made available to churches in search of pastors.

The SAAR Project

Continuing desire for a more rational organization led to the appointment of a Commission for the Study of Administrative Areas and Relationships (SAAR). Instructed by the General Council to study the existing patterns of administrative units, the commission recommended that the American Baptist Convention be divided into fifteen *regions,* subdivided into *areas,* with a core staff of specialists and area ministers. Beginning its work in 1962, the SAAR commission kindled interest in its plan, and the result was the formation of several regions, many of which represented combinations of states. Several city societies were reluctant to merge with a region, and in 1977 there were still thirty-seven groupings, which were referred to as region/state/city (R/S/C) units. Of these, eight were regions, twenty were state conventions, and nine were standard city societies.

SCODS Proposal Adopted

More fundamental changes were to result from a Study Commission on Denominational Structure (SCODS), appointed in 1968 at Boston. By then a number of factors had produced greater openness to changing the organization so as to achieve more efficiency and a better balance between the independence and interdependence of local congregations. As state conventions reorganized, and as commissions considered patterns of organization, there was evident a determination to take account of theological principles as well as historic Baptist concerns in designing a new system.

In 1969, at Seattle, "A Statement of Purpose" was adopted as a guideline for organizational proposals. The intent to subordinate merely pragmatic considerations to basic theological convictions was evident in the language of this document. Describing the American Baptist Convention as a "manifestation of the church universal," it expressed a belief that God's intention can be sought and followed "in local congregations . . . and in associational, regional, national, and world bodies." Thus the ecclesial nature of organizations larger than local churches with associations was affirmed. It also declared an intention to "seek such a balance of freedom and order as will keep all parts of the Convention open to the guidance of the Holy Spirit and at the same time enable them to work responsibly to carry out the common task of mission and ministry." Thus it stated that issues of freedom and order are to be considered in the wider church. It further expressed an intention to implement and not "to alter the objects of the corporation as stated in the Act of Incorporation." These objects were as follows:

—to bear witness to the gospel of Jesus Christ in the world and to lead persons to Christ
—to seek the mind of Christ on moral, spiritual, political, economic, social, denominational and ecumenical mat-

ters, and to express to the rest of society, on behalf of American Baptists, their convictions as to the mind of Christ on these matters
—to guide, unify, and assist American Baptists in their witness in the world, in preparing members for the work of ministry, and in serving both those within and outside the fellowship of Christ
—and to promote closer relations among American Baptist churches and groups within the whole body of Christ and to promote understanding with other religious bodies.

Thus attention was to be given to a biblical view of the church and to the continuity of earlier denominational objectives in formulating plans for the future. Further expansion of biblical concepts of the church and of Baptist tradition are set forth in a preamble to the SCODS proposals.[7]

Extensive changes resulted from the adoption of the SCODS plan at the annual meeting in Denver in 1972. The official name was changed from "American Baptist Convention" to *"American Baptist Churches in the U.S.A."* Before the new proposals were adopted, hearings were held in many parts of the convention territory to afford ample opportunity for reaction and input from clergy and laity. With respect to a suitable name, it was generally felt that "convention" is unsuitable for a church body, because it connotes a meeting rather than a continuing organization. There was considerable sentiment favoring "American Baptist Church," but many felt that this term had implications of a connectional system and a centralized authority that would threaten local independence. "American Baptist Churches" is an awkward term, but it was the name with the most support, and it does indicate both the national and the churchly character of the body, while making clear that churches are the constituency of ABCUSA. It suggests also the interdependence as well as the independence of the national organization and its churches.

---
[7]Final Report of Study Commission on Denominational Structure of the American Baptist Convention, May 1972.

At the heart of the plan was the creation of the General Board composed of representatives of all the churches, making this board the legislative body of the denomination and vesting it with authority to make decisions and to formulate policy. Thus, through elected representatives the churches could speak and act definitively on matters of common concern. Provisions were made to ensure that a *proportionate number of men and women, clergy and laity, ethnic groups, youth, and any other minorities would be represented on the General Board, by electing representatives-at-large as needed to provide balance.*

It might seem that the removal of authority to make decisions from the large annual meeting to the smaller group was a step away from democracy. In an analogous way to our American government, however, a more genuine representative democracy was made possible. The system resembles our American government also in its federalism, for the General Board takes actions in its semiannual meetings affecting the larger denomination, while leaving local churches free to act independently in local concerns (and also free to refuse to accept decisions of the General Board when they so desire). The older method of making decisions at an annual meeting had not been representative, as analyses of registration records show. At the typical convention, only one-third to one-fourth of the churches had delegates present, with the largest representation coming from the vicinity of the meeting. In 1971, for example, 3,249 delegates were registered out of a potential 21,000. Of those attending, 70 percent were pastors and their spouses, leaving the laity greatly underrepresented. Moreover, it had long been obvious that three thousand or more persons could not be a deliberative body.

Under the new plan there would be biennial meetings for celebration, inspiration, information, and fellowship. Delegates would elect officers of the ABCUSA and representatives-at-large to the General Board. Delegates could discuss, debate, and vote on statements of concern, and they retain power to make changes in bylaws.

Election districts were established for the purpose of choosing representatives to the General Board. These were to be made up, as nearly as possible, of forty to sixty churches conveniently located for such a meeting. Although it would have been desirable to utilize associations for election districts, they varied so greatly in number of churches and geographical expanse that they were unsuited to this purpose. Every church was notified of the time for an election and could send delegates to participate in the selection of a representative to the General Board. They also elected members for the Regional Board. In addition to local church delegates, the regional boards also sent delegates to election district meetings, to share in electing the representatives to represent regions as well as churches on the General Board. (This provision is further explained in the SCOR discussion later in this chapter.)

In addition to these representatives, one-fourth of the General Board members were representatives-at-large. They were elected at the Biennial Meeting, having been chosen for nomination so as to bring racial, ethnic, gender, or geographical balance, or to include persons with special expertise needed by the General Board or one of the program boards.

Six other persons are ex officio members of the General Board: the president of the ABCUSA, the vice president, the immediate past president, and the executive directors of American Baptist Women's Ministries, American Baptist Men, and the Ministers' Council.

A further step toward unifying the national structure was the provision that the members of related program boards (also called national boards) are chosen from the membership of the General Board, rather than by separate elections. The Board of Educational Ministries (BEM), Board of National Ministries (BNM), and Board of International Ministries (BIM) have about sixty-five members each, appointed from members of the General Board. The fourth related board, the

Organization of the American Baptist Denomination

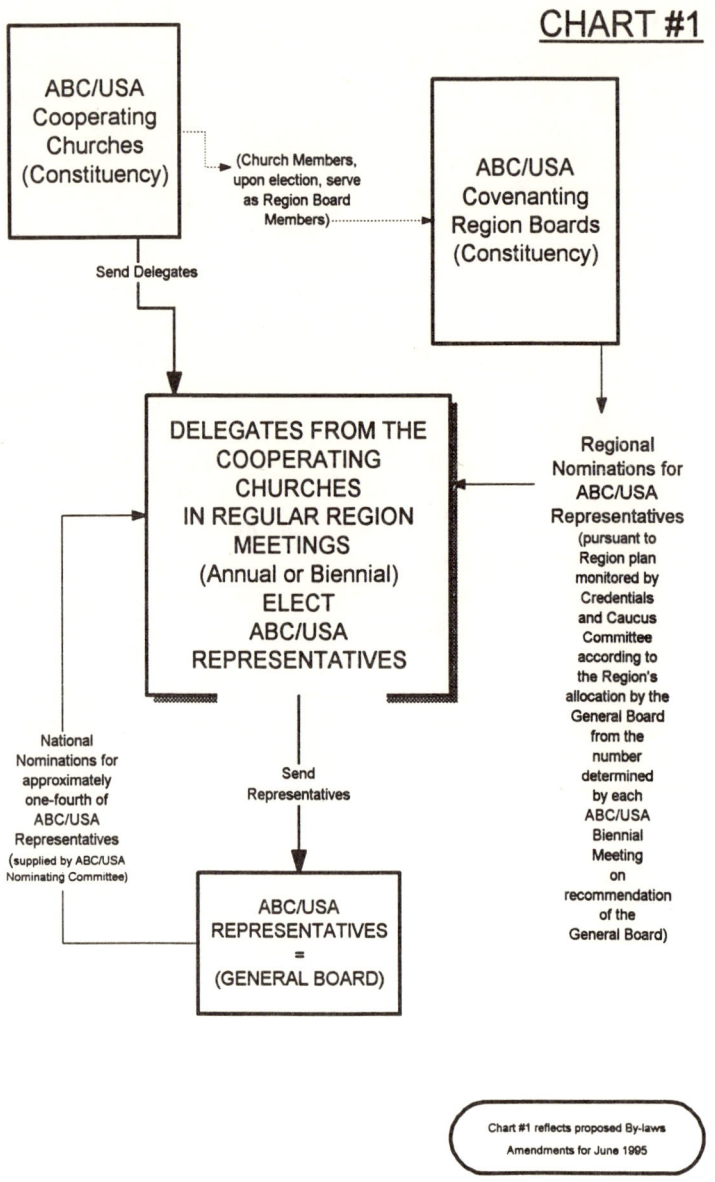

Charts on pages 214 and 218 are used by permission of the Office of the General Secretary, American Baptist Churches in the U.S.A.

Ministers and Missionaries Benefit Board (M & M), has twelve to eighteen members, some of whom are not members of the General Board. The chief administrative officer of each of these related boards is a national secretary of the ABCUSA. A typical General Board meeting includes plenary sessions and separate simultaneous sessions of the program boards.

The General Secretary of ABCUSA is invested with more authority and responsibility than has belonged to predecessors. Elected by the General Board, this officer has a four-year term of office, with no limitation on the number of terms served. As the administrative head of the denomination, the General Secretary coordinates the activities of the related boards, aids in personnel selection, has charge of ecumenical relations, and gives leadership and direction to American Baptist Churches in the U.S.A.

Culmination of Reorganization: SCOR

With the adoption of the SCODS plan, a national structure had been developed that made local churches constituents of a representative body. It remained unclear, however, what the relationship of the regional bodies (regions, states, and city societies) was to the national organization. Although the original instructions to the SCODS Commission had included the examination of relationships between R/S/C units and national agencies, lack of time prevented completion of this stage of the process. The SCODS report, therefore, recommended that another commission be appointed to consider this unfinished business.

Accordingly, in 1974, the Study Commission on Relationships (SCOR) was appointed by the General Board to draw up a plan by which the regional units might be integrated into the new structure. Proposals made by SCOR were presented in 1977 to the Biennial Meeting delegates at San Diego, who voted to change the Bylaws so as to implement the SCOR recommendations. The suggested changes were a logical extension of the principles embodied in SCODS, aiming to complete the process of making the American Baptist Churches, U.S.A., an inclusive body encompassing national, regional, and local levels.

The plan provided that the regional bodies (regions, state conventions, city societies) become constituent members of the American Baptist Churches, U.S.A. As such they might send representatives to the Biennial Meetings and to the General Board. This means that the *ABCUSA has a dual constituency—cooperating churches* represented through their elected representatives *and regions* through their representatives. In order to maintain the size of the General Board, however, it was decided that representatives of the churches would also serve as representatives of their respective regional bodies. Regional boards therefore also send delegates to election district assemblies, so that they will have a voice in the selection of the representatives who represent both cooperating churches and regional boards. These representatives are expected to make a conscientious effort to become informed about the opinions of their constituencies and to make periodic reports to them, but they cannot be instructed how to vote on particular issues.

Regional bodies have two roles—as a direct service to churches of their respective areas and as an integral part of the national body. They are intermediaries providing communications and coordination of the interests of churches with those of the national bodies. Each region has an executive minister and a regional board. Regional boards develop their own programs and make policies on matters clearly related to their own territories.

In aspects of mission which belong to the denomination as a whole, however, regional boards cooperate with the General Board. Executive ministers of regional bodies are elected in consultation with the general secretary of the ABCUSA, and the general secretary participates in the evaluation of executive ministers. The General Board designates functions of the regional boards, and it may evaluate their performance.

Contacts between regional and national agencies are largely through two councils. One is the *Regional Executive Ministers Council (REMC),* comprising the general secretary and the executive ministers of each of the regions. The other is the *General Executive Council* (composed of the general secretary, National Executive Council, Regional Executive Ministers Council, associate national secretaries, and executive directors of the American Baptist Assembly, American Baptist Historical Society, American Baptist Men, Commission on the Ministry, and Ministers Council). Through these two bodies regions have a voice in policy recommendations, evaluations, and other matters of concern to the constituents of the American Baptist Churches, U.S.A. Although the General Board has power to make decisions in most issues, matters supported strongly by regional executive ministers and other staff persons carry considerable weight with the General Board.

The Covenant Concept

A fundamental concept employed in SCOR as a basis for establishing and clarifying relationships of regional bodies to national agencies is that of "covenant." First, there was a "Common Budget Covenant," which had already been worked out and approved by all parties prior to SCOR. As a basis for relating regions to national organization, this was followed by a "Covenant of Relationships" and an accompanying "Statement of Agreements," designed to unite general, regional, and national boards with the former "affiliating organizations" which are now designated "covenanting regional boards." The covenant contains biblical and theological statements regarding covenantal relations to furnish a rationale for church groups to use this method as a foundation for cooperating in mission. Asserting that associations, regional units, or national bodies have an ecclesial nature, and that being faithful to the gospel requires cooperation in mission, it recognizes the authority of local congregations to order their own inner life. It states an assumption, however, that "the freedom of the congregation is genuine, but not absolute, since the nature of the body of Christ calls for interdependence between congregations in associational, regional, national, denomination-wide, or international expressions of the church." Operational assumptions follow, regarding the appropriateness of working together on a voluntary basis in a representative system, acknowledging that "representation flows from, not toward,

American Baptist Boards and Councils*

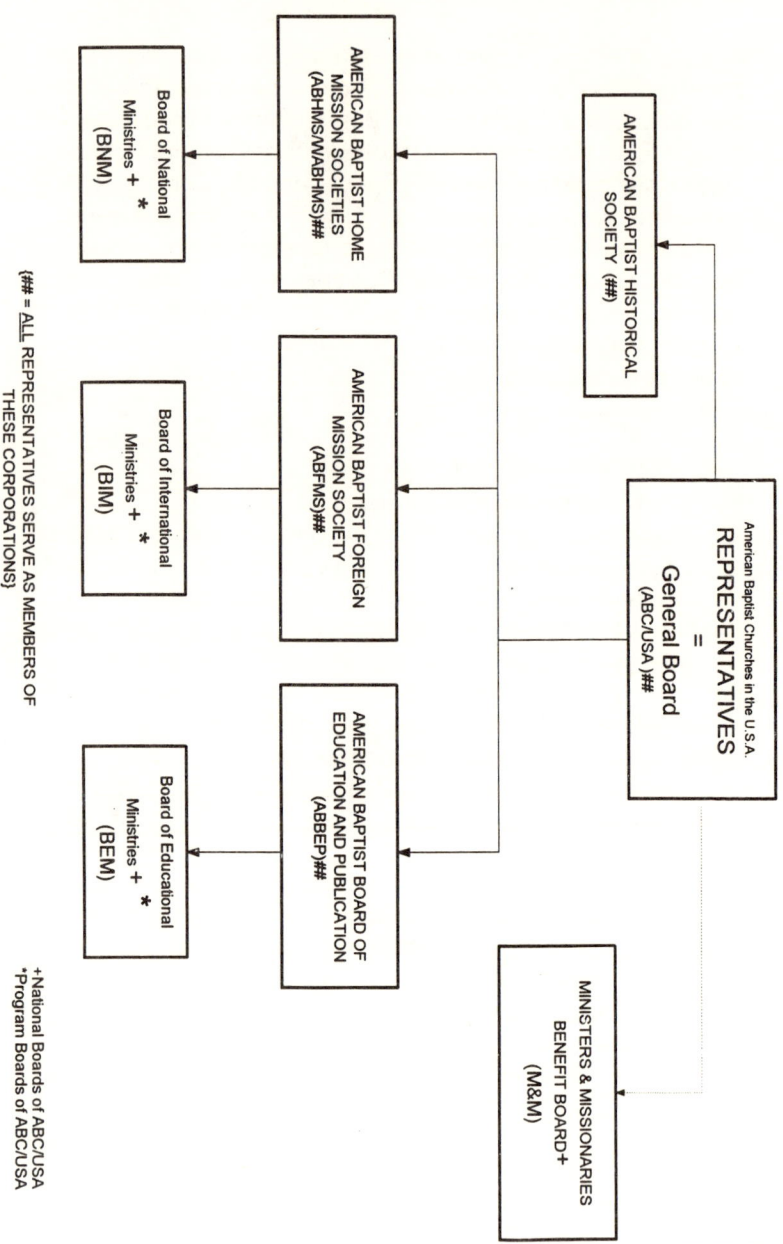

*Boards are made up of representatives elected by churches. Councils are made up of executives employed by denominational organizations.

the 'grass roots.' "[8] The accompanying statements of agreement contain an understanding of initial responsibilities and programmatic matters, as well as procedures for adjudicating differences that may arise between the General Board and regional boards.

There was some dissent to the SCOR proposals at the San Diego Biennial Meeting, but it was surprisingly small. A number of amendments to proposed bylaw changes were offered from the floor, most of them intended to retain a larger measure of autonomy in the regional bodies. After debating a few of the amendments and voting on them, it was apparent that the overwhelming majority of the delegates favored the trend toward integrating the regional bodies into the structure that had been set in motion with approval of the SCODS recommendations. Such an outcome would have been unthinkable ten or fifteen years earlier, but the growing concern for denominational unity and cohesiveness had led to a determination to restore the balance between independence and interdependence in a more unified organization.

Checks and Balances

As safeguards to the integrity of the regional bodies, there are certain checks and balances. The regional boards are represented directly on the General Board by representatives (regional). They are thus assured that the concerns of their respective areas will be heard. The provision for the executive ministers (regional secretaries) to be on the General Executive Council as well as the Regional Executive Ministers Council offers another means of voicing the concerns of cooperating churches and regions to the national entities. In case of differences between a regional board and the General Board or a national board, procedures are available for adjudicating the point at issue.

Some limitations are placed upon the authority of the General Board. Any proposal to merge with another reli-

---

[8] "The Covenant of Relationships and Its Agreements Among the General, National, and Regional Boards of the American Baptist Churches," 1977.

gious body, to amend the "Statement of Purpose of the ABC-USA," or to change the "free church" polity of the denomination requires ratification by two-thirds of the regional boards and two-thirds of the delegates at the Biennial Meeting. Decisions to inaugurate capital fund-raising campaigns require ratification by two-thirds of the regional boards, but not of the Biennial Meeting.

The national character of the denomination has been emphasized by many changes in nomenclature. There are now three sets of boards: general, national, and regional. Executive ministers of regional bodies are also, in their relationship to the General Board, designated as regional secretaries of the American Baptist Churches, U.S.A. There are also three councils: the General Executive Council, the National Executive Council, and the Regional Executive Ministers Council. Other new bodies are ABCUSA Nominating Committee, and the Biennial ABCUSA Program Committee.

The changes envisioned by the SCOR proposals were to take effect only after two-thirds of the regional bodies ratified the new system. On the first day of January following such ratification, the plan was to go into effect, provided that adoption be completed not later than October 31, 1978. None of the affiliating organizations was compelled to become a covenanting regional board, but by 1990 all of them had done so, and the process of reorganization had been completed, except for such continuing refinements and modifications as experience proved desirable.

At last, many converging influences had wrought a change in the consciousness of American Baptists and produced a radically different structure from the old, poorly defined Northern Baptist Convention. No one imagined, however, that the new plan would work without any problems, and provision was made for hearing criticisms and suggestions for such further changes as might become necessary. A Denominational Review Commission was appointed in 1983 to "consider the best means to enhance democratic decision-making in the denomination."

Recent Changes in the Representative Process of American Baptist Churches, U.S.A.

The Denominational Review Commission (DRC) initiated a number of improvements, including an overhaul of the bylaws and standing rules.

In June 1993 the General Board approved a number of proposals for changes in the denomination's representative process. This action was in response to recommendations presented in a report by the ABC's Representative Process Review Commission (RPRC), which had been asked to find ways to improve "efficiencies and economics of the representative process."

One basic goal of the RPRC recommendations was to minimize "distinctions among representatives based on how they were selected." Those recommendations were also designed "to enable our many separate units to function more interdependently as a denomination united in common mission."

At the Biennial Meeting of American Baptist Churches, U.S.A. in June 1995, responding to the changes proposed by the RPRC, delegates voted (790 yes, 263 no) to affirm six resolutions to amend the denomination's bylaws.

The election districts were invented in the 1970s for the sole purpose of electing three-fourths of the representatives who make up the General Board. The RPRC discovered that this process had not produced a General Board reflective of the denomination. The 149 election districts had not been asked to consider the overall balance of the representatives.

Under changes voted in Syracuse, three-fourths of the General Board representatives now are nominated by ongoing regional bodies that are knowledgeable of their particular constituencies. Each region designs the nomination procedures that work best in that particular region. Both diversity and planning to achieve it are overseen by the ABC Credentials and Caucus Committee. These "regionally nominated representatives," who are elected at their region's annual or biennial meetings, have replaced election district representatives.

Each election district representative was accountable only to an election district, which normally met only every four years. Now, both regionally nominated and nationally nominated representatives are responsible on an ongoing basis to the regions that elect them.

Previously, one-fourth of the total number of General Board members had been "at-large" representatives, selected by the ABC Nominating Committee not only to assure gender and racial/ethnic balance, but also to take advantage of specialized skills needed by the program boards or the General Board. In fact, however, the number of at-large representatives had never been adequate to correct the imbalance originating in the election district sector. Moreover, the attempt to achieve racial/ethnic balance through at-large nominations had virtually eliminated the opportunity to choose persons solely on the basis of their specialized skills.

The changes that were affirmed in Syracuse mandated that the same proportion of the total number of representatives—25 percent—were to be selected by the same ABC Nominating Committee for election by the regions. Because of the improved balance and racial/ethnic inclusiveness achieved through regionally nominated representatives, however, there is more opportunity now for consideration of specialized skills to be properly emphasized in the selection process of those who will now be called "nationally nominated representatives." In addition, the current nominating process mandates increased counsel from— and cross-validation by—both the regions and the denomination's caucuses, which will help to achieve appropriate nominations as well as the necessary balance and racial/ethnic inclusiveness.

Another significant change was the affirmation of a gradual reduction in the size of the General Board. The RPRC found that a top policy-making body as large as the ABC General Board was most unusual, and other denominations are reducing their boards to improve efficiency and effectiveness.

The commission's recommendation, affirmed in 1995, was for reducing by attrition the General Board membership from 211 to 160.

Previously, only the election district representatives were related to churches. Now, every General Board member—regionally nominated or nationally nominated—is assigned a constituency of churches. Those assignments are direct, not through the election district. Thus, the same total number of representatives as in the prior arrangement are responsible to specific churches because *all* Board members now relate directly to congregations.

Other Developments

American Baptists, like others, have been troubled about their blurred sense of identity, so that Dr. Robert C. Campbell, general secretary of American Baptist Churches, U.S.A. from 1972–1987, appointed in 1984 a Commission on Denominational Identity to "identify who we are as American Baptists." In its report, the commission concluded that what will unite us is:

> not a program but vision, a vision of the saving reign of Christ and of the discipleship that Christ demands. Discipleship is the discipline that makes us ready to announce the rule of God and to act in obedience to God's will. . . . Forgiveness, reconciliation, peace, and justice will distinguish the life and community of the people of God. . . . Our personal relationship to Christ and our spiritual nurture and growth are bound to the ministry of justice and peace in the world.[9]

Commission on Denominational Unity

In late 1995 the General Board voted to establish the Commission on Denominational Unity and named Robert Campbell chair.

In proposing the commission, the Board's Executive Committee noted: "Throughout our history, American Baptists have struggled with issues around which there has been considerable disagreement. We have been able to find ways to deal constructively with these issues and maintain our common commitment to the gospel of Jesus Christ and to ministries of reconciliation. At the present time, we are deeply concerned about the growing controversy surrounding the interpretation of Biblical passages regarding homosexual practice.

"The General Board has recently passed two statements which refer to homosexuality: one, in October 1992, the statement 'we affirm that the practice of homosexuality is incompatible with Christian teaching'; and two, in June 1993, a Resolution Calling for Dialogue on Issues of Human Sexuality, which includes the statement '. . . acknowledge that there exists a variety of understandings throughout our denomination on issues of human sexuality such as homosexuality.'

---

[9] American Baptists: A Unifying Vision, report of the commission on Denominational Identity, p. 11.

"Questions have been raised as to the implications of these two statements. These questions illustrate the urgency of addressing how we, as a non-creedal people in voluntary relationships make statements and commit to actions without fracturing our fellowship in regard to differences surrounding those statements and actions.

"Therefore, the General Board Executive Committee recommends to the General Board the establishment of a broadly representative Commission on Denominational Unity to gather information across the denomination, to engage in dialogue, study and prayer and to bring to the General Board any findings and recommendations that it considers necessary and/or helpful to advance our common commitment to the gospel of Jesus Christ and to maintain the unity of His body."

The commission's report to the Board was received in November 1997, with a second reading scheduled for June 1998.

Review Commission on Denominational Structure and Process

The General Board in June 1997 established the Review Commission on Denominational Structure and Process. Its Executive Committee's proposal noted: "As we stand at the edge of a new millennium and recognize that 'the local church is the fundamental unit of mission,' questions as to how we best work together to accomplish the mission of the Church seem to be surfacing at various places within our denominational family. Consequently, now appears to be the time to begin a process of assessing our current structure and process as called for by Standing Rule 11.2.6d which states that the General Board Executive Committee 'shall determine the time and procedure for regular General Board assessment of the structure and process of the ABC/USA.'"

The proposal called for the General Board to "establish a broadly representative Review Commission on Denominational Structure and Process. The commission's task will be to study, assess and make recommendations with respect to the present and future structure and process of the denomination. The commission is directed to seek input from staff and encouraged to seek assistance in its task from all sources that it deems appropriate both within and outside of the ABC family."

The commission will be representative of the makeup of the denomination as to race/ethnicity, gender, age, and geographic section and will include both laypersons and professional church leaders. The final report and recommendations of the commission will be presented to the General Board at its November 1999 meeting with interim reports as appropriate.

Relationships with Denominational Schools

Although the integration of regional, national, and local levels was effected, and a multiplicity of functions was incorporated in appropriate national boards, one area of relationship remained unresolved—that with denominational colleges and seminaries. Numerous American Baptist colleges and theological schools have been established over the years, beginning with Brown University in 1764. Many of them are no longer affiliated with the denomination, but quite a few retain some connection. Those that remain have entered covenant relationships with the Board of Educational Ministries, defining the expectations and commitments of the Board and the school. The Board is greatly limited in the financial support it can offer, and its service to the schools is provided mostly in other ways.

A denomination can derive cohesive power from its schools when strong mutual bonds exist between them. The schools need to be undergirded by substantial financial support, and there needs to be some kind of accountability to the churches that give the support. In the Southern Baptist Convention, the North American Baptist Conference, and the Baptist General Conference of America, colleges and seminaries and denominations have mutual obligations and both parties benefit from the relationships. As the experience of Southern Baptists shows, however, when a narrowly conservative party tries to control denominational schools the results can be devastating.

The ABCUSA has tried to provide financial resources for its schools to some extent, but available funds are very limited. For many years the denomination's Institutional Support Program has been the main church support. That plan provides that representatives of schools might approach churches in an assigned region to solicit funds, and some schools have been able to realize substantial help in that way. In 1988, it was reported that $3,567,000 had been raised for colleges, seminaries, and campus ministries.

The American Baptist Association of Seminary Administrators (ABASA), organized in 1975, recommended that each ABCUSA-related seminary enter into a covenant with the denomination. Consequently, mutual pledges were made by each party, and these have helped to develop a sense of direction for the denomination in relation to theological education. The financial resources of ABCUSA have been too limited to permit any significant increase in funding seminaries, but, as of this writing, a major campaign is contemplated to include this purpose. Some additional financial aid has been made available to students, with $200,000 in matching grants being given to seminary students in 1989–1990, and these are to be continued at this level for at least five years. Thus progress has been made to strengthen bonds with seminaries and colleges, although to some it seems painfully slow and inadequate.

Conclusion

Without a common vision of mission and a clear commitment to serve Christ and his church, organizational structures will not renew a denomination. On the other hand, motivation and vision may be hampered when structures are not available to realize the vision. To meet the challenges of our world and its need for the redemptive, transforming word of the Christian gospel, churches must be clear about God's purpose for the church and our responsibility as a part of that church. Given the motivation and commitment and vision, effective organizational forms can help to balance freedom and order, provide open communication, encourage creativity, accept diversity, and enable cooperation with other Christians of all denominations in realizing the vision of the kingdom of God.

11

Ecumenical Relationships

Up to this point, we have been largely concerned with relationships of Baptists to fellow Baptists. Few, however, would contend that such a treatment exhausts our interests or responsibilities as we approach the twenty-first century. Pastors and churches daily make contacts with those of other denominations. Through their responses to councils of churches, joint evangelistic endeavors, and community social services, Baptists are constantly determining the extent to which they will become involved in cooperative Christianity. Let us consider some of the major expressions of cooperation that provide a context for our involvements.

The Modern Ecumenical Movement

The twentieth century has witnessed a surge of interest in Christian unity, commonly designated "the ecumenical movement." Some have hailed this movement as "the great new fact of our era," while others view it with suspicion. Probably the majority of those at the grass-roots level of the churches, however, have only a hazy notion of what is meant by the term "ecumenical," and their attitude toward it has been largely one of indifference.

The Term "Ecumenical"

Why should Christians in our time be either hostile or indifferent to a movement of such great significance? In great measure both of these attitudes stem from a lack of information or from misinformation disseminated by opponents. The word "ecumenical" meant originally "the inhabited earth," but today it signifies the unity of the universal Christian church. The root word *oikos* means "house" or "household," and the Ephesian letter in the Bible speaks to those who are "members of the household of God" (2:19) who are being used as material to construct a holy temple "built together spiritually into a dwelling place for God" (2:22). Here, as elsewhere, the church is envisioned as a corporate entity, which includes all of God's people. The modern ecumenical movement has devoted a great deal of attention to seeking common doctrinal agreement and to giving visible expression to the unity of the Christian church. Today there is also strong emphasis upon Christian mission in the world, to which God has called the church. The ecumenical movement is not one specific organization, but a spirit or a movement embodied in many organizational forms.

On scriptural grounds one could hardly object to the idea that Christian unity should be made more visible by cooperation in doing the work of God. The essential idea of the church in the New Testament is of a body of people united with Jesus Christ as its head and engaged in his mission. Although the word "church" is most often used in the New Testament with reference to local congregations, yet there is always implicit the larger idea of "the people of God." Local fellowships represent the total church of God in their particular localities, but they participate in the larger household of faith. Jesus prayed that his followers in generations to come might "become completely one" (John 17:23). Paul urged the Ephesians to maintain the unity of the Spirit, reminding them that "there is one body and one Spirit ... one Lord, one faith, one baptism, and one God and Father of all" (Eph. 4:4-6). We have become so accustomed to the many divisions within the church that we take the present fragmentation as normal. It is unlikely that the writers of the New Testament would have considered it so, for they assumed a basic unity of the church.

Nor could anyone oppose an ecumenical emphasis upon the grounds of Baptist history, for the early Baptists were not sectarian. Their statements of faith affirmed that "there is one holy, catholic church." The attitude of General Baptists was reflected in their "Orthodox Creed" of 1678, the subtitle of which indicated that it was "an essay to unite and confirm all true Protestants." A nonsectarian spirit also characterized the Particular Baptists, as is shown by their major doctrinal statement. Desiring to express their closeness to others, they adapted the Westminster Confession, which with a few alterations had also been used as the Savoy Confession of the Congregationalists. The Baptists then made a few changes with regard to their doctrines of the church, baptism, the ministry, and the relationship of the civil government to religious matters. They deliberately chose to use these Presbyterian-Congregationalist documents in order to declare their "hearty agreement with them, in that wholesome Protestant doctrine, which, with so clear evidence of Scriptures they have asserted."[1]

Anyone familiar with the writings of Baptists in the seventeenth and eighteenth centuries will realize that they were not sectarians; they did not believe themselves to have an exclusive right to be called the church. They frequently asserted their identity as Protestants and recognized that their basic convictions were shared by others. They felt particularly close to Presbyterians and Congregationalists, but as John Smyth's party had stated in 1612: "All penitent and faithful Christians are brethren in the communion of the outward church, wheresoever they live, by what name soever they are known."[2] In America there were many occasions where Baptists cooperated with other denominations in missions to the Native Americans, Bible societies, and other matters. In the cooperative efforts of Christians, which multiplied in the twentieth century, American Baptists

---

[1] W.L. Lumpkin, *Baptist Confessions of Faith* (Valley Forge: Judson Press, 1959), page 245.

[2] *Ibid.*, page 137.

were partners of other Protestants. Baptists believed that they had certain convictions to preserve, but they did not pretend to have a monopoly on Christian truth.

The Theory of Denominationalism

The word "denomination" came to be applied to the diverse groups of Protestants in the eighteenth century. Baptists have referred to themselves as a denomination, implying that they considered themselves but a part of a larger body. "Denomination" means simply "called by a name," and the assumption underlying the theory of denominationalism is that there is a greater unity which binds all of the diverse groups called by different names into one entity. It recognizes that there are many differences in outward forms, in worship ceremonies, and even in doctrinal formulations, but that there is a basic unity in the acknowledgement of the lordship of Christ over his church.

To accept the term "denomination" presupposes several things. In the first place, it recognizes that in this world it is impossible to see eye-to-eye on everything. Brought up under different circumstances, conditioned by different experiences, people are bound to arrive at different opinions. Under the pressure of environmental circumstances, there will be different external forms of worship and practice. To accept the inevitability of such differences does not lead to a conclusion that differences are unimportant, but it simply accepts realistically the fact that there will be such variety. Because it is important to reach the truth as fully as possible, those who have different perspectives and opinions must come together to engage in dialogue with each other. Under the leading of the Spirit, it is to be hoped that there may be a meeting of minds, and that a fuller apprehension of the truth may be reached. Through conference, study, and prayer, the light of God's truth may break more fully upon people's minds. In the meantime, Christians must accept each other and work and pray together.

To accept this theory of denominationalism is to acknowledge that Christian fellowship is founded upon something more than agreement in doctrine. Theology is important, and Christianity does involve doctrines of God, Christ, humanity, sin, and salvation. However, our doctrinal formulations are affected by our experiences of God's revelation, and there is room for differing understandings. Therefore, the basis of fellowship is not simply assent to a set of propositions. Fellowship has a deeper source also than a common set of values, for it is more than an ethical system. The Christian faith at its heart involves new relationships with God and with other people, and that which binds us together is a common experience of God's grace. It involves a work of the Holy Spirit in our lives by which we become new creatures in Christ and "members one of another," as by faith we accept God's gracious offer of reconciliation and power. With all who claim such an experience and who confess Jesus Christ as Savior and Lord we are bound to work and pray together, notwithstanding differences which may exist among us.

Sometimes the unity of Christians in Christ has been obscured by magnifying institutional differences. Forgetting the true basis of fellowship, members of different denominational groups become so isolated from one another that they seem to lack any real unity. The consequence is that the world has often been more impressed by the divisions within the church than by our underlying oneness. Surely some visible expression ought to be given to the unity we have, so that the body of Christ may not appear to be divided and at war within itself.

The practical question, however, is: What form should such visible unity take? Ought organic unity of all or most Christians to be the goal? Should we aspire to a unity that leaves denominations intact but eventuates in a common understanding of the apostolic faith and mutual acceptance of one another's baptism, eucharist, and ministry? Or is it sufficient to establish councils which provide opportunity for denominational representatives to meet, acknowledging one another as Christians without seeking a doctrinal consensus but learning to worship together, and uniting in a common witness and mission? There is no unanimity among Christians as to what is most desirable and feasible. If we lived in an ideal world, unhampered by sinful individuals and structures, one world church might be a reasonable aspiration. As things are, however, we must settle for more modest aims.

Denominational divisions can be obstacles to Christian witness, and there is no reason to be complacent about them. Such is especially the case when they stem from barriers of race and color, socioeconomic differences, cultural conflicts, and other tensions within society. Then they become a reflection of the world instead of the church. Within the Christian community, it is the will of Christ to break down artificial barriers that divide people.

Where there are genuine insights that others seem to neglect, a denomination may need to preserve a particular emphasis. Denominations may even serve to check each other's pretenses, reminding us that all human institutions are fallible and stand under the judgment of God. There are nonetheless more divisions within the church of Jesus Christ than are warranted. Moreover, denominational loyalty is often stressed so much that members are encouraged to make that supersede their Christian identity.

Emergence of the Ecumenical Movement

The desire for church unity is not a new phenomenon. For centuries there had been one dominant church in western Europe, until the schisms of the Reformation. When Reformation churches proliferated in the sixteenth century, the divisions distressed many leading reformers. Martin Luther, John Calvin, and others sought ways to promote reunion among Protestants and even with the Roman Catholic Church, because Christian unity was important to them. In every century since that time, there have been efforts to foster unity among Christians.

The reasons for the renewed emphasis upon Christian unity in modern times are diverse. To some extent outward pressures have made the need for cooperation and fellowship more apparent. Fears engendered by communism, the Cold War, and the possibility of a devastating thermonuclear war were among the external pressures of the twentieth century. So were a rising spirit of nationalism and the resurgence of some of the oldest world religions, with increasing threats that doors to Christian missions would be closed. More important, especially since the collapse of communism in Eastern Europe, have been positive factors such as renewed interest in biblical studies after World War II, which brought a fresh understanding of the importance of the church in God's purpose for the world. A spate of books focused the attention of clergy and laity alike upon this subject as never before. A deepened appreciation of the nature and mission of the church made people more conscious of its divided state and the need for more cooperation and fellowship. The increasing secularism of the West and a rising tide of peoples breaking free from oppressive legacies of colonialism presented challenges and opportunities that called for a united witness and practical service,

New impetus was given to Christian unity by the Second Vatican Council (1962–1965). Under the leadership of Pope John XXIII, the doors were opened for Catholics to engage in dialogue with non-Catholics on subjects that previously had been forbidden territory. A surprising new interest in Bible study sprang up, in which both laity and clergy were affected, and which was often carried on in interfaith groups. An unprecedented removal of barriers encouraged greater mutual understanding and more cordial relations between Protestants and Roman Catholics. Dialogues between Protestants and Catholics proliferated in homes and churches. Several denominations arranged bilateral discussions over a five-year period, including Baptists, who engaged in discussions under the joint auspices of the Baptist World Alliance and the Secretariat for Christian Unity. Out of the new situation came many consultations, cooperative undertakings, mutual understandings, and a joint statement on mission.

The need for a common Christian witness and the perception of a common mission has been a powerful incentive for Christian cooperation. It was in mission areas that the need for unity and cooperation was felt most intensely in the first place. Here the ecumenical movement may be said to have been born. Early in the missionary experience, William Carey (the Baptist pioneer of the modern missionary movement) saw the need for cooperation. In 1810 he proposed that a "general association of all denominations of Christians from the four quarters of the world" be held every ten years.

Although his suggestion was not taken up at the time, the need for such meetings became more pressing. During the years after 1850, more and more regional missionary conferences were held. Cooperation was developed along several lines, such as joint translation projects, cooperative efforts in publishing, sponsorship of hospitals and schools, and comity agreements to prevent wasted effort through overlapping of mission fields.

In 1910 a very significant missionary conference was held at Edinburgh, Scotland. Here, 1,355 delegates representing missionary societies from all over the world met. They sought to discover by consultation how the churches could help one another, by pooling whatever knowledge and experience each had gained, instead of working competitively. Out of this conference emerged three new movements which paved the way for the forming of the World Council of Churches.

The first was the International Missionary Council, formed in 1921 to achieve a greater measure of practical cooperation among missionaries. Besides providing a small, permanent organization to carry on its work continuously, it held four great world conferences—at Jerusalem, in 1928; at Tambaram, India, in 1938; at Whitby, Canada, in 1947; and at Willingen, Germany, in 1952. Since this former mission organization merged with the World Council of Churches, its concerns have been continued in a series of major international conferences on missions and evangelism. A second movement developing from the 1910 meeting was the Faith and Order Movement. One of the purposes of this was to explore together the reasons why denominations differed from each other, when they worshiped the same Lord and used the same Bible. Faith and Order held world conferences at Lausanne, Switzerland, in 1927 and at Edinburgh, Scotland, in 1937. The third great movement stemming from 1910 was the Life and Work Movement, which had a world gathering at Stockholm in 1925 and one at Oxford in 1937. Its purpose was to make possible cooperative undertakings other than missions.

It was quite natural that these three movements, with different emphases but having many of the same people interested in each, should think of joining forces. Out of the meetings at Oxford and Edinburgh in the summer of 1937, there came a proposal to form a World Council of Churches through the merging of the Faith and Order and the Life and Work movements. Although the International Missionary Council continued its separate existence for more than two decades, it was fully cooperative with the World Council of Churches and became a division of the larger body in 1961.

Ecumenical Organizations

The World Council of Churches

Although plans for organization of the World Council of Churches (WCC) had been completed by 1939, the coming of World War II prevented their implementation. It was in 1948, at Amsterdam, that this organization finally came into being. The constitution began with a statement describing the nature and basis of this council: "The World Council of Churches is a fellowship of churches which accept our Lord Jesus Christ as God and Saviour." There are many who criticized this statement as inadequate. It was certainly inadequate for a full statement of doctrine, but it offered a minimal basis for fellowship and cooperative work. At the third General Assembly in 1961, a revised statement was adopted: "The World Council of Churches is a fellowship of churches which confess the Lord Jesus Christ as God and Saviour, according to the Scriptures, and therefore seek to fulfill their common calling to the glory of the one God, Father, Son and Holy Spirit." Assuming a great deal that is not said, it sums up the essential elements of the Christian faith by its affirmation regarding Scriptures, the triune God, and Jesus Christ. Each term is filled with implications, and the statement says a great deal in a few words.

A few words of clarification are necessary at this point. In the parlance of the World Council, the word "church" does not refer to an individual local church, but to a denominational body. A local church can be related to the World Council only through the membership of its denomination. The same is true of the National Council of the Churches of Christ, which is discussed later in this chapter.

The work of the World Council is conducted through an assembly, composed of delegates from member churches and meeting about every seven years, and a central committee made up of 150 members meeting annually, which serves as a governing body between assemblies. The assembly sets broad policies, which the Central Committee and its Executive Committee carry out. There are commissions and committees with permanent staff to maintain specific aspects of the work without loss of continuity. Through these instrumentalities member churches share in an enormous range of activities. As people meet and work together in common mission tasks, they become more aware of their kinship in Christ.

Among the objectives of the council, as stated in the constitution, are: "to support the churches in their worldwide missionary and evangelistic task" and "to express the common concern of the churches in the service of human need, the breaking down of barriers between people." In pursuing these and other aims, the council engages in a multiplicity of activities. It may sponsor a prayer meeting or provide relief for refugees or victims of famine. It may make theological education available where there has been none. It may confront multinational corporations on issues of moral import, work to protect human rights, and sponsor biblical and theological studies. An important part of the council's purpose is also "to support the churches in their task of evangelism," and significant world conferences have been held on these and other topics. Other interests include: concern for renewal of congregations, worship, social justice, combating racism, support for women in ministry, and dealing with environmental issues. A very important conference was held in Seoul in 1989 to seek ways to raise the consciousness of Christians in issues of justice, peace, and the integrity of creation (JPIC), drawing up a proposal for consideration of the assembly in Canberra in 1991. This document aroused considerable interest and holds potential for the long-range future.

Through fifty years of its existence, many changes have come in the World Council's size, composition, issues, and programs. There has been a significant increase in the number of representatives from churches of the Third World, particularly Africa, where the number of Christians has grown dramatically. Indeed, the newer churches from developing countries have gone from minority to majority status and voting power. It is not surprising that the different perspectives and needs of people from non-Western cultures should influence the agendas of the WCC. Inherent in its very nature is the motivation to support the aspirations of people struggling to overcome poverty and oppression and to attain more stable governments, opportunities for education, and higher living standards. It is not surprising either that the attempt to assimilate so many from diverse cultures should create tensions in the Council, as their perceptions of theology and justice issues sometimes conflict with many in the more affluent churches of the West.

The World Council has been the target of sharp criticism from several sources, much of it stemming from the Council's attempts to minister to fellow Christians in their struggle against forces that support the status quo. Some latent antiecumenical feelings had come to the fore by the 1960s, and they intensified in the next decades. The resurgent conservatism in the United States, evident in political and religious life, manifested itself often in a reactionary spirit that was hostile to the ecumenical movement, labeling it "radical," "left-wing," and "liberal."

Certain popular television ministries reached millions with an antiecumenical polemic, which helped to foment a hostile climate of opinion. Given the size and diversity of the World Council's membership and the multiplicity of its undertakings, it was inevitable that some of its public statements and programs would arouse controversy, especially those aimed at correcting social injustices. Although it has sometimes supported theological positions of dubious validity and programs of questionable merit, these represent but a fraction of the WCC's work. On the whole, the Council has been led by men and women, motivated by loyalty to Christ and the gospel, who have sought to strengthen the church in fulfilling its mission of proclamation, worship, teaching, and ministering to the spiritual and material needs of peoples of the world.

Negative criticisms, coupled with a good deal of indifference, have divided churches in the United States in their attitudes toward ecumenical organizations, and by 1980 ecumenical enthusiasm had waned, diminishing support for the WCC. Curtailment of funds necessitated retrenchment in programs and cutbacks in personnel. In the 1960s efforts had been made to broaden its fellowship by establishing better rapport with evangelicals in the United States, and these were stepped up in the 1980s. The purpose of the Council is to cultivate a deeper sense of Christian unity, to make possible cooperation in many areas, and to encourage Christians to fulfill their mission under God more faithfully. Such a goal would seem to merit sympathetic consideration among Christians as it aims to promote unity.

The forces at work in the world today in opposition to the Christian church are formidable. A fragmented Christian witness hampers the churches in coping with secularizing tendencies and in seeking to win back lost segments of the population to Jesus Christ. Once more we hear with seriousness the question, "Is Christ divided?" and we must answer it with a resounding NO! That answer must come not only in words, but in deeds that demonstrate the unity of Christians of all denominations through worshiping and witnessing together.

The National Council of the Churches of Christ in the U.S.A.

In addition to the World Council of Churches, there are agencies for promoting unity and cooperation on national and local levels. For Americans one of the chief means through which interdenominational Protestantism can be expressed is the National Council of the Churches of Christ in the U.S.A. Organized in 1950, it was the heir of a number of earlier movements, particularly the Federal Council of Churches. In the face of increasingly complex problems of an urban industrial society, a growing Protestantism in the late nineteenth century found ways to cooperate in evangelism, missions, Christian education, and social programs. Among these earlier interdenominational organizations were the

Y.M.C.A., the Y.W.C.A., the International Society of Christian Endeavor, the Evangelical Alliance, the International Uniform Lesson plan, the World's Student Christian Federation, and various others. In 1908 the Federal Council of Churches was constituted and became the main channel for cooperative work. At the same time there were separate agencies in which Protestants cooperated for special purposes, such as the Foreign Missions Council of North America, the International Council of Religious Education, the Missionary Education Movement of the United States and Canada, the National Protestant Council of Higher Education, and the United Stewardship Council.

In 1950, the Federal Council and most of these special-purpose organizations were merged into the National Council of the Churches of Christ in the U.S.A. The preamble states the basis of the new organization as follows: "In the Providence of God, the time has come when it seems fitting more fully to manifest oneness in Jesus Christ as Divine Lord and Savior, by the creation of an inclusive cooperative agency of the Christian churches of the United States of America to continue and extend the following general agencies of the churches and to combine all their interests and functions." In continuing the work of the agencies listed in the foregoing paragraph, its work was much like that of the World Council but carried out on a different level. In taking on the responsibilities of the Foreign and Home Missions Councils, it provided a useful means of exchanging information and coordinating activities of many denominations. Through a commission it called together representatives of the churches to plan the Uniform Lessons for Sunday church schools. Many practical interests were served through these departments of the National Council, and even some denominations that declined to join the NCCC cooperated in selected areas of interest.

Church World Service, begun in 1946 as a channel through which church organizations could assist refugees and people displaced by war, was another agency that joined the NCCC. It has been a major part of the Council, receiving about three-fourths of the funds channeled through it. Although there is no integral connection between the NCCC and the WCC, one purpose of the former is "to maintain fellowship and cooperation with the World Council of Churches and with other international Christian organizations." It also has maintained close working ties with regional and local councils in the United States and Canada.

By the fortieth anniversary of its founding, the National Council was having serious financial problems. Like the World Council, it was the target of criticism both from within its own ranks and from external sources. It shared the general distrust of a large segment of the American public toward ecumenical organizations in general. Ecumenism had been perceived as the concern of denominational leaders, clergy, and a minority of the laity. At the grass roots, commitment to the aims of the ecumenical movement had been limited, and many opposed the National Council because of its encouragement of activism in challenging social injustice. The organization was regarded as much more liberal than the majority of church members whom their delegates represented. Its policies were widely thought to be unfavorable to business, frequently critical of the United States, and more interested in social issues than evangelism.

Some of the criticisms were justified, but in general critics selected certain statements or programs which they found most objectionable, often out of context, using them to portray a distorted image of the NCCC. Part of the problem arose from the fact that the member denominations did not grant either funds or authority to the Governing Board, which had little control over public statements, programs, or appointments of the units or subunits. Consequently, a public statement on some controversial social or political issue emanating from a small committee might be highlighted in the media, giving the impression that the opinion reported was the official view of the National Council.

It was probably true that evangelism had been downgraded from its earlier priority status, but that was partly because denominations had their own approaches to this activity. There were criticisms of priorities given to some programs, but those choices were affected by the fact that denominations designated financial contributions for projects in which they were most interested. It is difficult to sort out how many of the charges against the Council were justified, but given the built-in difficulties, it is easy to excuse many of the shortcomings. On the other hand there were many faults, and dissatisfaction grew among the member churches.

Declining income led finally to a decision that changes had to be made. In 1984 a Presidential Panel Report called for a major overhaul of the organization. Consequently, a committee labored over plans for restructuring. Their proposals were finally adopted in 1990, and the restructured Council was to be functioning by January 1991. The aims were to make the organization more cohesive and efficient and all of its parts more accountable. Toward the former aim, the Council would conceive of itself as a "communion of communions," instead of just a "cooperative program agency." Member communions were urged to covenant with each other and ways were sought to encourage fuller participation of all delegates.

To achieve a greater measure of accountability for public statements, policies, and programs, the new General Board was given more authority to monitor and approve them. All of the former functions of commissions, committees, units, and subunits were subsumed under four new units (Unity and Relationships; Education, Communications and Discipleship; Prophetic Justice; and Church World Service and Witness), and new mission definitions were formulated for each of the units and subunits. Board members would serve on the four unit committees. Whether the restructured National Council will be able to serve the member communions more efficiently and responsibly, and with less negative criticism, will be tested during the decade of the 1990s.

ABCUSA and the Councils

American Baptist Churches in the U.S.A., in its various stages of development, had been a charter member of the Federal Council in 1908, and of the National Council in 1950. ABC had also become a member of the World Council of Churches in 1948. Individual ABCUSA churches have the option of being listed in the annual directory as "not approving affiliation with or providing financial support to the National Council of the Churches of Christ through the American Baptist Churches in the U.S.A.," and slightly over ten percent of them make that choice. While no provision is made for the NCCC in the Unified Mission Budget, program boards make allocations for specific services of NCCC agencies. Otherwise, the only ABCUSA funds that go to the Council are those designated for it. In spite of these conditions, which hinder American Baptists from contributing their fair share to the WCC and NCCC, there has been continued insistence by some that all ties with these councils be severed. As a result the General Board appointed an Ecumenical Relations Review Commission (ERREC) in 1984.

After four years of monitoring and critiquing the WCC and the NCCC, the commission reported to the General Board. Although the report acknowledged the shortcomings of these bodies, it also recognized the importance of their overall contributions and stated the belief that more would be lost than gained by severing connections. It recommended that the General Board reaffirm its relationships with the bodies in question and that the ABCUSA also become an official observer in the National Association of Evangelicals. Thereupon the General Board voted favorably upon the recommendations of ERREC. The vote included a continued monitoring and critiquing of policies and programs of the three bodies and provided for a periodic review of the denomination's ecumenical relations.

The National Association of Evangelicals

Another organization for cooperative Christianity is the National Association of Evangelicals (NAE), organized in 1943 as an alternative to the NCCC. Unlike the NCCC, in which only denominations can become members, the NAE accepts denominations, agencies, congregations, and individuals as members. It has a doctrinal statement which must be subscribed by all who would join its fellowship, and it does not admit anyone who belongs to the WCC or the NCCC. This latter restriction prohibited the ABCUSA from becoming a member, but an observer status is another option and they chose that course.

Although not completely parallel to the NCCC, the NAE

does have commissions on evangelism and home missions, Christian education, evangelical churchmen, stewardship, higher education, and social action. It promotes foreign missions through a closely related organization, the Evangelical Foreign Missions Association. Through its Office of Governmental Affairs it can represent the interests of evangelicals in Washington, and World Relief is an arm for humanitarian work.

Evangelicals share other channels of interest and action, which have no direct connection with the NAE. These have emerged since World War II as a significant force in American Protestantism. Fuller Theological Seminary was established in 1947 to represent what was called the New Evangelicals. In 1956 the magazine *Christianity Today* was founded and became the leading evangelical periodical. Evangelicals for Social Action was organized in the late 1970s to promote justice, liberty, and peace from a biblical perspective. American Evangelicals have sponsored world congresses on evangelism at Lausanne, Berlin, and Manila, as well as regional ones in the United States. Steps have been taken toward discussion and cooperation involving the WCC Commission on World Mission and Evangelism, the World Evangelical Fellowship, and the Lausanne Committee on World Evangelization. These are only a few of the many evangelical attempts to express concern for Christian cooperation in mission.

Local and State Councils of Churches

Many churches feel most comfortable working cooperatively with other Christians in their own community council of churches. Here individual Baptists can find fellowship with persons of other denominations as all work together on projects of local interest. There are many practical matters in which it is advantageous to cooperate, including both specifically Christian concerns and community needs and problems.

Some ecumenical concerns of the various denominations can better be expressed through statewide cooperation than through larger or smaller organizations. Membership in state councils usually consists of local councils of churches and statewide or regional denominational bodies. Typical of the work of a state council are such activities as the following: legislative seminars and political action at the state capital; ministry to migrant workers; chaplaincy at hospitals and at penal and welfare institutions; rural or inner-city ministries; programs of Christian education, such as weekday religious education; and statewide meetings by such council-related groups as Church Women United.

Consultation on Church Union

There are numerous other forms of ecumenical relationships, including a number of important mergers which have occurred in the second half of the twentieth century. Worthy of mention is the Consultation on Church Union (COCU), which began in 1962 as an effort to unite several old-line denominations in a new church which would be "truly catholic, truly evangelical, and truly reformed." Having overcome obstacles that had seemed insurmountable, it finally reached consensus on baptism, ministry, eucharist, and other matters. Many had high hopes that this vision was going to become a reality. By the 1980s, however, the movement, now called "Churches of Christ Uniting," was losing momentum. American Baptist Churches were observer-participants, but not full members, of this endeavor. There are other expressions of cooperative Christianity in the United States, but early dreams of bold ecumenical measures had somewhat faded by the final decade of the twentieth century.

Baptists and Ecumenism

The American Baptist Churches in the U.S.A. and the three National Baptist bodies are members of both the NCCC and the WCC. Baptists in Great Britain are also members of both the British Council of Churches and the World Council.

Southern Baptists and most, if not all, other Baptists in the United States remain unaffiliated with either of these organizations, but a few are members of the National Association of Evangelicals. Southern Baptists participated actively in the Home and Foreign Missions Conferences and the International Council of Christian Education for many years, until these merged with the NCCC in 1950. Although a substantial minority among them has favored a cooperative relationship with these larger fellowships, and some individuals take part in Faith and Order meetings, the official stance is strongly opposed to such relationships. As noted in chapter 5, Southern Baptist Theological Seminary served as host for a major consultation in 1979, sponsored by the WCC Faith and Order Commission, on the subject of infant and believers' baptism. Out of the meetings came the *Baptism, Eucharist, and Ministry* document, which defined areas of agreement between these two positions, without being able to accept each other's views entirely. Baptists have also engaged in extended discussions with both Roman Catholics and Lutherans.

With regard to state and local councils, there is a more receptive feeling among many Baptists than toward broader ecumenical bodies. In general Baptists cooperate more freely in these. Probably the reason for this tendency is that the need for cooperation is more evident on this level. Through such means they can work together in attacking problems that are rife in American communities. They have cooperated in interdenominational evangelistic efforts, in supporting or opposing legislation, in migrant ministries, and in numerous other areas of need.

A unique form of ecumenism on the local level is found in the North where many Baptist churches are related to other denominations through combinations called federated churches or union churches, where the congregation includes persons of two or more denominations. These are usually in situations where congregations are small and can benefit by sharing pastoral and other resources. In other situations there are dually aligned churches. While this status is usually held by Baptist churches that are connected with two Baptist bodies, in a few instances Baptist churches are affiliated both with the American Baptist Churches and with the United Church of Christ or some other denomination.

"Associated Relationships" with Other Denominations

One example of cooperation on a national level with another denomination is the special relationship between the American Baptist Churches and the Church of the Brethren, a denomination which practices believers' baptism and is strongly oriented toward issues of peace and justice and toward practical service. After conversations between 1961 and 1971 exploring the possibility of merger, it was decided to settle for an "associated relationship," which aimed at broadening areas of cooperation without giving up separate identities. Each of the two bodies has an "official observer" who attends the other's General Board meetings and the Interchurch Relations Committee. Opportunities are provided for the observer to offer feedback and suggestions as well as to bring greetings. Areas of cooperation have been most notable in theological education, where Northern Baptist and Bethany Seminaries have shared a campus, library, and instructional facilities.

A special relationship exists also between the American Baptist Churches and the Progressive National Baptist Convention, similar to that with the Church of the Brethren. Formed in 1970, this "associated relationship" affirmed a desire to cooperate without the loss of identity or autonomy. One feature of this relationship has been the promotion of dual alignments, meaning that churches may have an affiliation with both denominations. A new region, the American Baptist Churches of the South, was organized with 104 predominantly black churches and about 20 predominantly white churches. This relationship was marked by the shared conduct of the "Fund of Renewal" in the 1970s, which raised capital funds for economic and educational development for minority groups. Many pastors and laypersons from the PNBC have had leadership roles in organizations of the ABC-USA, and there is potential for closer cooperation between the two bodies. There have also been points of tension and conflicting goals, as the Commission on Denominational Identity discovered, but a new Commission on Denominational Inclusiveness began to address these concerns in 1991.

Cooperation with Other Baptists

In addition to agencies for interdenominational cooperation there are channels through which various Baptist groups work together. In the United States there are at least twenty-four organized Baptist groups. The largest is the Southern Baptist Convention, and next in order come the National Baptist Convention, Inc., the National Baptist Convention of America, the Progressive National Baptist Convention, and the American Baptist Churches in the U.S.A. These vary from 15,700,000 to about 1,500,000 in size. Others range in size from about 250,000 to as few as 50. There are also numerous Baptist groups in other countries around the world. In order to help maintain a sense of identity, to assist one another, and to share in mutual tasks, Baptists cooperate through various agencies.

The Baptist World Alliance

Baptist people in all parts of the Christian world are united under the banner of the Baptist World Alliance. Organized in 1905 in London, this federation has met about every five years. Its purpose is stated in the preamble to its constitution: "The Baptist World Alliance, extending over every part of the world, exists in order more fully to show the essential oneness of Baptist people in the Lord Jesus Christ, to impart inspiration to the brotherhood, and to promote the spirit of fellowship, service and cooperation among its members; but this Alliance may in no way interfere with the independence of the churches or assume the administrative functions of existing organizations." In its purpose of imparting inspiration through the infrequent meetings, and in affording links by which fellowship among Baptists can be strengthened, the Alliance has been most useful. At some points it has helped to safeguard and promote fuller liberty and respect for human rights. An executive committee and several commissions meet annually for study, exchange of ideas, and planning programs. With a minimum of permanent staff, however, its activities are limited.

Other Cooperative Baptist Agencies in the United States

There are other Baptist agencies through which certain kinds of activities are coordinated. In the United States, the most important one is probably the Baptist Joint Committee on Public Affairs. Nine Baptist bodies have jointly supported this enterprise, which is administered through a small permanent staff in Washington, D.C. In 1991, however, the Executive Committee voted to dissociate the Southern Baptist Convention from the Baptist Joint Committee and withdrew all support, but substantial increases from other Baptist groups and individuals offset much of the loss. Through a periodical called *Report from the Capital* the Joint Committee disseminates information concerning laws which have been introduced or passed that have a bearing on religious liberty or other religious issues. Because of their considerable expertise in this field of church-state issues, staff members have won the respect of many legislators and others and are frequently called upon to testify in hearings in this field. The Joint Committee's primary responsibility is to note potential threats to the cherished Baptist view of religious liberty and the First Amendment guarantees.

Greater cooperation among Baptists of the United States and Canada would be desirable, but their spirit of independence has been strong, and preoccupation with their own interests has hampered development of closer ties. In the 1980s a controversy between "conservatives" and "moderates" in the Southern Baptist Convention raised additional barriers to cooperative relations. The North American Baptist Fellowship, established in 1966 by Baptists of Canada, Mexico, and the United States, has offered prospects of more cooperative endeavors, but its achievements have been mostly in the area of fellowship.

Appendix 1

Some Significant Dates in Baptist History

1609 The first General Baptist Church formed by English refugees in Holland, under leadership of John Smyth

1612 The first General Baptist Church on English soil, led by Thomas Helwys and John Murton

1612 Plea for freedom of worship published by Helwys; the first claim for complete religious freedom in the English language

1638 The first Particular Baptist Church begun in England

1639 Baptist beginnings in America; congregation gathered by Roger Williams

1641 Practice of immersion became more general among Baptists in England

1650 Beginning of development of formal associations among Baptists; rapid growth of Baptists during Commonwealth period

1670 General Association of Six-Principle Baptists formed in America

1677 Particular Baptists adopted revision of Westminster Confession

1678 General Baptists adopted the "Orthodox Creed"

1707	Particular Baptists in America formed Philadelphia Baptist Association
1750–1790	Impetus to Baptist growth in America: particularly in New England and South by successive "awakenings"
1767–1786	Struggle for religious liberty, particularly in Massachusetts and Virginia
1780	Freewill Baptists organized in New England
1792	Baptist Missionary Society founded in England; sent William Carey to India; inspired similar movements by others
1812	Adoniram Judson sails for India and Burma
1814	American Baptists form Triennial Convention for foreign missions
1817	Purpose of Triennial Convention expanded to include home missions and education
1824	Baptist General Tract Society established (forerunner of the American Baptist Publication Society)
1832	American Baptist Home Mission Society organized
1832	Antimissionary movement among Baptists (Primitive Baptists) begins to crystallize
1833	New Hampshire Confession of Faith drafted
1845	Southern Baptist Convention formed; marked break between Baptists of North and South in missionary undertakings overseas
1870	Resolution of the Southern Baptist Convention to oppose efforts to unite boards of North and South
1871	Organization of Woman's Baptist Foreign Mission Societies (East and West); marked more active role of women in denominational life
1877	Formation of Woman's Baptist Home Mission Societies
1894	Fortress Monroe (Va.) Conference: agreement between Baptists of North and South recognizing territorial limits; eased tensions caused by work of A.B.P.S. and A.B.H.M.S. in South
1895	Organization of the National Baptist Convention of America, the first black Baptist body

APPENDIX 1

1905	Baptist World Alliance held first meeting in London: an agency to provide fellowship among Baptists of the world
1907	Formation of the Northern Baptist Convention; attempt to integrate work of various special-purpose societies
1911	Freewill Baptists merged with Northern Baptist Convention
1925	High-water mark of Fundamentalist-Modernist controversy of the 1920s
1943	Organization of the Conservative Baptist Foreign Mission Society; beginning of steps which led to secession from the Northern Baptist Convention in 1947
1943	Southern Baptist Convention received some California churches into its membership; marked beginning of breakdown of comity agreements and expansion of Southern Baptists into all of the United States
1944	Founding of American Baptist Assembly at Green Lake, Wis.
1948	Northern Baptist Convention became constituent member of the World Council of Churches; first Assembly held at Amsterdam
1950	Northern Baptists changed name to American Baptist Convention
1950	American Baptist Convention became constituent member of the National Council of Churches of Christ at first NCCC meeting in Cleveland
1954	First Theological Conference at Green Lake initiated series of movements reflecting and strengthening theological consensus and healing of old tensions
1961	Reorganization Plan adopted by American Baptist Convention (making the convention a more coherent and efficient denominational body)
1962	National offices of American Baptist Convention at Valley Forge occupied by the agencies of the denomination
1966	Forming of North American Baptist Fellowship
1966	Commission on Christian Unity established by General Council of American Baptist Convention
1968	In response to "demands" of a Black Caucus, the General Council of the A.B.C. provided for fuller participation in denominational leadership
1970	American Baptist Convention and Progressive National Baptist Convention entered into an "associated relationship"

1972 Implementation of recommendations of Study Commission on Denominational Structure (SCODS): General Council replaced by a more representative 200-member General Board, office of the General Secretary strengthened, and name changed to "American Baptist Churches in the U.S.A."

1977 Adoption of recommendations of Study Commission on Relationships (SCOR) at San Diego Biennial of ABCUSA, calling for covenants of relationship between congregational units and corporate structures of the denomination; new bylaws embodying these provisions became operative Jan. 1, 1979 after ratification by 2/3 of affiliating organizations

1979 Recommendations of a two-year study on Women in Ministry, commissioned by the Ministers' Council in 1977, approved by the Council

1987 Denominational Review Commission reported that reorganization of 1972–1977 had been successful in achieving its purposes and made minor adjustments

1988 General Board, after four-year study, reaffirmed membership in National and World Councils of Churches and adopted "official observer" relationship with National Association of Evangelicals

1995 Biennial Meeting delegates voted to change election district structure of the General Board to one in which three-fourths of Board representatives are nominated by ongoing regional bodies (regionally-nominated representatives) and one-quarter are selected by the ABC Nominating Committee for election by the regions (nationally-nominated representatives). Also approved was reduction by attrition of General Board membership from 211 to 160

1995 General Board voted to establish Commission on Denominational Unity. Dr. Robert C. Campbell, well-known educator, administrator, and general secretary of American Baptist Churches in the U.S.A. from 1972–1987, named chair

1997 General Board established Review Commission on Denominational Structure and Process "to study, assess and make recommendations with respect to the present and future structure and process of the denomination"

Appendix 2

Church Covenants

From the earliest period of Baptist history, it has been customary for churches to adopt covenants. The content of such covenants has varied from time to time and place to place. Some churches have preferred to limit the statement to a general Christian commitment to Christ and his church, while others have included more specific obligations. In any case, it would seem that only such matters as have universal validity for Christians ought to be included.

Three types of church covenant are printed below. One of them is an older and more general type of covenant, and the second is one in common use among Baptist churches today. The third was adopted in 1965 by the Drexel Hill (Pa.) Baptist Church.

Type of Church Covenant: A

Minister: It being made manifest by God's Word that God is pleased to walk in a way of covenant with his people, God promising to be their God and they promising to be God's people;

People: We, therefore, desiring to worship and serve God,

and believing it to be our duty to walk together as one body in Christ, do freely and solemnly covenant with God and with one another, and do bind ourselves in the presence of God, to acknowledge God to be our God and ourselves the people of God; to cleave unto the Lord Jesus, the great head of the church, as our only king and lawgiver; and to walk together in Christian love, the Spirit of God assisting us, in all God's ways and ordinances as they have been made known or shall be made known unto us from the holy Word; praying that the God of peace, who brought from the dead our Lord Jesus, may prepare and strengthen us for every good work, working in us that which is well pleasing in God's sight, through Jesus Christ our Lord, to whom be glory for ever and ever. Amen.

Type of Church Covenant: B

Having been led, as we believe, by the Spirit of God, to receive the Lord Jesus Christ as our Savior, and on the profession of our faith having been baptized in the name of the Father, and of the Son, and of the Holy Spirit, we do now in the presence of God and this assembly most solemnly and joyfully enter into covenant with one another, as one body in Christ.

We engage, therefore, by the aid of the Holy Spirit, to walk together in Christian love, to strive for the advancement of this church in knowledge, holiness, and comfort; to promote its prosperity and spirituality; to sustain its worship, ordinances, discipline, and doctrines; to contribute cheerfully and regularly to the support of the ministry, the expenses of the church, the relief of the poor, and the spread of the gospel throughout all nations.

We also engage to maintain as far as possible family and secret devotion; to teach our children the Christian truths; to seek the salvation of our kindred and acquaintances; to walk circumspectly in the world; to be just in our dealings, faithful in our engagements, exemplary in our deportment, and zealous in our efforts to advance the kingdom of our Savior.

We further engage to watch over one another in Christian love; to remember each other in prayer; to aid each other in sickness and distress; to cultivate Christian sympathy in feeling and courtesy in speech; to be slow to take offense but always ready for reconciliation, and mindful of the rules of our Savior to secure it without delay.

We moreover engage that, when we remove from this place, we will as soon as possible unite with some other church where we can carry out the spirit of the covenant and principles of God's Word.

Type of Church Covenant: C

Having been led by the Spirit of God to profess our faith in Jesus Christ, and having been baptized in the name of the Father, the Son, and the Holy Spirit, we do now solemnly and joyfully affirm our covenant with God and with each other.

We pledge to serve Christ in the fellowship of this congregation. We shall endeavor to love one another, to remember one another in prayer, to share in each other's joys, and to sustain each other in times of distress. We aspire to be a fellowship of the concerned, where the lost may find Jesus Christ, sinners may find pardon, seekers may find meaning for their lives, and where all who come may find welcome. We shall strive to be responsible church members, through faithful attendance, study, and giving.

We shall seek to be obedient to Christ in our daily living. Within our homes, in our labor, and while at leisure we shall strive for attitudes and actions which will reflect God's spirit working through us. Believing that our bodies are temples of the Holy Spirit, we shall endeavor to avoid experiences and habits which defile the body and hinder our witness.

Bound together in a fellowship of faith with all who confess Jesus Christ as Lord and Saviour, we shall pray and labor for a spirit of unity among all Christians.

Believing that our call to be a church is a call to witness in the world, we dedicate ourselves anew as servants of the Lord of all life. Whenever people are in bondage to ignorance, poverty, fear, or prejudice, we shall strive for justice, freedom, dignity and peace. Whenever people are separated by barriers of hostility and distrust, we shall be ministers of God's reconciling love. As we pledge our support to the work of our missionaries throughout the world, we commit ourselves to the mission to which God calls us all.

Acknowledging our human frailties and ever seeking forgiveness, we profess our need of the Holy Spirit, and commit our lives to Jesus Christ, and through him to the care, the judgment, the deliverance, and the mercy of Almighty God. Amen.

Appendix 3

Suggested Constitution and Bylaws

For Churches with Multiple Boards

Constitution of the _____ Baptist Church

Note: Wording appearing in brackets [like this] offer optional variations. This constitution is designed for a large church but may be adapted for a smaller church by combining offices and functions.

Article I—Name

This church was organized in _____ and is duly incorporated under the laws of the State of _____ as the _____ Church.

Article II—Purpose

The purpose of this congregation is to give visible form to that faith and fellowship to which God has called God's people. We acknowledge ourselves to be a local manifestation of the universal church in and through which Jesus Christ continues to minister to the world by his Holy Spirit. We seek to fulfill this calling through corporate services of worship, programs of Christian education and nurture, proclamation of the gospel by word and deed, and ministry to human need in the name of Christ.

Article III—Polity

Recognizing Jesus Christ as the only Head of the church, this congregation seeks to ascertain and obey the will of our Lord in all matters of faith and practice. Authority to govern the spiritual and temporal affairs of this church being given to us by Christ, we hold that such authority and responsibility is vested in the membership of the congregation.

In carrying out the wider ministry for which Christ has made his church responsible, we adhere to membership in the ___[name]___ Association [Cluster], the American Baptist Churches of ___[name of region],___ and the American Baptist Churches in the U.S.A.

This church shall not withdraw from any of these bodies, except by a duly adopted amendment to this Constitution, introduced upon petition for such withdrawal signed by two-thirds of all the members of the church; nor shall such action be taken until at least thirty days have elapsed following a consultation thereto by the Boards of Deacons and Trustees of this church with the Moderator of the Association and the Executive Minister of the American Baptist Churches of ___[name of region].___

This church shall also cooperate with the larger Christian fellowship through local and other councils of churches and with other informal agencies of cooperative Christianity.

Article IV—Doctrine

The church accepts the Scriptures of the Old and New Testaments as the inspired witness to God's revelatory actions in human history and as the authoritative basis for its doctrine and practice.

[Optional: The confession of faith drawn up and adopted by this church is regarded as an expression of the essential doctrines of grace as set forth in the Scriptures. This document shall be subject to revision by the congregation as new insights from the Word of God shall indicate ways in which our faith and life may be brought into fuller accord with the mind of Christ.]

[Or: This church also accepts the Apostles' Creed as a convenient summary of basic elements of the gospel, which is useful for instruction and witness.]

[Or: This church has no statement of doctrine other than the Scriptures.]

This church also has adopted the following covenant as a means by which its members express their intent to accept the lordship of Jesus Christ in the life of the church and in the affairs of daily life:

[See Appendix 2 for alternative covenants, or the church may develop its own. It is reiterated here also that an illuminating discussion of the history of Baptist usage of covenants and an extensive collection of Baptist covenants is to be found in: Charles Deweese, *Baptist Church Covenants* (Broadman Press, 1990).]

Article V—Membership

Section 1. *Admission of Members.* Persons may be received into membership by any of the following methods, upon the recommendation of the Pastor and the Board of Deacons and the vote of the congregation:

A. *By Baptism.* Anyone who confesses Jesus Christ as Savior and Lord and who is in essential agreement with the doctrine and practice of this church may be received into the fellowship of this congregation following believers' baptism by immersion.

B. *By Letter.* Any person who is in substantial accord with the doctrine and practice of this church may be received by letter of commendation from any other Baptist church.[1]

C. *By Christian Experience.* Any believer who has formerly been baptized upon a profession of faith, and who

---

[1] Many churches admit persons from other denominations to full membership upon reception of a letter, or upon a statement of former Christian experience, when the Deacons are satisfied that such persons manifest a genuine commitment of their lives to Christ. (See chapter 5 for a discussion of "open membership.") In such circumstances the word "Baptist" would be omitted from this paragraph, and the reference to baptism would be omitted from the next paragraph.

for sufficient reason cannot produce a letter from a church, but who is in substantial accord with the faith and practice of this church, may be received upon satisfactory statement of Christian faith.
- D. *By Restoration.* Any person who has lost membership in this church for neglect or other violation of covenant obligations may be restored to membership upon recommendation of the Board of Deacons and vote of the church.
- E. [Optional Paragraph: *Associate Membership.* Any person professing faith in the Lord Jesus Christ and giving evidence of Christian commitment may be received as an associate member. Associate members shall be considered as regular members with all privileges and responsibilities except that they may not serve as deacons or trustees and may not vote on any motion affecting transfer or sale of church property, or the affiliation of this church with the American Baptist Churches in the U.S.A.]

Section 2. *Dismissal of Members.* Persons may be dismissed from membership by any of the following methods:
- A. *By Reason of Death.*
- B. *By Letter.* Any member in good standing may receive a letter of dismission and commendation to any other church, following recommendation of the Board of Deacons and vote of the church. The name of the church to which membership is being transferred shall be named in the request, and the letter shall be sent to the pastor or clerk of that church. Such letter shall be valid for only six months after its date, unless renewed, and this restriction shall be stated in the letter.
- C. *By Request.* If a person expresses a wish to resign from membership, he/she should put the request in writing. Upon recommendation of the Board of Deacons, his/her name shall no longer be included among the members. The pastor shall acknowledge the request in writing and express the church's continuing concern for the individual.
- D. *By Removal.* Upon recommendation of the Board of Deacons, the church may vote to remove the names of

persons who have been on an inactive list for at least two years.
E. *By Exclusion.* Should a member be guilty of persistent breach of covenant obligations, the church may terminate her/his membership. Only after due notice and a hearing before the Board of Deacons, and after faithful efforts have been made to bring about repentance and reconciliation, should such action be taken.
F. *Inactive membership list.* When a person has manifested a lack of interest in the life of the church for a year by failure to attend services, to communicate with the church, or to contribute to its support, his/her name may be placed on an inactive list upon recommendation of the Board of Deacons and vote of the church.
  1. Persons whose names are on the inactive membership list shall not be counted or reported as members and shall not take part in church business meetings or be eligible to hold office.
  2. Any person whose name is on the inactive membership list may be reinstated to active membership by vote of the Board of Deacons without further action of the church.

Article VI—Dissolution

In the event of the liquidation, dissolution, or winding-up of the affairs of the church, no manager, trustee, or officer of the church or any private individual shall be entitled to share in the distribution of any of the corporate assets, but the assets shall be distributed exclusively to the [choose one] American Baptist Churches of ___[name of the region],___ one of the national program boards of the American Baptist Churches in the USA, or a combination of these organizations.

Article VII—Amendments

This constitution may be amended at a regular or called meeting of the church upon two-thirds vote of those present and voting. Before such a vote can be taken, however, notice of the proposed amendment must have been given to each member by letter at least one month in advance of the time when action is to be taken. If any change in affiliation is involved, the provisions in Article III shall apply.

See also pages 69–70 for further suggestions concerning provisions on denominational relationships.

Bylaws of the _____ Baptist Church

Article I—Officers of the Church

Section 1. *Pastor.* The pastor shall be the leader of the church in all of its activities and shall preach the gospel, administer the ordinances, have charge of the stated services of public worship, and direct the spiritual welfare of the church. He/she shall be a member of all boards, committees, and auxiliary organizations of the church. She/he shall be elected by the church upon recommendation of the pulpit committee, as provided in Article V, Section 1, and may be removed from office only by resignation or as provided in Article V, Section 2.

Section 2. *Moderator.* A moderator shall be elected at each annual meeting to serve for one year. This officer shall preside at all congregational business meetings, shall serve as chairperson of the Church Council, and shall be an *ex officio* member of all boards and committees.

Section 3. *Clerk.* A clerk shall be elected at each annual meeting to serve for one year. This officer shall keep a record of proceedings of church meetings, which shall be read and approved at the next church meeting, and shall also serve as secretary of the Church Council. He/she shall maintain a record of the names and addresses of members, with dates and manner of admission and dismission; also, a record of baptisms and a record of those on the inactive list. She/he shall notify all officers, committee members, and delegates of their election or appointment. He/she shall issue letters of dismission and recommendation as voted by the church, preserve on file all communications and written reports, and give legal notice of all such meetings as required by this constitution. He/she shall also assist in preparing denominational reports. Immediately after the election of a new clerk the incumbent shall deliver to that person all books and records for which he/she has been responsible.

Section 4. *Treasurer.* A treasurer shall be elected at each annual meeting to serve for one year. He/she shall have custody of the funds of the church and all deposits made in the name of the church, and all checks drawn shall be in the name of the church. He/she shall keep separate accounts of all funds raised or contributed for particular purposes, and no funds shall be disbursed except for the purposes for which they were raised or contributed. She/he shall have custody of the securities, investments, title papers, and other valuable documents of the church.

Funds received for the support of the church and for the reduction of church indebtedness shall be disbursed only on order of the Finance Committee or by vote of the church.

The treasurer shall present to the church an itemized report of receipts and disbursements, showing the actual financial condition of the church at each annual meeting, this report to have been audited previously by the Auditing Committee elected by the church. Such other financial reports as may be required by the church shall be presented.

[Some churches also have a benevolence treasurer who handles all funds contributed to the World Mission Support of the American Baptist Churches in the USA and any other outreach projects of the church.]

Section 5. *Financial Secretary.* A financial secretary shall be elected at each annual meeting to serve for one year. It shall be the duty of this officer to furnish each member of the church a pledge card and envelopes for contribution to church expense and benevolence; to keep a record of all pledges made; to collect all money contributed; and to keep a correct account thereof between the church and its members. He/she shall deposit such collections, weekly, in the bank selected by the Finance Committee, and render a statement thereof to the treasurer. At the end of each fiscal year a report shall be made to the Finance Committee, giving an account of the matters pertaining to this office. Periodic statements of account shall be sent to contributors.

Section 6. *Church School Superintendent.* A church school superintendent shall be elected at each annual meeting to serve for one year. In conjunction with the Board of

Christian Education the superintendent shall be responsible for direction of the Sunday church school. This person shall be a member of the Board of Christian Education, and with it shall select and appoint church school departmental superintendents and teachers.

[Note: The foregoing section is for use only if the church chooses not to make the superintendent an appointee of the Board of Christian Education, as provided in Article II, Section 4 of these suggested bylaws. If this section is omitted, the following section will be renumbered as Section 6.]

Section 7. *Limitation of Terms.* With the exception of the pastor and the clerk, elected officers may serve six consecutive one-year terms, after which one year must elapse before they are again eligible for reelection to the same office.

Article II—Boards of the Church

Section 1. *General Provisions.* Members of church boards shall be elected from the membership of the church at the annual meeting for terms of three years, arranged so that one-third are elected each year. A member may serve for two full terms, but then may not be reelected until one year has elapsed. Each board shall form its organization promptly after the annual meeting, choosing a chairperson, vice-chairperson, and secretary. Each board shall meet regularly each month. Special meetings may be called by the chairperson or the pastor. A majority of the elected members shall constitute a quorum. Each board shall report on its work in writing at each annual meeting of the church.

Section 2. *Board of Deacons* [or Diaconate]. The Board of Deacons shall consist of [three, six, nine, twelve, or more] members. It shall in every way assist in the work of the pastoral office, including the following:

- A. Consider with the pastor all applicants for church membership and all requests for letters of dismission and make appropriate recommendations to the church.
- B. Cooperate with the pastor in providing supply ministry and other leadership for Sunday services and other meetings in the pastor's absence.
- C. Provide for the Lord's Supper and aid in its administration.

D. Maintain and administer a Fellowship Fund for meeting special humanitarian needs, receiving funds at each communion service and delivering them to the treasurer.
E. Visit the members and care for sick, needy, and distressed persons of the church or community.

Section 3. *Board of Trustees.* The Board of Trustees shall consist of [three, six, or more] members. [Where there is no separate Finance Committee, the duties of such a group may be added to the Board of Trustees, in which case a larger board may be needed.] Its responsibilities shall include the following:
A. Hold in trust all church property and take all necessary measures for its protection, management, upkeep, and improvement.
B. In consultation with other boards and committees, establish guidelines for the use of church property for all purposes and programs planned by church groups as well as by groups from outside the church.

Notwithstanding the above, this board shall have no power to buy, sell, mortgage, lease, or transfer any real estate property without specific vote of the church authorizing such action.

Section 4. *Board of Christian Education.* The Board of Christian Education shall consist of [three, six, or nine] members. It shall be responsible for organization and administration of the entire educational program of the church, including the following:
A. Develop and interpret to the church the educational goals and objectives.
B. Study the educational needs of the church and make decisions concerning (1) time schedule, (2) educational use of space and equipment, (3) addition or elimination of classes or organizations, and (4) evaluation and selection of curriculum materials.
C. Appoint a Sunday church school superintendent and cooperate with him/her in the selection and appointment of departmental superintendents and teachers and in the direction of the school [omit this section if Article I, Section 6 is used].

D. Discover, enlist, appoint, and train educational workers.
E. Approve and coordinate programs of support conducted by groups and organizations under its jurisdiction (such as home-church cooperation, community relations, and cooperative educational activities with other churches).
F. Prepare and administer the educational budget of the church.

Article III—Church [or Advisory] Council

There shall be a Church [or Advisory] Council composed of the pastor, moderator, clerk, treasurer, financial secretary, Sunday church school superintendent, the chairpersons of each board, and two members-at-large from the congregation.

This council shall serve as a coordinating and planning body for the church. All matters of importance should be considered by it before being presented to the church. It shall appoint a nominating committee each year and shall have an opportunity to review the report of the nomination committee prior to its submission to the church for a vote.

Article IV—Standing Committees of the Church

Section 1. *Nominating Committee.* The Nominating Committee shall be appointed at the annual meeting [or by the Church Council within thirty days after the annual meeting] of the church. During the year, as vacancies in offices may occur, it shall present nominations for filling these to the Church Council, which shall have authority to appoint persons to fill out the unexpired terms.

Prior to the next annual meeting, it shall prepare a list of qualified persons to fill the various offices for which elections are held. It shall interview each nominee proposed and ascertain his or her willingness to serve if elected. The committee shall nominate one or more persons for each office to be filled and report the names to the Church Council for its review at least two weeks before submitting them for election by the church. This list of nominations shall be made available to the congregation one week before the election of officers.

Section 2. *Pastoral Relations Committee.* The Pastoral Relations Committee shall be composed of five members. Because of the sensitive nature of this committee's work, the members shall be appointed by the moderator and confirmed by the Church Council. Their terms of office shall be three years.

The purpose of this committee is to foster constructive communication between the congregation and its pastoral leadership, and to implement the congregation's responsibility for the pastor's professional and personal well-being. The specific functions of the committee shall be the following:

A. To strengthen pastor-people relationships through mutual exploration of the role of pastoral leadership.
B. To act as an additional channel regarding congregational reactions to the pastor's leadership and for the pastor's reactions to the congregation's response to his/her leadership.
C. To counsel with the pastor regarding a continuing education program.
D. To conduct an annual performance review with the pastor.
E. To review annually the church's responsibility for the pastor's compensation, benefits and professional expenses; and, after consultation with the pastor, to prepare and submit recommendations to the Finance Committee.

To perform its task, the committee shall avail itself of resources provided by the denomination from the associational, regional, and/or national offices.

Section 3. *Evangelism and Missions Committee.* The Evangelism and Missions Committee, in conjunction with the pastor, shall plan and supervise all evangelistic efforts of the church. It shall also seek to inform the congregation about, and promote interest and support for, world missions support, ecumenical relationships, and affiliations with outside organizations.

Section 4. *Community Outreach and Public Mission Committee.* The Community Outreach and Public Mission Committee shall be aware of opportunities within the community for service to people with special needs or problems, and shall seek to elicit the interest and support of members of the congregation in responding to those needs. It shall also sponsor consideration within the church's program of moral issues and social concerns, in an attempt to help members view social issues from a Christian perspective and act out of informed and sensitive consciences.

Section 5. *Worship and Music Committee.* The Worship and Music Committee, a subcommittee of the Board of Deacons, shall cooperate with the pastor in selecting an organist and choir director and in the arrangement of the music in the church services. It shall also take an interest in the entire musical program of the church and in whatever matters may contribute to appropriate worship services.

Section 6. *Finance Committee.* The Finance Committee shall be composed of the treasurer, the financial secretary, the chairpersons of the Boards of Trustees and Deacons, and two members-at-large from the congregation.

This committee shall have responsibility for preparation of the annual church budget, submitting it first to the Church [or Advisory] Council and then to the congregation for approval. It shall coordinate the gathering of information pertaining to budget requests, and it shall have responsibility for administering the budget. Any emergency or special offerings shall be approved by the Finance Committee.

The committee shall enlist and train personnel for the annual financial canvass. It shall also enlist persons to count the weekly receipts.

The committee shall also authorize the church treasurer to pay bills, after proper signatures on vouchers have been obtained from authorized persons. It shall provide for its chairperson and one other member to be eligible for access to the safe deposit box. It shall designate the banks where the funds shall be deposited and shall be responsible for the proper recording and depositing of church funds.

The Finance Committee shall have authority to transfer monies from the various special or subsidiary funds to pay for projects within the scope of the original intent of the donor, after said projects have been approved by the church.

[Note: In some churches this committee is combined with the Board of Trustees.]

Section 7. *Auditing Committee.* The Auditing Committee, elected at the annual meeting of the church, shall audit the financial records of the church at least once a year and shall make a written report of the same to the church at the time of the next annual church meeting.

Section 8. *Other Committees.* The congregation or the Church Council may establish new standing committees from time to time as needed, such as social and recreational, fellowship, long-range planning, publicity and communications, ushering, etc.

[For discussion of officers, committees and boards—their purposes, functions, and composition—see chapter 7.]

Article V—The Pastorate

Section 1. *Calling a Pastor.* When the pastorate has been vacated, a Pulpit Committee composed of [five to twelve, depending on the size of the congregation] members shall be elected by the church [or appointed by the Church Council]. The composition of this committee should be representative of age, gender, organizational, ethnic and other diversities represented in the congregation.

This committee shall secure names of prospective pastors, working in full consultation with the area minister and/or executive minister of the region and American Baptist Personnel Services. In reviewing and examining candidates, it shall carefully consider their personal qualifications, experience and record, education, theological views, spiritual discernment, concept of the church and ministry, and abilities as a preacher, administrator, counselor, and leader of worship, as well as other abilities pertaining to the special needs of the church.

When the committee has selected one candidate based on credentials and interviews, it shall invite that person to visit the church, arranging opportunities for members to become acquainted with their prospective pastor. He/she shall be asked to preach in at least one service. If, after this visit, the members feel led to issue a call, and the candidate indicates an interest in such a call, a time shall be appointed for the congregation to vote by secret ballot. An affirmative vote of three-fourths of the members present and qualified to vote, provided there be a quorum present and voting, shall be necessary to make the call valid.

Section 2. *Termination of Pastorate.* A pastor's term of office may be ended upon ninety days' notice on the part of the pastor or of the church, or upon shorter notice upon mutual agreement of the pastor and Board of Deacons.

Termination of the office by the church may be voted at a regularly called business meeting, provided that its purpose has been read from the pulpit on two successive Sundays. A vote by secret ballot of two-thirds of the members present and qualified to vote, provided there shall be a quorum present and voting, shall make valid the termination of such office.

Article VI—Elections

Section 1. *Time.* The annual election of officers shall be held during the annual meeting of the church.

Section 2. *Qualification of Voters.* All matters pertaining to the purchase, sale, or mortgaging of property shall be voted on only by members in good standing and who are of legal age. On all other matters members in good standing who are fifteen years of age or older are entitled to vote.

Section 3. *Procedure.* At least one week before the election the Nominating Committee shall present to the church the names of one or more persons for each office to be filled. At the time of the annual meeting it shall be the privilege of any member present and qualified to vote to place in nomination the name of any eligible person for any office not so nominated. A majority of the ballots cast is necessary for the election of any officer.

Section 4. *Vacancies.* Vacancies occurring during the year may be filled for the unexpired term by the Church Council from names recommended by the Nominating Committee.

Article VII—Meetings

Section 1. *Worship Services.* Public services of worship shall be held each Lord's Day.

The Lord's Supper shall be observed on the first Sunday morning of each month, or at such other times as the Board of Deacons may determine. Other occasional meetings may be appointed by the pastor at his or her discretion, by the Church Council, or by vote of the church.

Section 2. *The Annual Meeting.* The annual meeting shall be held on a date selected by the Church Council, not more than one month after the end of the church year, for the purposes of receiving annual reports of individual officers, boards, and committees of the church and its auxiliary organizations, electing officers, transacting necessary business, and discussing issues vital to the life and witness of the church. [Quarterly meetings shall be held on _____.]

A quorum for the transaction of business shall be ten [or other] percent of the members.

Special business meetings may be called at any time by the pastor or the moderator, or upon the written petition of three members of the Church Council or 10 percent of the church membership. Notice of such meeting, and the object for which it is called, shall be given from the pulpit at least one week in advance of the date of the meeting. At any of the regular meetings of worship, however, the church may, without notice, act upon the reception of members, the dismission of members to other churches, and the appointment of delegates to councils or denominational meetings, but not upon other types of business.

Article VIII—Church Year

The fiscal year of the church shall be the calendar year.

Article IX—Amendments

The bylaws may be amended by a simple majority vote of those present and voting (assuming that there is a quorum present). A notice of the intention to recommend such amendment(s) must be given at least two weeks in advance either from the pulpit or in a letter to each member.

Variations for a Single-Board Church

The following plan is offered as an alternative to the preceding bylaws. It provides for a single board, responsible for the entire life of the church, which operates through departments that exercise functions in specific areas. Names for the single board vary. It is called the Church Board here, but it may be known as Board of Managers, Board of Stewards, Church Council, or Board of Deacons. If the latter, it restores responsibility for the whole life of the church to the

Deacons, but in this case some other term (perhaps Diaconate) is needed for the department which cares specifically for the church's spiritual life. The single-board plan is easily adapted to the needs of small congregations as well as larger ones and is being used increasingly in the American Baptist Churches in the U.S.A.

The constitution for a single-board plan of organization would be the same as for a multiple-board church, except perhaps for minor editorial changes. The principal differences would be in Articles II, III, and IV of the bylaws, which would be replaced by the following:

Article II—Church Board

Section 1. *General Provisions.* There shall be a Church Board of [six, nine, twelve, or more] members, three of whom shall be designated as trustees of the church property and authorized to sign legal papers at the direction of the church or the Church Board. The Church Board shall be divided into three classes of equal numbers, each class to serve three years, with terms of office so arranged that one class shall be elected each year at the annual meeting. Members shall not serve more than two consecutive full terms.

The pastor and the Church Board, subject to the approval of the church, shall direct all the various activities of the church in accordance with its purpose, polity, and doctrine as stated in the Constitution. They shall be responsible for the services and meetings of the church, its program of Christian education, its evangelistic and missionary outreach, its witness to the community, the raising of funds, the care and maintenance of the property, and the administration of the finances of the church.

The Church Board shall carry out its responsibilities through several committees and subcommittees. The various aspects of the work of the church shall be divided into [four, five, or six] departments [commissions, standing committees], and a committee shall be responsible for each department. The chairperson of each of these committees shall be a member of the Church Board, but the other members of the committees and subcommittees may be drawn from the church at large and they shall be appointed by the

Church Board. In the election of the Board consideration should be given to the selection of persons who would be suitable to serve as chairpersons of the several departments.

The Church Board shall meet regularly each month, and at the first meeting after the annual meeting of the church, it shall choose a chairperson, vice-chairperson, and secretary. When the chairperson of a particular committee cannot be present for a meeting, another member of the committee should be designated to attend, with power to vote. Each department committee shall report its activities to the Church Board each month and shall make recommendations for action by the Board.

Section 2. *Nominating and Auditing Committees.* In addition to the above committees of the Church Board, the church at its annual meeting shall elect a nominating committee and an auditing committee to function for the ensuing year.

Section 3. *Departments.* All activities of the church shall be assigned to the following departments: (1) Evangelism and Missions; (2) Christian Education and Nurture; (3) Worship and Music; (4) Property and Finance; (5) Community Outreach and Public Mission; and (6) Pastoral Relations. [Other titles may be preferred.]

[The number of departments can be increased or decreased to meet the needs of the local congregation, but it is best to keep this number fairly small. In the rest of the sections under this article, the specific departments ought to be listed, the areas of responsibility assigned to each department stated, and the number of persons on the department committee given.]

Appendix 4

Selected Bibliography

American Baptists: A Unifying Vision, Study Document and Commentary, by the Commission on Denominational Identity of the ABCUSA (Valley Forge: Judson Press, 1988). An accompanying Leader's Guide is also available. Concern for mission in a changing world prompted this description of Baptist identity. Focusing more upon mission challenges, it highlights core elements of "convictional genes" and biblical imperatives which furnish a basis for unity that overrides our diversities. Intended for study in local churches.

American Baptist Quarterly, 1982–, published by the American Baptist Historical Society. This journal is successor to *Foundations.* Usually focusing each issue on a theme, it is devoted to Baptist studies, relating Baptist heritage to practical and contemporary issues. Some specific issues are cited in footnote references in this book. An important resource.

Ammerman, Nancy T., *Baptist Battles* (New Brunswick: Rutgers University Press, 1990). Reared a Southern Baptist, the author examines the current conflict in the SBC from the viewpoint of a sociologist of religion.

Baker, Robert A., *The Southern Baptist Convention and Its People, 1845–1972* (Nashville: Broadman Press, 1974). A detailed outline of the history of Southern Baptists.

Baptist, Eucharist, and Ministry, Faith and Order Paper No. 111 (Geneva: World Council of Churches, 1982). The fruit of years of interdenominational study, this is the text of a final draft authorized for circulation among the churches for their study, critiques, and proposals for further study and/or changes.

Baptist History and Heritage, 1965–, a quarterly published by the Southern Baptist Historical Society. A useful resource dealing with Baptist themes, especially pertaining to Southern Baptist life.

Beasley-Murray, George R., *Baptism in the New Testament* (Grand Rapids: Wm. B. Eerdmans Publishing Co., 1973). Originally published in 1962, the book was later published in this paperback edition. A thorough, comprehensive study of baptism, stating a Baptist point of view.

Blazier, Kenneth D., and Linda R. Isham, eds., *The Teaching Church at Work, Revised* (Valley Forge: Judson Press, 1993). A manual describing the work of the Board of Christian Education in a local church.

Brachlow, Stephen, *The Communion of Saints: Puritans and Separatist Ecclesiology* (Oxford University Press, 1988). By a Baptist church historian, this book is a thorough investigation of discussions of church polity by Radical Puritans and Separatists in England. It has special significance for Baptists, as this is the matrix from which the Baptists emerged.

Brackney, William H., ed., *Baptist Life and Thought: A Source Book, Revised Edition* (Valley Forge: Judson Press, 1998). A valuable resource, with documents and commentary on major strands of Baptist life and thought.

_____, *The Baptists* (Westport: Greenwood Press, 1988). The second volume in the *Denominations in America* series is organized around what are perceived as five major "vertices" of Baptist history, especially those in the United States. Part Two comprises useful sketches of Baptist leaders. There are also helpful bibliographical resources.

Campolo, Anthony, *A Denomination Looks at Itself* (Valley Forge:

Judson Press, 1971). A Baptist sociologist analyzes trends in the ABC, based upon data gathered by the Roper polling organization. Some good insights are still helpful for present and future.

Carr, Warren, *Baptism: Conscience and Clue For the Church* (New York: Holt, Rinehart and Winston, Inc., 1964). Raises questions concerning the confused baptismal theology reflected in practices of the baptism of children, but without finding very persuasive solution.

Deweese, Charles W., *Baptist Church Covenants* (Nashville: Broadman Press, 1990). Good historical survey of Baptist usage of covenants; many examples drawn from different periods of history and various parts of the world.

Dictionary of Baptists in America, edited by Bill J. Leonard (Downers Grove, Il.: InterVarsity Press, 1994).

Dictionary of Christianity in America, edited by Daniel G. Reid, R.D. Linder, Bruce L. Shelley, and Harry S. Stout (Downers Grove: InterVarsity Press, 1990). An excellent encyclopedic dictionary of persons, ideas, organizations, and history of Christianity in the United States.

Evangelical Dictionary of Theology, ed. by W. A. Elwell (Grand Rapids: Baker Book House, 1984). A helpful resource covering ideas and organizations of evangelicals in the U.S.

Final Report of Study Commission on Denominational Structures of the ABC, May 1972. Detailed report of the structure proposed for a reorganization of the American Baptist Convention (SCODS), approved at the Denver Convention in 1972.

Fitts, Leroy, A History of Black Baptists (Nashville: Broadman Press, 1985). A fine survey of the history, traditions, and characteristic emphases of black Baptist churches, based on wide reading and research.

Foundations, A Journal of History and Theology, 1958–1982. Launched at a time when the ABC was engaged in the task of defining its identity, clarifying its theology, and unifying its aims, this journal contributed many fresh insights into Baptist history and ethos and helped bring about a renewed vision of the church and its mission. A valuable resource.

Gardner, Robert G., *Baptists of Early America: A Statistical*

History, 1639–1790 (Georgia Baptist Historical Society, 1983). Based on exhaustive researches, this work gives background commentary, analyses, and many tables illustrating the growth and composition of Baptist churches in the U.S. to 1790.

Garrett, James Leo, Jr., ed., *Baptist Relations with Other Christians* (Valley Forge: Judson Press, 1974). Contributors from many parts of the world describe the diverse Baptist attitudes to and relations with other church bodies.

George, Timothy, and David S. Dockery, *Baptist Theologians* (Nashville: Broadman Press, 1990).

Gilmore, Alec, ed., *Christian Baptism* (Valley Forge: Judson Press, 1959). A fine scholarly biblical, historical, and theological study of baptism by British Baptists.

Hamilton, Charles V., *The Black Preacher in America* (New York: Morrow & Co., 1972). A sociopolitical study of the black preacher, based largely upon interviews with contemporary preachers, though also covers earlier periods.

Hudson, Winthrop S., ed., *Baptist Concepts of the Church* (Valley Forge: Judson Press, 1959). Baptist historians examine ecclesiology of Baptists at various times and places, showing how a substantial doctrine of the church became eroded.

_____, *Baptists in Transition* (Valley Forge: Judson Press, 1979). Traces changes in Baptist understandings of the church, associationalism, and the ordained ministry, putting present ideas and institutional arrangements into perspective.

Johnson, Emmett V., *The Work of the Pastoral Relations Committee* (Valley Forge: Judson Press, 1983). Practical book on functions of this committee.

_____, *Church Growth—ABC Style* (Board of National Ministries, ABC, n.d.). The ABC Director of Evangelism explains this approach to church growth, indicating differences from the Church Growth Movement.

Leonard, Bill, *God's Last and Best Hope: the Fragmentation of the SBC* (Grand Rapids: Wm. B. Eerdmans Publishing Co., 1990). A Southern Baptist church historian puts the takeover of the SBC by fundamentalist conservatives in the light of history and culture. A perceptive and well-written book.

Lumpkin, William L., ed., *Baptist Confessions of Faith* (Valley

Forge: Judson Press, 1959). Useful collection of historic Baptist confessions, with commentary.

_____, *Baptist Foundations in the South* (Nashville: Broadman Press, 1961). A good account of the impact of the Great Awakening on the growth of Baptists in the South and of the development of the Sandy Creek traditions.

Massey, Floyd, Jr., and Samuel B. McKinney, *Church Administration in the Black Perspective* (Valley Forge: Judson Press, 1976). Explanation of black Baptist traditions and their bearing upon church life. Practical guidelines for church organizations by well-informed ministers.

McBeth, H. Leon, *Women in Baptist Life* (Nashville: Broadman Press, 1979). Puts roles of women in Baptist churches into perspective.

_____, *The Baptist Heritage: Four Centuries of Baptist Witness* (Nashville: Broadman Press, 1987). Comprehensive coverage of Baptists around the world, with special emphasis upon the U.S. Based upon intensive and extensive research. An excellent work, but recent coverage of the SBC is better than that of ABC.

McLoughlin, William G., *Soul Liberty: the Baptists' Struggles in New England 1630–1835* (Providence: Brown University Press, 1991). A painstaking study of the gradual formulation of a doctrine of religious liberty and the separation of church and state, utilizing original research done earlier for his three-volume work on a similar subject.

Miller, Glenn T., *Religious Liberty in America* (Philadelphia: The Westminster Press, 1976). A useful study of the development of a tradition of religious liberty in the United States amidst the changing culture, and its bearing upon modern issues.

Moody, Dale, *Baptism: Foundation for Christian Unity* (Philadelphia: The Westminster Press, 1967). Excellent survey of baptismal theology and practice among major Protestant traditions and of Roman Catholics.

Morikawa, Hazel T., *Footprints: One Man's Pilgrimage: A Biography of Jutsuo Morikawa* (Jennings Associates, P. O. Box 358, Berkeley, CA 94701, 1990). Moving story of an American Baptist leader whose vision influenced the ABCUSA. See also

American Baptist Quarterly, XII (June 1993). This issue honors the memory of Jitsuo Morikawa; it contains articles and sermons illustrative of his theology and statements by persons acquainted with him and his impact on the ABC.

Olson, Adolph, *A Centenary History as Related to the Baptist General Conference Of America* (Chicago: Baptist Conference Press, 1952). Useful account of this church body.

Payne, Ernest, A., *The Fellowship of Believers*, rev. ed. (London: Carey Kingsgate Press, 1952). A historical study of Baptist doctrines of the church, the ministry, baptism and the Lord's Supper, worship, and spiritual discipline, by a British Baptist church historian. Special attention is given to the formative period of the seventeenth and eighteenth centuries.

Randolph, C. F., ed., *Seventh Day Baptists in Europe and America* (Plainfield: American Sabbath Tract Society, 1910). Outdated, but somewhat useful.

Recommended Procedures for Ordination, Commissioning, and Recognition for the Christian Ministry in the American Baptist Churches (Valley Forge: 1980). Statement approved by Commission on the Ministry and the Ministers Council.

Russell, C. Allyn, *Voices of American Fundamentalists* (Philadelphia: The Westminister Press, 1976). By a Baptist church historian; includes biographical accounts of several Baptist ministers. Well done.

Shelley, Bruce L., *A History of Conservative Baptists* (Wheaton: Conservative Baptist Press, 1971). A good account by a church historian of that denomination.

Shotwell, Malcolm G., *Renewing the Baptist Principle of Associations* (Ann Arbor: University Microfilms International, 1990). An excellent study of associationalism, past and present, with a proposal for renewal today and its testing out by five associations.

Shurden, Walter B., *Associationalism Among Baptists in America* (New York: Arno Press, 1980). A helpful study of the history of associations.

_____, ed., *The Life of Baptists in the Life of the World: 80 Years of the Baptist World Alliance* (Nashville: Broadman Press, 1985). A sourcebook containing addresses by presidents of the Baptist World Alliance and other world Baptist leaders.

Stewart, Howard R., *American Baptists and the Church* (Lanham, Md.: University Press of America, 1997). Advocates recovery of associational life by American Baptist Churches in the U.S.A. as a means of adjudicating difficult issues and promoting denominational unity. Historical, biblical, practical approach.

Torbet, Robert G., *A History of the Baptists* (Valley Forge: Judson Press, 1978, 10th printing). First published in 1950, this was the first general history of Baptists of the world of consequence. Updated periodically, it continues to be useful.

_____, *Venture of Faith* (Philadelphia, Judson Press, 1955). A history of the American Baptist Foreign Mission Society and of the Woman's American Baptist Foreign Mission Society.

_____, *Ecumenism . . . Free Church Dilemma* (Valley Forge: Judson Press, 1968). Written by a Baptist church historian who also served as the ecumenical officer of the ABC, it highlights the peculiar difficulties experienced by the free churches in full participation in the ecumenical movement.

Torbet, Robert G., and Samuel S. Hill, Jr., *Baptists—North and South* (Valley Forge: Judson Press, 1964). Compares and contrasts American Baptists with Southern Baptists, taking account of differences in history, culture, theology, and ecclesiology.

Tull, James E., *Shapers of Baptist Thought* (Valley Forge: Judson Press, 1972). The thought of nine representative Baptists, who played important roles in significant movements affecting Baptists and others, by a Baptist theologian. A substantial, useful volume.

_____, *A History of Landmarkism in the Light of Historical Baptist Ecclesiology* (New York: Arno Press, 1980). Traces development of Landmarkist ideas and their inconsistency with earlier Baptist doctrine of the church. Important because it exposes the errors in a movement which has had wide and detrimental effect upon Baptists north and south.

Washington, James M., *Frustrated Fellowship: The Black Quest for Social Power* (Macon: Mercer University Press, 1986). Valuable historical insights into the black religious experience.

White, Barrington, R., *The English Separatist Tradition* (Oxford: Oxford University Press, 1971). Study by British Baptist church historian of separate congregationalism, out of which the first Baptists emerged.

Wilmore, Gayraud S., and James H. Cone, *Black Theology: A Documentary History, 1966–1979* (Maryknoll: Orbis Books, 1979). Wide range of articles and documents pertaining to development of black churches and black theology, with introductions to each main section by one of the editors.

Woyke, Frank H., *Heritage and Ministry of the North American Baptist Conference* (Oakbrook Terrace: North American Baptist Conference, 1979). Useful historical summary of German Baptists in the United States.

Zeman, Gerald K., *Baptists in Canada: Search for Identity Amidst Diversity* (Burlington: G. R. Welch Co., 1980).

Index

Administrator, pastor as, 108
Advisory (Church, Executive) Council, 67, 142, 266
African American Baptist churches, 55, 109, 128, 200–202
Amending constitution and bylaws, 261–262, 271
American Baptist Churches in the U.S.A. (ABCUSA), 4, 69, 73, 115, 203–225, 241–248
American Baptist Convention, 203–204, 206–207
American Baptist Men, 136, 142 fn, 213
American Baptist Ministers' Council, 112, 213
American Baptist Quarterly, 171 fn, 191 fn, 207
American Baptist Societies, 185, 187–188
American Baptist Women's Ministries, 136, 142 fn, 213
Ammerman, Nancy, 109 fn
Anabaptists, 11
Area ministers, 63–64
Associate membership, 72, 91–92
Associational principle, 17, 39–40, 41–44, 173–194
Associations, 175–179, 187, 196
Auditing committee, 140, 268–269, 273
Authority in local church, 3, 7, 52–53, 258
Authority of pastor, 109–111
Authority of Scriptures, 7, 57–58, 65–66, 258
Autonomy of local church, 8, 46, 54–55

Baker, Robert A., 198 fn
Baldwin, Thomas, 182
Baptism, 145–161
  Administrator, 158–159
  Believers', 4, 7, 9, 10–16, 38–39, 43, 51, 87, 91, 93–94
  Immersion, 3, 7, 9, 85–89, 91, 95, 150, 157–158
  Meaning of, 150–156
  Minimum age, 74–75, 159–160
  Role of church in, 158 ff.
  Subjects of, 156–157, 159–160
Baptism, Eucharist, and Ministry (BEM) Document, 92–95, 150, 170–172
Baptist General Conference, 202
Baptist Joint Committee for Public Affairs, 138, 248
Baptist World Alliance, 233, 247
Baptist Youth Fellowship, 141–142
Baptists
  Distinctive emphases, 5, 6–10, 16–18
  General, 15, 16, 40–41
  Particular, 16, 41–44
  Misleading definitions, 6–10, 46
  Need for clear sense of identity, 3–6, 10
  Origins, 10–16
Barnes, W. W., 179 fn
Barth, Karl, 151
Barth, Markus, 147
Beasley-Murray, George, 146–147
Bible study, 56–58
Bi-vocational pastors, 117
Blazier, Kenneth D., 131 fn
Board of Christian Education, 125, 131–135, 265–266
Board of Educational Ministries (BEM), 142 fn
Board of International Ministries, 136
Board of National Ministries, 122 fn, 136, 137
Bread for the World, 137
Brown, J. Newton, 46
Brunner, Emil, 29

Call to ministry, 113–114
Calling a pastor, 69–70, 140, 269

283

INDEX

Calvin, John, 37, 45
Carey, William, 233–234
Carr, Warren, 151
Charleston Baptist Association, 179
Christian education, 32–33, 54, 56–58, 265–266
Christian unity, 35–36, 52, 86, 227–235, 238
Christian vocation, 81–82, 102–103
Christopherson, K. E., 171 fn
Church
    Baptist concept of, 16–17, 38, 49–50
    Biblical doctrine of, 19–33, 49–50
    Definition of, 44
    Fellowship, 28–30
    People of God, 22, 26–28
    Universal, 40–44, 174, 187–189, 210
    Visible and invisible, 17, 37–38, 174
    Servanthood of, 30, 51–52
Church clerk, 124, 262–263
Church *completed*, 68, 97
Church council, 67, 142, 266
Church councils, 185–187
Church *essential*, 68
Church growth, 135–136
Church meeting(s), 55–60, 270–271
Church membership
    Admission to, 72–73, 259–260
    Duties, 76–82
    Preparation for, 73–75
    Privileges of, 82–83
    Termination of, 83–85, 260–261
Church of the Brethren, 246
Church offices
    Basis for determining, 50, 97–101
    Pastor, 98, 105–118
    Other offices, 121–144
Church power, 17, 52–55, 66–67
Church school superintendent, 125, 263–264
Church World Service, 137, 239–240
City societies, 185, 205, 215
Clark, Neville, 154
Commission on Denominational Identity, 4, 53, 223
Common Budget Covenant, 217
Communications Committee, 141, 269
Communion—see Lord's Supper
Community Outreach, 136–138, 267–268
Confessions of Faith, 40–44, 46, 65–66, 166, 174, 229, 258
Congregational approval of new members, 75–76
Congregational polity, 3, 7, 52–55, 58–61, 122
Congregationalists, 11, 12–18
Conservative Baptist Movement, 200
Counseling, 108
Constituting local churches, 63–70

Constitution and Bylaws for local church, 66–70, 121–144, 257–273
Consultation on Church Union (COCU), 244
Councils of churches, 235–244
    Baptists and, 244–246
    Local, 243–244
    National, 238–241
    State, 243–244
    World, 235–238
Covenant of Relationships, 217, 219
Covenants, 65–66, 76–85, 253–256, 259
Criswell, W. A., 109
CROP Walk, 137

Dates significant for Baptist history, 249–252
Deaconess, 99–100, 129–130
Deacons (Diaconate), 75, 97, 116, 126–130, 138–139, 142–143, 264–265
Deacons' Fund, 127
Democratic procedures, 54–55
Denominational affiliation, 66–67, 69, 258
Denominational schools, 224–225
Denominations
    Meaning of, 230–232
    Value of, 6
Deweese, Charles, 76 fn, 259
Dewolf, Delavan, 187
Discipleship classes, 73–75
Dissolution of a church, 261
Dual alignment, 245

Ecumenical movement, 227–246
    Agencies for Baptist cooperation, 247–248
    Christian unity, 52
    Encounter with, 5–6
    Interchurch cooperative organizations, 235–244
    Modern ecumenical movement, 227–230, 232–235
Ecumenical Relations Review Commission (ERREC), 241–242
Edwards, Morgan, 179
Elders, 100
Eldership, 109
Election districts, 212–213, 216, 221
Evangelicals for Social Action, 134
Evangelism, 31, 54, 135–136, 190, 267
Exclusion of members, 84
Executive Ministers (ABCUSA), 62–63, 69, 216–217

Finance Committee, 139, 140, 268
Financial secretary, 125, 263
Fitts, Leroy, 201 fn
Foundations, 147 fn, 175 fn, 183 fn, 207
Fuller, Andrew, 110, 152–153

INDEX

285

Gathered churches, 12–13, 14
General Board (ABCUSA), 212–215, 216–217
General Council, 209
General Secretary (ABCUSA), 209, 215
Gilmore, Alec, 154 fn
Glasser, Arthur F., 134
Graves, J. R., 46
Grow By Caring, 135
Guidelines for drafting constitution, 122–124

Habitat for Humanity, 137
Hand of fellowship, 75–76
Hauerwas, Stanley, 112 fn
Helwys, Thomas, 15
Hiscox, E. S., 46, 188
Hoadley, Frank T., xvii, 188 fn
Hodges, Sloan S., 202 fn
Howell, R. B. C., 127
Hudson, W. S., 102 fn, 110 fn, 175 fn, 183

Immersion—see Baptism
Inactive members, 84–85, 261
Independence of churches, 8–9, 40–41, 52–53
Infant dedication, 156–157
Interdependence of churches, 8–9, 40–41, 217, 219

Jesus and the Church, 22–24
Johnson, Emmett V., 135 fn, 138 fn
Johnson, William B., 183, 197–198

Keach, Benjamin, 76

Laity, 81–82, 97, 101–103
Landmarkists, 46, 196
Lay preachers, 119–120
Leonard, Bill J., 160 fn, 160, 199 fn
Lewis, C. S., 20–21
License to preach, 115, 119–120
Local churches
  Authority of, 17, 43–44, 48, 52–55, 66–67
  Autonomy of, 8–9, 46
  Characteristic marks, 50–52
  Organization of, 55–70
  Procedure for organizing, 63–70
Loftis, John F., 127 fn
Lord's Supper, 161–172
  Administrator, 169–170
  BEM Document, 170–172
  Church ordinance, 166–167
  Frequency, 167
  Meaning, 162–166
  Occasional, 168
  Open or closed, 170
  Private home or hospital, 168–169

Lumpkin, William L., 39 fn, 40 fn, 41 fn, 42 fn, 166 fn
Luther, Martin, 7, 45, 52, 102

McBeth, H. Leon, 9 fn, 11 fn, 198 fn
McCoy, Isaac, 185
McKinney, Samuel B., 110 fn, 128 fn
Manning, James, 180
Maring, N. H., 187 fn
Massey, Floyd, Jr., 110 fn, 128 fn
Meeting house, 28
Membership Committee, 75
Mennonites, 11, 15
Ministerial education, 112–113, 115
Ministerial ethics, 111–112
M & M Board (ABCUSA), 209, 215
Mission of the church, 1–3, 30–33, 51, 133–135, 136–138, 196, 197
Missions Committee, 267
Moderator, 60–61, 124, 144, 262, 271
Moody, Dale, 151
Morgan, Carl H., 98
Morikawa, Jitsuo, 207
Multiple-board organization, 67, 126, 257–271
Music Committee, 139, 268

National Association of Evangelicals, 67, 242–243
National Baptist Convention, Inc., 201–202
National Baptist Convention of America, 201
National Council of the Churches of Christ (NCCC), 62, 238–241
National Executive Council (ABCUSA), 217, 220
Nelson, Reuben E., 208
New Hampshire Confession of Faith, 46, 77, 189
Nominating Committee, 139, 266, 273
North American Baptist Conference, 202
North American Baptist Fellowship, 248
Northern Baptist Convention, 189, 203, 204–205

Oldham, J. H., 36
Olson, Adolph, 202 fn
Open membership, 85–87
Ordinances—see Baptism and Lord's Supper
Ordination, 115–120
  Associations and, 190
  Meaning of, 117–118
  Procedures, 115–117
  Recognition of, 116–117
  Withdrawal of, 118–119
  Standards (ABCUSA), 115, 117
Organization of local churches, 55–70, 97–101, 257–273

Pastoral office, 98, 105–120, 269–270
  Authority of, 109–111
  Call, 113–114
  Moderator, 60–61
  Necessary to church, 104
  Ordination, 115–119
  Qualifications, 111–114
  Roles of, 106–109
Pastoral Relations Committee, 138–139, 143, 144, 267
Payne, E. A., 44 fn, 151 fn, 154
Peck, John Mason, 185
Pendleton, J. M., 46
Personnel Services (ABCUSA), 64, 69
Philadelphia Baptist Association, 175–179
Philadelphia Baptist Confession, 42, 97, 119, 149, 189
Policy Statement on the Ministry (ABCUSA), 110–111
Polity, criteria for, 20, 49–50, 101
Polity defined, 1–3
Preaching, 107
Priesthood of believers, 7, 101–103, 110
Progressive National Baptist Convention, 201–202, 246
Pulpit Committee, 140
Puritanism, 12–13

Rebaptism, 94–95, 159–161
Reception of members
  Baptism, 72, 75
  Experience, 72
  Letter, 72
  Restoration, 72
Regenerate membership, 9–10, 18, 38–39, 45, 51, 71–72, 89–90
Regional and national organizations, 195–205, 215–220
Religious liberty, 7, 9, 14–15, 137, 248
Report from the Capital, 138, 248
Responsibilities of church members, 76–83
Rice, Luther, 181, 182
Robinson, John, 14 fn
Rules of Order, 61–63

Sacraments, 145–172
Separation of church and state, 7, 9, 17, 248
Shelley, Bruce, 200 fn

Shotwell, Malcolm G., 193 fn
Single-board organization, 67, 126, 142–144, 271–272
Smyth, John, 14–15, 229
Social issues and church, 1–3, 30–33, 133–135, 136–138, 267–268
Society method, 180–185, 187–189, 205
Soul liberty, 8
Southern Baptist Convention, 3, 61, 73, 74, 109, 128, 191, 197–200, 244
Stancil, Bill, 130 fn
Standing resolutions, 67–68
State conventions, 183–184, 205
Statement of Purpose (ABCUSA), 210
Statements of Concern (ABCUSA), 137
Study Commission on Denominational Structures (SCODS) (ABCUSA), 210–215
Study Commission on Relationships (SCOR), 215–220
Study of Administrative Areas and Relationships (SAAR), 209–210
Symbols, 55, 148–150, 158

Teaching, church and, 32–33, 107–108, 131–133
Terminating membership
  Letter, 83–84
  Request, 84
  Exclusion, 84
Torbet, Robert G., 9 fn, 11 fn
Treasurer, 124–125, 263, 266, 268
Triennial Convention, 182–183, 184, 186
Trustees, 69, 128, 130–131, 265

Ushering Committee, 139, 269

Vatican Council II, 233

Wamble, Hugh, 174 fn
Watchcare, 72
Wayland, Francis L., 46
Whitley, W. T., 17 fn
Williams, Roger, 16
Women in Ministry, 114, 129
World Council of Churches, 67, 235–238
Worship, 30–31, 55–56, 106–107, 268, 270
Worship Committee, 139, 268
Woyke, Frank H., 202 fn

Younger, George D., 191 fn